Web Site Design Goodies

by Joe Burns, Ph.D.

Pearson Technology Group
201 West 103rd Street Indianapolis, Indiana 46290

Praise for *Web Site Design Goodies*

Those looking for design templates and HTML "how-to" will be disappointed. And a good thing, too. Instead, Joe Burns provides refreshing honesty and opinion, with intelligent advice on the key elements of Web site design; advice which will still stand you in good stead long after HTML is a distant memory—a Web design guide for life.

Give a man a design template or code list and you've fed him for one Web site. Give him this book, and you've set him on his way to building as many different Web sites as he needs. Instead of a paint-by-numbers approach, Joe uses his personable, conversational style to encourage self-development and design confidence.

At the same time, he provides in-depth comment on important Web site design issues, such as colors, technical wizardry, link placement, fonts, focus, and so on. He uses numerous examples, surveys, and site reviews to back up his points. Anyone who thinks they've done a good job with their Web site would do well to read this book and then reassess their work.

—*Mark Brownlow, VP Content, Internet Business Forum, Inc.;* `http://www.ibizHome.com/`

Praise for Author Joe Burns' HTML Goodies Web Site

From the Web Site Visitors

"Thanks for the beautiful pieces of work. I salute you."

—*John J. Lacombe II;* `jlacombe@cpcug.org`*; Organization: Capital PC Users Group*

"This is not only a first-rate page, but is also a huge help to me, and, my guess is, many, MANY people like me. These tutorials have helped me create my own page. Once again, thank you. You're terrific."

—*Rose Dewitt Bukater;* `renatab@webspan.net`

"Wow! Either I'm not as dumb as I thought or you are a very good teacher! I think it's the latter."

—*Greville Hulse;* `hulsegrevgeh@access1.net`

ii

"You probably get dozens of thank-you notes each day, but I just wanted to add my own to the lot. Since I'm a just starting out in the HTML world, I've been visiting your tutorials a lot. Just wanted you to know I've learned more from your site than from any of the books I've bought!"

—*Dawn C. Lindley;* `lindley@usa.net`

"Dear Mr. Really Smart cool-happening dude, I would like to thank you because I have made the transition from FrontPage 98 to HTML all because of you. I spent months trying to learn HTML before I learned of your site, and at age 14 I fully understand the ins and outs of HTML 4. My page is in the works and I owe it all to you. =)"

—*Taylor Ackley;* `ackleyx@hotmail.com`

"I just wanted to let you know that you are doing an amazing service to all of us weekend Web masters. Thanks a million! P.S. My Web page looks and feels a thousand times better since I have been following your tutorials."

—*Aaron Joel Chettle;* `ajchettl@learn.senecac.on.ca`*; Organization: Seneca College Engineering*

"WOW!!!!...I was always interested in setting up a Web page, but was afraid that it would be too difficult for me to comprehend...So my first introduction to HTML were actually YOUR primers...and WOW!!!!!!! I went through ALL of them this very morning with my mouth hanging wide open...I am still so surprised that I cannot gather any words to describe to you how I feel at this moment."

—*Ludwin L. Statie;* `ludwinl.statie@curinfo.an`

"I'm an old dog learning new tricks. I will be taking a Web publishing college course come August. I used your primer as a jumpstart. I really enjoyed your primer and thought it would...help me. I now feel prepared for the college course and not so afraid to 'run with the big dogs.'"

—*Patricia Cuthbertson;* `desertratpat@thegrid.net`

From the Media

"If you are just learning, or already know HTML, this site is the only place you'll need. Expert tutorials make learning Web design quick and easy. Definitely check this site out."

>—*HTML Design Association*

"Dr. Joe Burns offers help at all levels—from novice to the expert."

>—*Signal Magazine; January 26, 1998*

"Great stuff. Probably the best overall site reviewed here."

>—*NetUser Magazine*

"If you're looking for information on HTML, you'll find it here."

>—*USA Today Hot Site; March 23, 1998*

"His is a technical site that appeals to an exploding piece of the Internet pie—people building their own Web site."

>—*PCNovice Guide to Building Web Sites; 1997*

"We would like permission to use your Web pages [HTML Goodies] to help teach [building] Web sites."

>—*San Antonio Electronic Commerce Resource Center; February 10, 1998*

2 Before You Write a Word   31

3 Begin the Design   71

4 Your Site and Your Server   111

5 Text and Color   135

9 Outside HTML

About the Author

Joe Burns, Ph.D., is a professor of communication and Web design at Southeastern Louisiana University. Originally from Cleveland, Ohio, Joe started Web programming as a graduate student at Bowling Green State University. The result of his playing with Web design and programming was HTML Goodies (`http://www.htmlgoodies.com`), one of the most popular HTML and design sites on the Web. In addition to the HTML Goodies site, Joe also writes the weekly "Goodies to Go" and the "Web Design Goodies" newsletters to an audience of more than a quarter-million readers. He has spoken at numerous conferences regarding HTML and Web design and is often asked to beta test and critique Web sites for businesses and individuals. Joe lives near New Orleans with his wife Tammy and his two cats Mardi and Chloe. His is the only house in the development with a blooming magnolia tree, three producing pear trees, a blueberry bush garden, and two 100-year-old live oak trees. He's really proud of that.

Dedication

Over the past year, I undertook two projects: writing this book and designing an online art gallery for my wife. Those two events met at just the right time to produce a far better book than I could have written without putting what I wrote into practice.

For allowing me to use her business idea as part of my own research and write about every aspect of the journey no matter how personal, I dedicate this book to my wife Tammy.

Just by her thirst for knowledge and her asking me hundreds of questions along the journey of creating a Web site from the ground up, she helped write more of this book than she could ever know.

It is said to want nothing and you'll have everything. I have her. That's enough.

Acknowledgments

First and foremost, a big fat thank you to everyone who allowed me to critique, screen capture, and just generally complain about their Web site for this book. I only wanted to critique amateur sites for this book and I know how hard it is to offer your Web baby up to another for criticism. You are all saints in my eyes and I hope you'll not be constructing Joe Burns dolls to stick pins in anytime soon. They sell them in New Orleans, you know.

On the publishing side of things, Victoria Elzey, who made writing this book a joy, Todd Green, who seems open to every stupid idea I can come up with, and the stunning Lindy Humphreys who can come back and content edit HTML Goodies anytime she wants.

The EarthWeb crew of Tim Ryan, who seems to always be the rock in the middle of any storm, Murray and Jack, Amita, Erika, and anyone else who curses my name when I call out of the blue with a problem.

Big thanks go out to Win Welford, Karen Fontenot, Dean John Miller, Jack and Lynn Wellman, Mike Applin, Bill Parrill, Joe Mirando, Terri Miller-Drufner, and anyone else who sat on the committee that hired me at Southeastern Louisiana University.

You all understood that the Web is a massive part of my life and hired me to teach both communications and the Web. By allowing me to put classes online, you allowed me to fulfill both of my loves, teaching and the Internet. Here's to the first semester we start teaching the Master's program. I'll deliver a solid series of Communication technology classes.

Patty Steib for taking my HTML class, helping me to get grants, and being my wife's first online customer.

Josie Walker for allowing me to teach HTML in the Southeastern MBA program.

Thanks to Marcus, Jordan, and Devon at GIS for not only taking my money, but also actually delivering what they promised after taking it. They never laughed at our design ideas...at least not to our face.

Thanks to my mother and father for acting as my northeastern sales force.

Finally, thanks to my aunt Jeanne who acted as a beta tester for my wife's Web site. She understood we needed both negative and positive feedback. She didn't spare her nephew's feelings one bit. If she didn't like it, she told me all about it.

As Elvis once said, "Thank ya'. Thank ya' very much."

Tell Us What You Think!

As the reader of this book, *you* are our most important critic and commentator. We value your opinion and want to know what we're doing right, what we could do better, what areas you'd like to see us publish in, and any other words of wisdom you're willing to pass our way.

As an Associate Publisher for Que, I welcome your comments. You can fax, email, or write me directly to let me know what you did or didn't like about this book—as well as what we can do to make our books stronger.

Please note that I cannot help you with technical problems related to the topic of this book, and that due to the high volume of mail I receive, I might not be able to reply to every message.

When you write, please be sure to include this book's title and author as well as your name and phone or fax number. I will carefully review your comments and share them with the author and editors who worked on the book.

Fax: 317-581-4666

Email: feedback@quepublishing.com

Mail: Dean Miller
Que
201 West 103rd Street
Indianapolis, IN 46290 USA

Introduction

So, you've decided to buy a Web design book, huh?

Good for you. I'm glad to see that you're taking an interest in the overall design of your Web project. That's commendable. All too often, people, businesses, students, organizations, or the Weekend Silicon Warrior take to the Web without any manner of code and without once considering the overall plan, what my father calls "The Big Picture."

If you've already bought this book for one reason or another, this should be a good introduction regarding what's ahead. If you're standing in a bookstore trying to get a feel as to if you should plunk down a few bucks then hopefully I can sell you right here.

What Makes YOU Such an Expert?

By "You" I mean "Me," of course.

That's a good question. What does make me an expert? This is a big problem any time someone writes anything that sets him or herself up as a base of knowledge. I guess I could list the books I've written and the sites I've designed and all the times I've been brought in to consult for sites and the fact that I write a design newsletter, and blah, blah, blah.

Suffice to say, I've been doing Web design since 1995 and over those years, I've done a lot of it.

The audience of a book, the readers, often tend to split along popularity lines no matter what the author's background. If a reader likes the author, then the reader most often agrees. If the reader dislikes the author, then the reader most often disagrees. I'm quite familiar with that concept from my last two programming books, *HTML Goodies* and *JavaScript Goodies*. (See how I snuck those in there?)

When the discussion of my writing a Web design book came up, I knew that because design offers no real hard and fast rules, my opinions would stand as simply the opinion of one person. Oh, I may have years and years of background, but I am still one person. That makes my opinions fairly easy to disregard.

I needed some support for what I was saying. You can pretty easily wave off a single opinion. It's far more difficult to wave off the opinions of 500 people.

We Polled the Web for This Book

Well, we didn't poll the whole Web. No one can do that. What EarthWeb and I did do was set up a series of four questionnaires, each covering a different aspect of Web design. They were

- Overall Web Concerns
- Image and Color Questions
- Text and Link Questions
- New Technology Questions

Each of the questionnaires contained between 28 and 35 questions. Each questionnaire was posted for as long as it took to gather 500 responses.

Because polling on the Web almost completely disallows for a random choice of participants, we decided to set up the polling so that the respondents would be chosen in a purposive manner, yet randomly given the ability to respond to the questionnaire.

The questionnaire was offered on the HTML Goodies Web site, which was, at that time, bringing in close to 500,000 unique visitors per month.

We chose to offer the questionnaire on HTML Goodies first because the audience would be a group of people who would not only be interested in Web design, but would have most likely performed some design themselves. HTML Goodies is a site dedicated to teaching Web page construction. We felt there was correlation.

Every seventh visitor was given the ability to take the questionnaire. That visitor could simply choose to not take the questionnaire and he or she would not be bothered with it again. The questionnaire remained posted until 500 visitors responded.

It normally took just under two days for the 500 visitors to offer their responses. The number of respondents that answered each question is noted in the book's text. Often the number was under 500 because not every respondent answered every question. The response rate usually fell between 480 and 495 respondents per question. Each new questionnaire was offered on the Monday following the completion of the last questionnaire. The four surveys were posted over four weeks during February and March of 2000.

I was the author of the questionnaire. Two editors read and commented on my wording. Each question was written to elicit as unbiased a response as possible. I asked questions in as specific a manner as I felt I could in order to use the results as part of the discussions I wanted to undertake in this text.

As you read through this book, there are numerous places where I make a point and then back it up with the results from the survey. And before you ask, yes, there were many times that I received poll results that differed from my own thoughts on Web design. You'll also get to read those results as you move through the book.

Please understand that this was not a random sample. It was purposive in nature and the results cannot statistically be said to represent the entire Web population. However, as are many purposive samples, the results are transferable to the population that gave the answers. That population was made up of those who not only surf the Web but also write for the Web.

I am confident that the result from this series of questionnaires has strong merit and can be used as support for the statements I make regarding Web design.

Where I'm Coming From...

If you're expecting that by reading this book you'll receive a set of templates that you can quickly alter and post to the Web, you won't. If you expect that within this book there are a set of hard and fast rules you can simply follow and, when finished, have a perfectly designed site, there aren't.

There are no such things as design templates that work for all sites. There are no such things as strict rules for design. If you pick up a book offering either of these quick fixes, put it down. In terms of design, the quick fix does not work.

Design is performed mainly before the first piece of text is coded. Design is site specific. What works for one site may be death to another site. Design is topic specific and because of that, there are no right or wrong design choices as long as the design goes to helping the site's purpose for being.

Now wait, maybe I did just lie to you. There is one hard and fast rule to design. It's the most enjoyable work you'll ever do when building a Web site. I say that because design is wide open. You are limited only by what your brain can imagine. In addition, I'll bet for a lot of you, this is the first time you've ever sat down and, without any other help, created your own place, your own little corner of the Web. You're going to love it.

Within the pages of this book, you're going to see a few overriding design concepts coming up again and again. I hit them pretty hard because I feel they're the basis for designing good pages.

#1. Your Web Site Is for Your Visitors, Not You

In all aspects of design, you must constantly think about the visitor. Just because you feel an element is pretty cool, doesn't mean it's right for the page. Yes, that includes personal pages. Even a personal page wants visitors, right? Then think of them when putting up your personal site.

#2. There Are No Incorrect Design Choices As Long As That Choice Goes to Help the Site's Specific Purpose

That's part of the design process. What will be your site's specific purpose and how can you design elements on a page to all point to that purpose?

#3. Content Is the Single Most Important Part of Your Web Site

This book is constructed in such a way that as it goes on, the elements discussed become less and less important to the site. That means that what's written first is most important. That means that if you find yourself agonizing over a concern addressed in Chapter 2, "Before You Write a Word," you're probably spending your time wisely. If you're agonizing over something in Chapter 8, "Hello? Anybody Here? How Many?," then maybe you're putting a little too much thought into an element that probably won't add much to your site's purpose anyway.

Design is personal. Design is specific. Design is done for your site, for your visitors.

At every step of the way, you need to make the decision whether to incorporate an element. I'm sorry to say, I can't offer a specific yes or no at any point of the process. That decision is up to you because you know your site, you know your visitors, and you know what you're trying to accomplish by posting the Web site.

I'm telling you the truth when I say you'll enjoy designing a Web site so much more when it's you concerning yourself over a decision rather than relying on a template to make the decision for you. It is a much more gratifying and much more intelligent choice. Why? Well, for one, the template doesn't know you or your site from Santa Claus. You do.

You are the person who should make the decisions. My job, and thus this book's job, is to lay out the plan and the steps you need to follow in order to make those decisions.

A Word About URLs

It is the way of the Web for sites to change and to come and go quickly. Because of this speed, it is impossible to accurately portray a Web site in a static medium such as a printed book (written and printed, mind you, weeks, oftentimes months, before it arrives in your hands). However, this is not to say that even outdated Web sites can't be of use. It is the principles that matter, not the longevity of the actual site presence.

Therefore, figures within this book are simply snapshots of Web sites when I first saw them. I am using them to make a point more than to have you visit the site itself as an example. I offer the URLs to the sites for your reference and convenience. Some of these sites still exist but have been tweaked, updated, or completely overhauled. In these cases, study the critiques and determine for yourself if these sites have improved and in what ways. For those sites that may be gone completely, you can only learn from their everlasting images in these pages.

That's the Pitch

There is, or by now there was, a commercial that uses the tag line, "I'd never work this hard for anyone by myself."

Web design is like that. You're about to build something out of nothing. You're about to put something to the Web that is from you. The decisions are yours but they affect the people who visit you.

Okay. Let's make a site.

Chapter 1

Judge Not Lest Ye Be Judged

Here is the basic conundrum in a nutshell:

> No matter what I tell you, it's wrong. Furthermore, no matter what I tell you, it's right.

If that sounds like a rather contradictory method of starting a book, you're right. Read on. I explain what I mean in the next few paragraphs.

I was in New York City one day, sitting in the offices of EarthWeb when the idea of my writing a Web design book came up. I had just finished off my second programming book and thought a change of topic would be good. By writing a design book, I could get away from page after page of computer code and begin to deal with the aesthetic aspects of the Web. Basically, I thought this would be an easier book to write.

No such luck. Now the conundrum comes into play.

The main problem in undertaking a design book is that there is really no such thing as a "rule." Teaching HTML or JavaScript programming is easier than teaching design in that I provided you the code, told you what it did, and that pretty much wrapped it up. The code would work tomorrow, next month, or a year from now. Code is code.

Design is a much more elusive animal. In fact, one of the main complaints I hear regarding my HTML Goodies site (http://www.htmlgoodies.com) is that I don't offer much design help. That's done on purpose, believe it or not. I decided to not offer a great deal of design help because I believe that HTML and Web page design is an art form. It's not at the Picasso level by any stretch, but it's an art form nonetheless. Instead of paint and paper, you have images and text manipulation. Of course, some of my earlier designs might have actually looked like a Picasso piece. I bet some of yours did, too.

Templates

The largest percentage of the complaints about my lack of design help on HTML Goodies note that I don't offer any Web page templates. Ugh. I think templates are terrible. You see, if I offered templates then users would believe that they could simply plug in a few words, a couple of images, and they'd have a well-designed Web site. Why? Well, the template came from HTML Goodies; thus, it has to be a good template and thus create a good site. There's logic, huh?

I've never understood template-format thinking. I think it goes, "design equals template, template equals design." My guess is that there's some serious rationalization in there. Design is hard because, as I said before, there aren't any hard or fast rules. The moment I say that one element is bad, someone jumps up and proves to me that the element works just fine on his site. There just isn't a right answer.

Whatever I tell you is wrong. Whatever I tell you is right.

Now let me add to that statement:

> Whatever I tell you is wrong if it harms your design.
> Whatever I tell you is right if it aids your design.

When a user can generate a Web site via a template, he can bypass the difficulty of design and go right to the coding. He can also blame someone else if the design stinks, which it will. Well, maybe that's harsh. Maybe the design won't stink. However, what will stink is that the user isn't the only person grabbing and completing the template. Hundreds, maybe thousands, of others did the same thing. Now you have a bunch of sites that all look exactly the same. That stinks.

The lack of templates on HTML Goodies is on purpose. If I offer fill-in-the-blanks templates then what I am basically saying is that there are hard and fast rules to designing a Web site. There aren't. Keep the conundrum in mind. One template does not cover all Web site formats. "So, offer multiple templates," some might say. Nope. Same problem. Templates are Web site design intended for speed with little or no concern for what the site does, who visits, or future updates and additions. Besides, this is art, remember? It's not really your painting if I do 80% of the work. How many paint-by-number pieces hang in the Louvre?

What works for one site probably won't work for another site. What doesn't work for you might work like a dream for someone else. Plus, when you post using a template, and someone else posts using the same template, what sets your site apart? Is it some text, an image or two? That's not enough. Your site will look like it came out of a cookie cutter mold because, basically, it did.

Liquid Design

That said, yes, there are some basic tenants of Web design. These are general thought processes that, in most cases, serve to better a site, but in every case, even the worst design can be perfectly acceptable inside the correct set of parameters.

For example, you probably don't want 17 or 20 animations all running on the same page. That would be confusing if not really ugly, right? But what if you are running a site that offers GIF animations for downloading? Then this particular design might be "correct."

Okay, fine. You certainly wouldn't want a black background with pink letters, now, would you? That's pretty awful I would say. For the most part that's true, unless you are running a site for a punk band and those are their adopted colors or your site has a 1950s look to it. Back then, that color combination was seen as being "rock-n-roll." As Elvis would say, "Thank ya'. Thank ya' very much."

Aaaaaaauuuuugh!

See the problem? The moment I create a template and say that the template is good; I stop your creative process and plant your feet firmly in cement. "So," you say, "create a template that I can manipulate and choose colors and pick images and set different fonts and design the page so that it shows more of 'me' than the template." This was actually written to me, I swear. My response:

> "Why don't you just design it?"

Those who want to get a site up and on the Web often want it fast and often templates are the way they go about it. The problem is that the person posting the Web site never once thought about his audience, what the site is for, or why he even wanted to put up a site in the first place. The reasoning would probably be something like "Everyone else has a site so I wanted one."

So, why put up a Web site? Well, as I said in the text, don't just put one up because someone else has one or because you simply feel you need one to be up with the times. Think for a moment. Why do you need a Web site?

Better yet, what makes you...you? What makes you great? What makes your business or company great? What is it that you want to shout from the rooftops about yourself or your organization?

I believe wholeheartedly that the Web is a form of communication. Have you ever joined a conversation just because you could? You most likely joined because you had something to say, something to share with others.

That something you have to say—that's why you should put up a Web page. Furthermore, that's what makes your Web page great.

That's the wrong reason to put up a site. I had a gentleman write to me in order to ask direction in creating a site for his business. I asked him why he needed a site in the first place. His answer was because his 13-year-old son had a site and if that kid can make a site then so can he. I bet that kid can also eat an entire box of Oreo cookies and then run two miles without turning green. Do you want to do that, too?

When "you" make the decision to put up a Web site, "you" need to understand that "you've" undertaken more than just some fun coding in order to kill a couple of hours on the weekend. Putting up a Web site involves a little planning, a little research, and a little creativity. Please don't let that word "creativity" frighten you.

A template gets you up and running, yes, but I guarantee that if you're at all interested in your site past the initial posting, or beating your 13-year-old kid to the punch, you'll spend the vast majority of your time trying out new blips of code and moving page elements around until you get just the look you want. In short, you'll be designing. You'll be destroying the template you wanted in the first place. Let me save you a month or two. Think design first. Leave the templates for someone else.

Just so you don't think I am totally against templates, let me offer a suggestion as to when you might want to use them. I helped a person put up a site that offered a ton of images. Each image was the same size and each would be sitting on a page that looked just like the last one. In that case, a template was required. It would have been insanity to design a new look for every page.

Here's another example. My wife and I put together a site that sold art. Every page that displays a piece of art looks like every other page that displays a piece of art. We set up the system so that a template was used by the system to create the page when a user clicked to view a painting. The computer put in the correct image, title, and price along with a few other elements. It was a template I designed and used again and again.

When I rage against templates, I do so because I want the designer of a Web site to enjoy the concept of putting together something of his or her own creation rather than simply putting up a Web page because he or she can.

Besides, Web site design is the fun part. Too often students dive right into coding. They throw copy-and-paste blips of code into a document, the page displays, and that's that. Too bad. The fun part is sitting down and designing the look, drawing a thousand possible visions, picking the right one and having it come to life.

Design is fun, design is good, and design is constant.

I had a professor one time that lived by the phrase, "Done is Good." She constantly had her eye on the end of the project and then moving along to the next project. I think that many people have the same goal-oriented feeling regarding Web design. Done is good. Well, I'm here to tell you, you'll never be done. Design is an ever-evolving art that takes you on a journey of basically raising a Web site. Your first design will be much like the infancy of the site. If you stay with the site and continue to update and better it, you'll watch it grow and develop into a mature, functioning site dedicated to yourself, the users, and their wants and needs.

Here's another thing to keep in mind. The design is what takes the most time. I have told students from the beginning of my teaching career, "The code is quick. The design is rough." I can spend hours with pieces of paper drawing out how I want a Web page to appear. Once I land upon the look I want, coding that look is lickety-split. I usually complete it in under an hour. Then comes the real time consumption. I sit and stare at the page because I don't quite like it. I move an image and then move it back. I change a font and then change it back. I move a line and shorten it, then elongate it, and move it somewhere else. The next thing I know it's five hours later, I haven't eaten or showered and David Letterman is on. I often emerge from my office to a sarcastic, "Welcome back," from my wife.

You are about to embark on a journey that never ends. Design is fluid. The moment you put up a page, the indicators you used to design it begin to change. Maybe you designed your site to appeal to an equal number of men and women visitors. Then, when the site is finally up and running, you find that your topic appeals mainly to women. Maybe some elements slow the page too much. Maybe some of the images need to be shuffled around. Maybe you just grow tired of the look.

Shucks. It's time to look at your design again.

Web Alive

If you do your design work correctly, after you put up your initial site, the redesigns will probably be little more than tweaks and other small changes, but they have to be made. The Web is alive. I guess I should say the Web audience is alive. It is a living, breathing, growing, changing thing that moves in and out of the site you've just posted.

As the book goes along I talk about how to gather information about your audience, what they like and dislike, and how you can design for it. Here's an example.

I talked to a woman at a design conference who asked how she could direct the audience away from a smaller part of the site back to the bigger parts. It seems that eight out of every ten visitors to the site were going to what she considered a minor portion. She wanted that to stop and for those users to stay within the main pages. I asked why she wanted to stop people from making the site a success.

It was all design. She had spent time on that bigger section so, darn it, that's what people should be looking at. Sorry. The audience has spoken. They have singled out what they like and it isn't what you thought it would be. It's time to rethink the design. It looks like that smaller portion has just moved up the ranks and become more than an afterthought.

The audience comes to your site and they judge it with their mouse clicker. Correct design assists them. They easily navigate, easily find what they're looking for, easily purchase, and enjoy what they see. That might mean a return visit. Poor design usually means the first visit is the last.

Isn't that really the point? When you post a Web site, what do you really want? Visitors. On the Web, they're called users. You want a lot of users. That's the first question anyone asks after finding out I have a Web site. They want to know how many users come to the site. The number of users is of paramount importance to Web designers. How many sites have you been into that have a counter on every page? That counter is the Web designer allowing him or herself to answer the question, "So, how many people come to your site?"

Isn't It the Idea More Than the Design?

This question comes up at least once every time I teach a class in Web design. The student makes a logical conclusion that if the thing that the site is offering is good enough then people will visit. The thinking can be boiled down to a combination of "If you build it, they will come" and "Build a better mousetrap and customers will beat a path to your door."

My answer to that question allows me to go back a few years to my days in radio. A radio station has to have an audience to survive. The way you gather up an audience is a two-step process. First you have to get the audience to sample you. That means audience members make the decision to turn their radio dials and listen to you over what they are currently listening to. Once the listeners have turned the dial and given you a listen, then it's your job to hold the listener. In short, keep them coming back for more. The relatively easy part was getting people to sample the station. If you spend enough money and create enough of a commotion, people will come and take a look. We did it through big contests, advertising, and live broadcasts inside a Cherry Picker, 80 feet above the highway (really). The audience wants to see what all of the fuss is about. Once there, now it's up to your music and your personalities to keep them.

It's the same thing on the Web. There are thousands of dot-com sites out there vying for the audience's attention. How do they get you to sample the site? Usually it's through a blitz of advertising or through a major promotion, usually a big money giveaway or the like. Smaller sites that don't have cash fight to get themselves onto search engines and to trade links with other, more established sites. The noncash method is slower but still effective.

Do users go to new sites? Sure. Why not? It doesn't cost any money and people are always looking for a new site to play with. Once the user is within your site, the design of the site becomes paramount. Now it's up to the site to help the user, guide the user, and make the user feel comfortable. The user subconsciously answers many different questions such as

1. Was it easy to get around?
2. Did the pages load quickly?
3. Did I understand what the site was doing?
4. Did I run into some programming I couldn't run?
5. Did the site ask for any of my personal information?
6. Did they tell me why they needed the personal information?
7. If I bought something, was the transaction easy?
8. Did I feel safe in the site?
9. Did the site offer me anything new?
10. Will I be back?

Let me get back to the topic for a moment. Sure, the topic of the site is very important. Fans of *Buffy the Vampire Slayer* always want to see a new Buffy site. They're looking for something new, something different, something that the sites they are used to going into don't offer. They want a site to appeal to them, to be easy to get around in, and help them get from point A to point Z. Offer your users something new, some good design, and you have a solid shot at keeping them. Don't and you won't.

Once the user arrives, brought there by the topic, the design is the single most important element of the site.

The Art of Critique

It is my opinion that the single most important thing to help you become a better Web site designer is to learn the art of critique.

I stated previously that there are no hard or fast rules to Web site design. Every design choice is good if used correctly. Every design choice is bad if used incorrectly.

What's a designer to do?

Critique. I feel it is so important to critique that I finish each chapter in this book with the critique of three different Web sites. These are not professional Web sites either. Amateur designers like you have created each of these sites. It wouldn't be fair if I only critiqued professional sites and then expected you to look at amateur sites. Besides, the professional sites have teams of designers working on them. They should be well designed, although often there are problems.

If you are going to design a Web site, you must critique other sites. You must look at what others are doing and make judgments about those doings.

Simply put, critiquing design teaches you more about design than I, or this book, ever could.

For example, would you rather take your car to be repaired by a person who has been fixing automobiles for ten years or to someone who's been reading about fixing your car?

I rest my case.

You're going to become a designer! Get in there. Get your hands dirty. Put yourself knee deep in design and all the concerns that come along with it. You'll simply be a better designer because of it.

This is one of those assignments that students almost have to be forced to do, yet after they've done it a couple of times, they end up liking it. I call this section, "The Art of Critique" because the ability to critique a Web site is an art form rather than a simple attack on the site at hand. Critique is constructive. Critique is not simply listing bad points in order to put down one site to lift yours up.

In the art of critique, one must remain objective at all times. A site that is in direct competition with you isn't doing everything wrong simply because it is vying for the same audience as you. Offering a poor critique because of personal feelings doesn't help. Stay objective. Learn from both what is good and what is bad. And speaking of bad...

There are no bad design elements as long as they are used within the correct parameters. That's important to keep in mind. When you set out to critique a site, it's important that you learn about the site before you begin saying what's good and what's bad.

Yes, you must make a point of also saying what is good about a site. Too often, the word critique takes on a bad connotation. People think that if they are going to be critiqued, they are going to be torn down and only poor elements will be brought out. If that happens, it's not a critique. It's an attack. Don't do that.

What Sites Should You Critique?

To begin with, critique sites that deal with topics you understand. Remember that design is dependent upon a lot of different factors—that's why templates don't work very well. They don't take into account what the site is trying to accomplish. Stick with sites that deal with topics you know and understand. At first you may only want to stick with sites that are dedicated to topics similar to the site you want to create.

The reason is so that you have some footing from which to make your judgments. When you critique, you state that this element is good and this element is not so good. If you don't really understand the topic of the site you're critiquing then your opinions can be easily brushed aside by those who do.

When you critique a Web site, you must first take the time to look at the entire site and get a feel for it. Ask yourself what the site is attempting to do. Get a general feel for the purpose of the site.

Once you understand what is going on, or at least what should be going on, get out of the site and clear your cache. It's time to critique.

The Steps

Why leave the site? Why clear the cache? Besides...what's a cache?

A cache is a section of the hard drive where copies are kept of every page your browser displays. Have you ever noticed how the second time you enter a site it comes in very quickly? That's because the images and text are not actually being read from the Web, but are actually being read from your hard drive, from the cache.

If you clear the cache, you start fresh with no cached images.

Load time is very, very important to a Web site. By leaving the site and clearing your cache, you re-enter with the slate wiped clean and can then get a feel for the site as might a first-time visitor.

Note

In Internet Explorer, clear your cache by clicking **Tools** and choosing **Internet Options**. Click **Delete files**. You are asked if you want to delete all the files in your Temporary Internet Folder. Click **OK**. The hard drive will buzz a bit. You're done. If you haven't cleared your cache in a while, or ever, there may be a lot of files to delete so don't be alarmed if this takes a little while. Close the box.

In Netscape Navigator, click **Edit** and choose **Preferences**. Click the little plus sign next to the header **Advanced**. It's along the left side of the box that opened. After you click the little plus sign a menu drops down, click the word **Cache**—it is the first element listed. Finally, click the **Clear Memory Cache** button. You're done. Close the box.

After each step of this critiquing process, you need to take the time to stop, look at what you've found, and ask yourself, "How can this help me?" or "How can I avoid doing this?"

That's the real purpose of these critiques. I am not asking you to help someone else's site. I want you to help yourself create a better site and avoid pitfalls before one of your users has to deal with them.

1. Time It

Look at a sweep second hand and log in at the top of the next minute. Stay with the homepage until it loads completely. You know it's done loading when it reads, "Document Done" down in the lower-left section of the browser's status bar.

Jot down the time. Did the site load quickly? If so, why? Was it a lack of images, or were the images small enough to load quickly?

How long was it until you could actually begin reading and navigating the site? Were you allowed to begin reading and clicking before all the images had come in? If so, jot that down. That's a positive comment. Remember: You're looking for positives as well as negatives.

Ask yourself, "How long would I have waited for this site to load before leaving the site?" If the site loaded fast enough for you then jot that down. If not, make a note of that, too.

Now, how can you use what you've found to make a better page for yourself? How can you avoid the pitfalls you ran into?

2. Display

How does the page look on your screen? Does it fit? If not, is it too big or too small? Do the elements on the page line up nicely or has your screen setting appeared to do bad things to the design?

Make a note of what you found and how you can use or avoid what you saw.

3. Try Another Browser

This is all too often overlooked when designing a Web site. The site looks great in Internet Explorer, but in Netscape Navigator, it's the pits.

Open the page in that other browser. Do all the elements display? If not, make a note of which do not and try to figure out why they don't display.

How can you use this information on your site?

4. Write Down the Concept

Write down what the site is trying to accomplish in one sentence. Then, ask yourself if that accomplishment is being met or if the site is falling short. If you cannot denote what the site is trying to do in one sentence then the site is not meeting its goals.

5. Offer Praise to the Site

At this point, you should be moving through the site and looking for general ideas and elements.

Because it is so easy to be negative, start with praise. Make a point of writing down at least one thing you feel the site is doing well. Ask yourself how you can possibly incorporate that into your own site.

6. Offer Concerns

Next, begin writing down the concerns you have about the site. Spell out the concerns as clearly as you can. Make a point of explaining why you have these concerns, not only that you have them. If you feel something is wrong, just don't say that it is a concern; tell why it is a concern.

Does the concern inhibit users on the page? Does it confuse users? Is it something that crashes the browser? Tell the concern and why it is a concern.

7. Offer a Suggestion

It is one thing to find fault, it is truly another to find fault and then offer a suggestion on how to better the page.

Do that. For every concern you find, offer a suggestion on how that negative can be turned into a positive.

8. Write an Overall Evaluation

When you have finished the critique, write a two-paragraph evaluation of the site. Give an overall grade to the site and discuss what should happen to make the site better.

There's no set number of sites that you should critique. Do as many as you feel comfortable doing. Do as many as you need to in order to get a better feel for your own work.

Speaking of your own work, once your site is up and running, you should make a point of critiquing your own site. Be honest. Be truthful. Be your own worst critic. It can only help you.

Maybe you could get someone else to critique your site. It's a process called beta testing.

Now, that I've gone over the format I suggest you follow when critiquing sites, I'd like to offer some critiques of my own. I follow the previously outlined format.

Each chapter in this book ends with the critique of three sites. Those who have read my critiques before have stated that it's the critiques that taught them the most about Web site design. I hope they help you, too.

Just remember, my critiques are only the beginning of the process. Once you understand what should be done, you need to make a point of critiquing some sites yourself. You'll build better Web sites because of it.

Web Page Versus Web Site

One More Thing...

Don't you hate when a teacher or professor says that? You're sure he or she was done and then they say, "one more thing."

Here's a hint. That "one more thing" the teacher or professor discusses...it will be on the test. I guarantee it. Before I get into my first critiques, here's "my one more thing." If there were to be a test, this would be on it.

You may have noticed that I am making a point of writing that you are designing a Web site rather than a Web page. I do that on purpose, because it's true. You are not designing individual Web pages; rather you are designing a Web site. It's very important that you keep that in mind throughout this process.

It's fairly easy to tell when a person has designed Web pages rather than a Web site. The resulting site usually looks like one of the following two examples.

The Great Homepage

The Great Homepage site is just as it states: The site is blessed with a fantastic homepage. The colors are well thought out, the images are placed nicely, the links are up high, and the look is warm and inviting. The problem comes when you start to venture into the site. Every link goes to a page that often pales in comparison to the homepage. Maybe the author has made a point of carrying the background color or an image across the pages, but for the most part, that's about all. The subpages are usually just text, or contain the dreaded "Coming Soon!" line. Worse yet, the page isn't there at all and the user is greeted by a nasty "Page Not Found" error.

The Great Homepage site also manifests itself when the author fails to rely on his or her subpages. This occurs when the author attempts to put the entire site on just that one homepage. The result is often a very long page with multiple sections requiring the visitor to scroll down from portion to portion. I find that homepages that fall into this trap often put the few links that they do have toward the bottom of the long page. That way the author believes they can force the user to scroll through the information. Once the links do arrive, they are usually the basics, a list of favorite links, a Guestbook, and a photo album. The subpages usually aren't very interesting because they aren't needed. The homepage has done it all. There really wasn't any need for the subpages.

Both of these problems arise when the author sets his or her sights on building a page rather than building a site. All the effort went into the homepage because, logically, that's the most important page. What little creative effort that was left over went to the subpages and they suffered.

I am as guilty of this as anyone else. My first Web site consisted of one page—the homepage. I had no subpages. Every link took the user right off site. It was just a page, but man, did that homepage look good.

Great page. Lousy site.

Many Pages—One Site

The second major problem that pops up when an author sets his or her sights on designing a page rather than a site is the concept of "Many Pages—One Site." This is simply the problem mentioned in "The Great Homepage" taken to the extreme. In this case, the author has built a homepage and multiple subpages, each a work of art in and of itself. The problem is that the homepage and the subpages have nothing whatsoever to do with one another.

For example, the homepage is blue with black text and yellow links. The first subpage has an orange background with blue links. The second subpage now has an image background and green links. The next subpage has a stripe down the left side that really doesn't do anything.

The site is made up of individual pages that can stand alone. Other than the fact that they are within the same Internet service provider (ISP) account, the pages have little to do with each other. In fact, the user can get quite confused and think he or she has left the site altogether.

That's not good.

Remember, you are setting out to build a Web site. The pages that make up the site should carry some element of consistency from page to page. Maybe a color, some images, or some other elements, but something must be there to hold the site together.

In addition, no one page should be seen as being any less or more important than any other page. The homepage is probably the most visited page on the site; that doesn't mean you should give it the lion's share of the attention.

When you design your site, which you start to do in Chapter 2, "Before You Write a Word," you need to make a point of deciding what subpages will accompany your homepage. Once you've made the decision to include that page, you must make a point of giving that subpage page equal attention in order to make it as well designed as any other.

Now let's look at the first three critiques.

Site Critiques

Over the years, I've been asked to review and critique numerous Web pages and sites. I've made a good many friends in the Web business and they often write to me and ask if I could tell them what I think of a new beta site design. It's always fun to get to see a site before anyone else sees it.

I asked the readers of the HTML Goodies "Goodies to Go!" newsletter to submit their sites for critique and for possible inclusion in this book. I expected to get around 100 submissions. I had to stop accepting after 1,500.

I'd like to tell you that the sites I review will always be there for you to go and visit, but most likely they won't. The Web is ever evolving and this book is pretty stable. The reviews contained might change or go away completely. Take the critiques for what they are, a snapshot of the site when I went in to see it.

The sites you see here run the gamut of programming ideas and levels. Every Web site has good points and every Web site has points that can be improved upon.

I offer these critiques as examples of the whole. I might touch on subjects here that have not come up in the book yet. That's fine. You'll recognize and understand them all the more when they do pop up.

The Funky Five (No Specific Author Listed)

`http://www.8op.com/thefunkyfive/`

Load Time: 57 Seconds, 57kps modem, cleared cache, 5/22/00 7:43AM.

My Screen Size: 1,024×768

Browsers Used: Internet Explorer 5 and Netscape Navigator 4.5

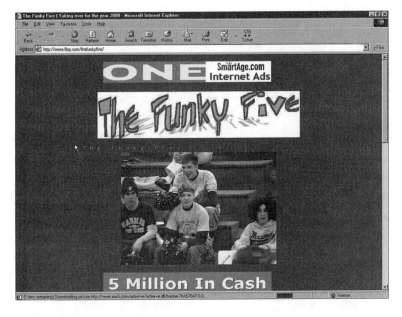

Figure 1.1
The Funky Five—showing only the Funky Four for some reason. (Color Plate C.1)

Concept: I chose this site first because it represents a great many sites out there on the Web. People want personal sites. They want to create their own little piece of the Web. In this case it's five guys who call themselves the "Funky Five—the most elite organization on earth. Its members are the epitome of greatness."

These five high school freshmen have put up a site that they want to represent them and their thoughts and beliefs. Good for the Funky Five. I mean that. Now, let's see if you can clean the site up a bit.

Praise: The site claims to be what it is and does not attempt to pull any punches. This is about the Funky Five, built by the Funky Five, and for fans of the Funky Five.

The information is geared to the site's purpose (which I will call the killer app very soon). The colors are good and the text and background color choices complement well. I can read every word.

Best of all—nowhere on the site did the young men get dirty or at all off-color. This is a clean site that had the potential to be a little blue. I compliment you for that, gentlemen.

Concern: The first thing I noticed upon entering the site was the page leads with an ad banner. No, the Funky five aren't selling space; this is an ad from a banner exchange service meant to drive traffic.

Now, I'm not against that, but I am against the placement. People's eyes move across a Web page from top to bottom, left to right. That ad banner is the first thing they see—thus—they perceive it to be the most important. This is why a lot of businesses put their logo in the upper-left corner. It's the first thing people see and it's the item they perceive as most important.

Suggestion: Lose the ad banner first and get your name up there. You can always snug that ad banner in on down the page.

Concern: The identifier image that reads "The Funky Five" is too large. The font (which I think I recognize as the "Ren and Stimpy" font) is blown up so large the letters are pixelating.

Suggestion: Go smaller on the letters or on the image itself. Don't blow an image up larger than it is supposed to go. If you want to enlarge then do it in an image editor so that the letters can stay true.

Concern: There's another ad banner. Why? You have one up top. Why are you giving a surfer the ability to leave your site twice? Does his leaving your site help your traffic? If you say yes because banner exchange sites give links to your site if people click your ad banners, go back and read the fine print. Usually you must have someone click twice on your page's ad banners to get one display of your page's ad. If everyone clicks every ad banner then two people must leave your site before one will come. You do the math.

Suggestion: Lose the second ad banner. There are better methods to getting more traffic than slowing your page with two ads.

Concern: Can you see, in the screen capture, the words "The Funky Five" next to the cursor? That's a DHTML effect that makes the letters snake around after my mouse. It was interesting for about a minute and then it became a real pain to work with. And guess what? It doesn't work in Netscape.

Suggestion: Lose it altogether. It does nothing for the page.

Concern: Where are the links? I see no way of moving around your site. I scroll a bit here...ah! There they are, well below the gatefold (the bottom of the browser window as shown in Figure 1.2).

Suggestion: Links go up high. They should be visible when the page loads. Hiding links is not assisting your users with their navigation of the site. Help your users. Don't make them have to search for anything.

Figure 1.2
The links are within an Inline Frame.

Concern: The inline frame format is actually a nice touch. It allows the user to stay on the same page. That allows great consistency, but it also creates one huge problem. The inline frame code simply does not work on Netscape Navigator.

> **Note**
>
> By the time of this book's publication, a version of Netscape may be out that supports inline frames, but I would still warn against using them without allowing for the problem. Just because a browser comes out that can support a certain effect does not mean you should immediately use the effect. Earlier versions of the same browser will still not support the command. You'll read that a few times in this book.

Suggestion: Try a traditional link system going from page to page.

Concern: There is yet one more banner trade ad banner on the page. That is simply too much for any surfer to handle.

Suggestion: Lose it altogether.

Concern: Each of the links open inside that inline frame. I'm proud of the designer because he (they are all guys, so I'm assuming it's a he) did keep each linked page small enough that it displayed pretty nicely inside the frame.

Suggestion: Again, traditional links let all Web surfers play with the site.

Overall: The site is not as bad as you might feel I am making it out to be, on the contrary. This site has great potential.

The people who keep the site update it and the information that they provide might actually be of interest to their demographic. If they stay with their purpose and continue to use this as a personal page to their group, I think they could have a nice little piece of the Web here.

The site needs to be better designed, though. This homepage is guilty of what I call stacking. Too often, first-time designers make a point of simply placing one element on top of another, on top of another, on top of another. That stacking makes for a long page that requires the audience to scroll. That's not good. Here's a rule of thumb:

> In terms of a Homepage: People don't mind clicking—they do mind scrolling.

Take a look at the site—is there a way you could get the text to be next to the snapshot image so that there is some left-to-right eye-movement across the page? Try it.

Do what you can to get the page onto one browser screen. If you cannot get it all onto a single browser screen, do not allow the scroll to go longer than two browser screens. Try not to allow the page to scroll more than one full browser screen, two total browser screens.

Oh, and one more thing...spellcheck that site. There are a few nasty misspellings. I didn't put this as a concern previously because it's happened too many times that I've told people that something was misspelled, when in fact it was misspelled on purpose. The author was following some form of hip lingo that I was simply too old to understand.

Take a look, fellahs. Are the words misspelled on purpose or because of a typo? If it's a typo—fix it!

Good luck, Funky Five. Keep up the good work and get rid of those ad banners.

Falcon Arrow—Anarchy Pro Wrestling (by Jonathan Cole)

`http://www.methane-inc.com/falcon/`

Load Time: 21 Seconds, 57kps modem, cleared cache, 5/22/00 9:10AM.

My Screen Size: 1,024×768

Browsers Used: Internet Explorer 5 and Netscape Navigator 4.5

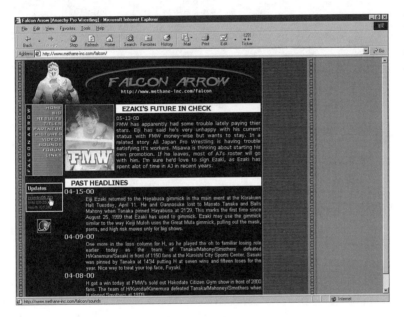

Figure 1.3
The Falcon Arrow wants to keep you up to date! (Color Plate C.2)

Concept: This is a fan page dedicated to wrestling. The topic may not be your cup of tea, but to those who enjoy the sport…er…entertainment, this page can be a winner.

Praise: Visually, this page is great. There is an identifier (you'll start to read that word a lot) in the top-left corner that the author carries across all pages. The text identifier is also carried across pages. It is very easy to know that you are still within the site while you move around.

There is also a secondary page shown in Figure 1.4.

The author has done what a lot of designers are doing lately. He has built a shell of sorts. The top and background remain the same. Only the middle section changes when people change pages, but this is not a frame setup. The images that carry across pages load very quickly because they are in the cache from the homepage and give the surfer reason to believe that everything else is going to follow just as quickly.

Figure 1.4

Subpages carry the same look and feel as the homepage.

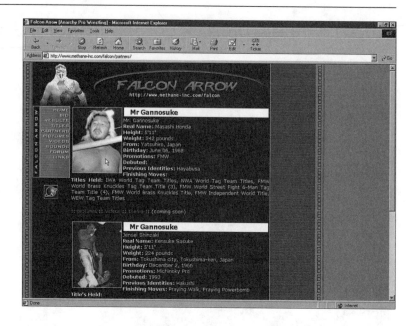

The author has made a point of setting every image's height and width within the inline image command, like so:

```
<IMG SRC="image.gif" HEIGHT="25" WIDTH="200">
```

That allowed the page's text to load very quickly. It looked like Figure 1.5 when the homepage first loaded.

That's very good, but it also leads me to my first concern.

Concern: The inline image flags do not have an ALT attribute included so there are no yellow ToolTip boxes that pop up. I know some people don't like the ToolTip boxes because they feel the boxes obscure the image. There may be some truth to that, but you need to use the ALT attribute so disabled-assistant (Americans with Disabilities Act (ADA) compliant) browsers and those persons browsing without the inline image turned on can also enjoy the site.

Suggestion: Use an ALT attribute in the inline images, like so:

```
<IMG SRC="image.gif" HEIGHT="25" WIDTH="200" ALT="wrestling picture">
```

Concern: You have no text equal to the image links in the main navigation block. Those who cannot see or use images can't successfully venture further into your site.

Suggestion: Put text equals, or maybe go with hypertext links fully.

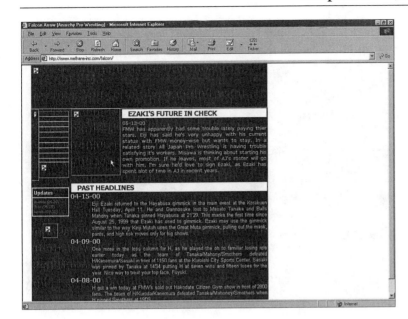

Figure 1.5
Every image is given its own space to load in.

Concern: There are rollovers on the text links (Updates) under the main block of navigation links, but there are no rollovers on the main navigation links.

Suggestion: Choose all rollovers or no rollovers, one or the other.

Overall: This is a good-looking site. When it loads, it loads fast and allows the user the get starting reading and clicking quickly.

The homepage does not scroll a great deal. That's very good. I still think you could get it all onto one screen, but that may be asking a bit much because the amount of text on the homepage does vary with the story.

A fan of this wrestling league could have a field day roaming around this site. Keep up the good work. Keep archives. This could be *the* site for this wrestling league if you keep it fresh for the audience.

Zaga Doo.com (by Ed Nichols)

`http://www.zagadoo.com/`

Load Time: 12 Seconds, 57kps modem, cleared cache, 5/22/00 10:28AM.

My Screen Size: 1,024×768

Browsers Used: Internet Explorer 5 and Netscape Navigator 4.5

Figure 1.6
What does Zaga Doo?
(Color Plate C.3)

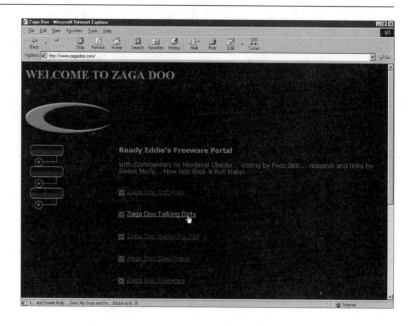

Concept: This was one of the very first sites to be submitted for critique. As soon as I saw the name, I knew I had to go and look at this thing. Anyone who would name a site Zaga Doo can't be all bad. The site offers reviews, downloads, and input on all kinds of software. The reviews I read were quick, to the point, and fairly helpful.

Praise: As I said previously, most of the stuff I read was helpful. The site is very easy to navigate. It is not held back by large images or overt navigation. It was easy to surf and the pages came in lightning fast.

Concern: I have the caption "What does Zaga Doo?" under the previous screen capture because it took me a little bit of time to figure out exactly what Zaga Doo did. The page loaded, I knew there were links to reviews of some kind, but past that I wanted to know more specifics. You certainly have space to provide more specific information.

Suggestion: At the top of the homepage, put a 20- to 30-word statement explaining exactly what the page is for. Don't make me click to learn about the site. Tell me right up front. State the site's killer app blatantly and immediately.

Concern: I don't get the three boxes that flow down the left side of the page. I've clicked, rolled over, and looked at source code. What do they do? I'm given the impression they're for some higher purpose because of their placement, but I get nothing.

Suggestion: It's confusing. Turn the images into links or add some text to explain it.

Concern: Why is there a new text scroll in the status bar on every page? In fact, why is there a text scroll in the status bar at all? The scroll doesn't help with the page's purpose. In fact, the scroll is a little annoying to those of who like to lay their pointers over the links and read the names of the pages and see if any of the links take them off site before they click.

Suggestion: Lose the scrolls, or make them much shorter and have them only scroll through once.

Concern: Why is this page so tall? There's no reason why this page has to be this long. There is a tremendous amount of whitespace to fill. Either fill it or take steps to eliminate it.

Suggestion: Scrunch it all together so that everything is on one screen. And make a link to the disclaimer rather than posting it in larger blocks of text than the links themselves.

Concern: The last two elements you have on the page are by far two of the most important, the updated stamp and your email. (Note: Neither of these is visible on the screen captures.)

Suggestion: This is a site that must stay fresh and let its users know how fresh it is. Get that stamp and that email up there higher so I see it right off.

Overall: Ready Eddie has a good purpose here that can be helpful. The writing on the sub-pages was quick and to the point. I understood it all.

The homepage needs to be reworked, though. At the moment it's a stacked page. Every element is on top of the next. Yes, there is some text next to the crescent image, but for the most part, the text just stacks up with a great deal of whitespace (made black by the background).

Pull it all together and post a statement explaining exactly what the site is for. Your users will love you for it.

Before You Write a Word

Freeze! Put the computer down! We have you surrounded!

Sorry for the startle, but if you're going to truly design a Web site you're going to need to get a few things straight first.

Here's what I would like you to do. This may seem a bit strange for some of you, but turn the computer off and grab yourself a pencil and some paper. If you're like me, you have absolutely no lined paper lying around the house, so just grab a few sheets out of the printer tray.

After years of working with HTML Goodies and designing too many sites to remember, I have found that the actual creation of the site goes much smoother if you first answer a few questions. There are five questions to be exact.

The Five Questions You Must Answer Before Beginning a Web Site

Let me point out once again that you are designing a Web site and not a Web page. Okay? Okay!

Too often I receive letters from people who have been charged by a boss or other superior to design and keep a company Web site. The boss gives no guidance and a deadline of sometime later that afternoon. The frantic email asks me to quickly describe what to write.

...is usually a list of questions. What is your business? What does the boss ...ite to do? Are you selling anything? How did you get chosen for this job? What ...the meaning of life? The reply often comes back with a few quickly drawn up answers that basically tell me little more than what I knew from the first one. The boss wants a Web site. He wants it by five.

I can't tell you how many letters I've received from military personnel asking for help because his superior wants a Web page...before nine. I guess the sergeant wants the site before nine because the army does more before nine a.m. than anyone else. (Rimshot sound effect goes here. Thanks, folks...I'm here all week.)

After helping a lot of people get started with a slew of business, military, organization, and personal sites, I've succeeded in creating a first step to Web page design. The following are five questions that you simply must answer fully before writing one word of text or HTML code.

If you don't know the answers to these questions then you're going to put up a site that doesn't represent you and a site that doesn't do what you want it to do. It will be a site that you're going to have to rewrite numerous times before hitting on the formula you should have laid out in the first place.

Sites that are coded before a plan is laid out become just what they are—code. The pages become testimonies to every trick the author knows. Text is bold or italic because, well, it can be. An image is animated because it can be. The background is bright pink because, well, I don't know. I can't think of a stunning reason for a background to be bright pink right off. However, I know there's a good reason because right now, somewhere on the Web, is a site with a glaring pink background that looks great. I'll bet that site took the time to choose that background color rather than just do it because, well, they could.

At this point, I don't care if you already have a site you're looking to redesign of if your site is simply a twinkle in your cyber-eye. Stop. Put the computer down. Take up a writing utensil, and write out good full answers to the following five questions.

Question One: Who Is Your Site For?

Yes, that is terrible English grammar, but it's a great question. Let me illustrate a bit further. The first time I taught HTML in a class setting, the group of students had to put together a final project, which was to build a Web site. I'm sorry to say I taught the class incorrectly. I never really delved into the design of the site itself. I simply threw a lot of coding at the students and said that they should use it and build their own site.

When I began grading those final projects, I ran into a lot of poorly built sites. I found page after page of images and colors that had no bearing whatsoever to the site's purpose. I remember one page distinctly. It had a pink background color, a butterfly, multiple dog and cat images—some animated—and an ad banner for a heavy metal band.

It looked horrible, like the person put no thought into the page. It looked like the author simply put together any and all elements that she liked for the entire world to see.

I had to ask her why she put such a page together. I was right. Her answer was something like, "I just liked all that stuff."

Ah, the message is starting to come in clearly. Can you see it yet?

In the same class, a young man put together a page devoted to his favorite musical group. I don't know why young men go for those black backgrounds, but in every class I teach, at least half of the young men go for the black backgrounds. Mind you, I don't have a thing against black backgrounds. They're very striking if done correctly. His wasn't. Over the background the young man had dark blue text. I couldn't read it. I squinted and blurred my vision and grabbed the side of the computer to attempt to stop the dark blue letters from moving around on the black background, but to no avail.

I thought that no one could enjoy this page. I marked off some points for the mistake and went on. When the student received the grade, he was upset and contacted me. He said that he put the text into dark blue because that's the way he liked it. I told him that it was very hard to read. That didn't matter. That was the way he liked it. See the problem? Using the student's logic, one could basically do anything on a Web site and as long as the author likes it then it's correct. Right?

Wrong!

Design Goodies Survey

Goodies Survey Question: Whom do you primarily design your Web sites for?

Me	45.2%
My visitors	21.5%
Clients	19.5%
Client Customers	4.5%
No Response	10.0%

N=485

I'd like to turn these results around so that all Web designers understand that the wants of their audience must come first.

Whom is your site for? If your answer is "My site is for me" then stop reading. You don't need me. In fact, you don't need anyone. If your site is just for you then design concerns are out the window. Design to please yourself and don't worry about what anyone else thinks.

Please don't think this is a bad thing, either. Many people might be happy with designing a site just for themselves. I'm not, but you might be. Personally, I'd like people to come to my Web site. So, my answer to the question, "Whom is your site for" is "my visitors."

That's who really matters, isn't it? Aren't you designing for them? Isn't the real concept of having this page to attract visitors and keep them happy while they're in your site so that they'll return sometime soon?

Yes, it is.

The Web Is Not a Mass Medium. The Web Is One to One

This is a point that you need to understand. If you can get this idea in your head, you'll end up building much better Web sites.

I think the reason a lot of Web designers tend to design the way they do is because they believe the Web is a mass medium. A mass medium is a medium, like television or radio, where one signal is being broadcast to a mass of people. Take television, for example. It is a mass medium. You have no say over what is on Sunday nights at 8 p.m. The network decides that. You simply decide to watch or not. If you watch, you are part of a mass audience.

You may think the Web is mass because you create a site and an audience comes and looks. It is not. Think about it. When you surf, who is in charge? You are. Who decides what topic is covered during that particular surfing session? Who decides how long you stay in a site? Who decides what is good and bad about the sites you look at?

You do. The Web is not mass to the surfer. It is one to one—one surfer to one designer's site.

I often tell students that the average time a surfer waits for a site to load before leaving is 15 seconds. Some students act almost offended. I talk about how an audience member leaves a site if he cannot easily read the text. I talk about how most surfers report that they leave a site if background music starts to play.

One time a student said that the audience was really petty and lazy. No, they're not. They're not petty and lazy. They are in charge. They are in charge of their own destiny and once you force something upon them that they don't like, they are gone from your site.

Think about your own surfing habits. I'll bet you've left a site because of something that you disliked that was very minor. You weren't petty and lazy, were you? Nope. You were in charge.

So, whom is your site for? Your visitors. Why? It's because they are in charge.

Super! We've made a breakthrough. Now...

Who Are Your Visitors?

Now that you've established that your site is for your visitors, let's delve further. Who exactly are your visitors?

On that piece of paper, write out one sentence that describes your most common visitor. Here are a few parameters you may want to include:

1. Is the visitor male or female? Could the visitor be either?

2. What is the visitor's age range? Try to keep this within a 15-year range. At least decide whether your most common visitor would be under or over 30 years of age.

3. Are the visitors coming because of business or leisure activity?

If you can answer just those three questions, you'll pretty much have the answer. Yes, I know you can delve far deeper into the question of who would come to your site, but I'm not looking for rocket science here. I want to know generally who will be coming to your site.

By the way, here is the answer you're not allowed to give:

> Anyone on the net is a possible visitor to my site.

No, they're not. There was a time when the answer was true. I remember people putting pages around 1995 or 1996 that contained nothing more than a résumé, some commentary pages, a couple of pictures, and a list of favorite links. They would draw visitors with just that. Of course, at that time the Web was new enough that anything was worth visiting. My most visited page at that time was dedicated to my two cats and their goofy quirks. Times have changed. The Web is growing by tens of thousands of pages per day. Just throwing up a site aimed at no one in particular is not enough anymore. The people who come to the Web can no longer be quickly categorized into male tech-heads who dig anything cyber. Have you got it? Did you write down the sentence? If not, do it now. Take some time. I'll still be here when you get back. (Waiting...waiting...waiting...)

Okay, now that you have a general description on who will come to your site, what does that person want? Don't get specific here, just stay general at this point.

Too often someone rushes forward without taking the time to decide who will make up the bulk of his audience as you are doing right now. That usually results in a page that contains every new whiz-bang thing out there. There are search engines and bulletin boards, chat rooms and Guestbooks, under construction images and pictures of the family dog, plus all the author's thoughts on how the military is somehow spying on his innermost thoughts.

I see these types of sites all the time. It's a mish-mash of every cool coding trick under the sun, posted with little or no regard for the audience. The author saw someone else had a new trick and he had to have it. Forget about if anyone would actually use it or not. That's secondary to a lot of Web designers. The author's main concern was to have his coding done first and attract visitors later. Let's not do that. Instead, let's look at your answer to the first question. Will your site draw predominantly men, women, or both?

I'd love to be able to take the time to write out all the things men like in a Web site and then all the things women like in a Web site, but I can't. Sure, I can give you a pretty good snapshot of how things are at the time I was writing this book in May of 2000, but the Web changes so often that what I tell you now will probably not hold up for six months. Here's a case in point.

In November 1999 through May 2000, the number of women making their way onto the Web had increased by nine million. Five years before today, women made up only 10 percent of all online users. Today it's even-Steven. Men and women are equally represented on the Web. No longer can a Web designer go online and simply assume the vast majority of his audience will be male. Women have entered the Web with a vengeance and they don't like the same things that men like.

According to a survey by the Pew Internet and American Life Project, men like Web pages that are full of factual information. They want quick statistics. Men surf mostly for scores, stocks, and other financial information.

Women, on the other hand, surf for far more long-form information covering religion, family, and especially health.

Men see the Web as something they do alone. Women see the Web as a community and they want to interact with that community. One of the biggest sites on the Web attracting women is iVillage.com (see Figure 2.1).

Figure 2.1
They don't call it a Village for nothing.

I don't know whether you can read the main headings across the top of the figure. They are Join Free, email, chat, boards, experts, games, feedback, membercenter.

See how the site is playing to a female audience? Each one of the previous elements is geared to community. They are all asking someone to join or get in touch with another person.

Whoa! Some of you might be laughing at me right now. I listed games as being a heading, but games are a man thing. Women don't play games, right?

Wrong.

In fact, according to the same Pew survey, women play more online games than men do. Really. Yahoo! Internet Life magazine did an entire cover story on just that fact. If you had gone with your stereotypical thinking, you would have missed that little, but important, tidbit of information.

> **Note**
>
> Please note that in this discussion about a site being geared to male or female, I am speaking in generalities gathered from my own research and in terms of the two sites specifically mentioned here. The concept that a perfect line is drawn between the likes and dislikes of male and female is never black and white. There are always shades of gray. Just please take this discussion as a starting point for you to recognize that there are differences between a male- or female-dominated audience.

Okay, so what about a site geared to men? How about ESPN.com (see Figure 2.2)?

Figure 2.2
Get me the info I want and get it fast.

If you notice nothing else, notice the number of links and the use of darker colors. That indicates strength. The iVillage.com site used more pastel shades. The ESPN site is geared to getting users to the sport they want quickly. Information is presented in table format. Scores and statistics just lend themselves to a fast quantitative display. So, will it be men or women?

I also asked you to write down if the common visitor to your site was under or over 30. Why? Because it's been shown that up until around the age of 30, men and women's Web habits are fairly equal. Past the age of 30, how men and women use the Web start to diverge. That kind of kills the whole man or woman discussion if you are aimed at a very young audience, huh? Isn't this fun?

Let me stop here because all this information I'm giving you will probably be useless to you once this book has been out a year. Things move that fast on the Web. The point I am trying to make in this first section is that you must first determine whom your site is for. Once you have that, you simply must make a point of finding out the habits, likes, and dislikes of those who will be coming to your site. That way you can build your site for your visitors.

But where do you get the information?

It's time to do what I call "using the beast to describe the beast."

The Web is overflowing with sites that want to tell you all about the Web and those that use it. If you are interested in building a Web site, have the sites shown in Figures 2.3-2.6 bookmarked for future use.

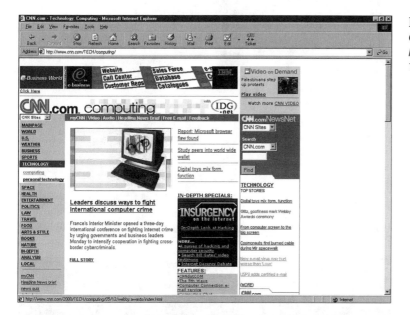

Figure 2.3

CNN Technology:
`http://www.cnn.com/`
`TECH/computing/.`

Figure 2.4

USA Today Tech:
`http://www.usatoday.`
`com/life/cyber/.`

Figure 2.5
ZDNet:
`http://www.zdnet.com/.`

Figure 2.6
Wired:
`http://www.wired.com/.`

The reason I like those particular sites is because I always find reports on surveys done by other groups. Those Web surveys are often the best place to gather information about how those who use the Web...use the Web.

There are also a great many sites that perform and then post the results of their surveys on their Web sites. There are others but the ones shown in Figures 2.7 and 2.8 are my favorites.

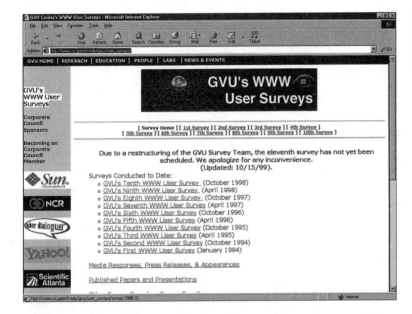

Figure 2.7
GVN:
`http://www.cc.gatech.`
`edu/gvu/user_surveys/.`

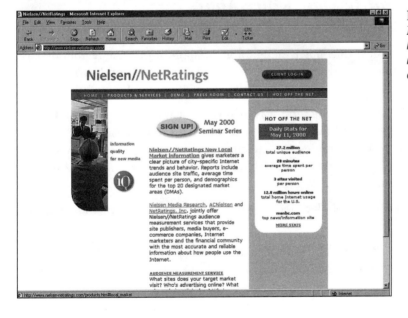

Figure 2.8
Nielsen Netratings:
`http://www.`
`nielsen-netratings.`
`com/.`

I don't expect you to read everything every day at these sites. I am offering them as a way for you to gather general information regarding your most common visitor. Once visitors start coming to your Web site, they should become your main source of information regarding what people who come to your site want from your site. Ask. Allow users to give feedback and take that feedback seriously. Don't bask in the glory of a nice comment and dismiss a negative comment as the ramblings of a jerk.

Yes, I know you want to start writing and I know you want to get pages to the Web, but take my word for it at this point you've done more for your Web site than you can imagine. You now know whom your Web site will be geared toward. You have a general mental picture of your visitor.

If you believe your site will be visited by mainly male or female then gear the content that way. If you believe the site will be visited by male and female equally then gear the content by age. If you believe the entire Web population will be drawn to your Web site, try again. Your description isn't quite specific enough. You will have an audience. Gear your site toward it. Read how users use the Web. Ask people who fall into your user description what they like in a Web site. Research. I know it's a word that makes people think of boring hours in a quiet library, but it's the best way to go about picking and describing an audience.

Okay—Question One is behind us. There are four more to go.

Question Two: What Is Your Killer App?

Your first question might be, "What in the world is a killer app?"

Here's how I explain it. The term *killer app* is slang for great application. The telephone has a killer app. It allows you to talk to people all over the world. The television has a killer app. It brings programming into your home. The stove has a killer app. It cooks your food.

Yes, I know this isn't exactly the way the term was used when it was first created, but I am co-opting it for my own purposes. I find it's a title that students can understand. They can get their brains around the subject. Besides, the meanings of words and phrases change over time. Remember when "bad" meant "bad." Thanks to Michael Jackson, I think it means "good" now. Go figure.

Because the term is geared to the Web, let's look at very popular sites and their killer apps (see Figures 2.9–2.13).

I want you to notice one thing about each of these sites. They are all very popular for, I believe, one reason. They have only the one killer app.

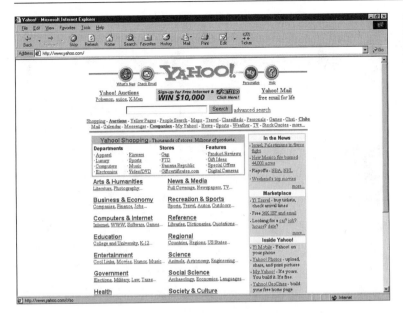

Figure 2.9
Yahoo.com Killer App: It catalogs and searches the Web for you.

Figure 2.10
eBay.com Killer App: It sets up auctions.

Figure 2.11

NAPSTER.com Killer App: It helps you find music on the Web.

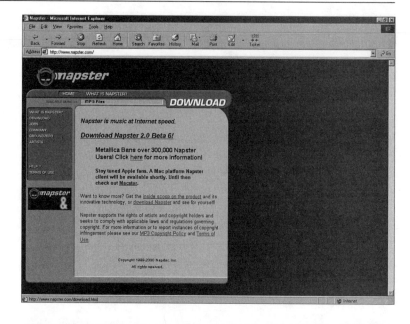

Figure 2.12

AutoByTel.com Killer App: It helps you buy a car.

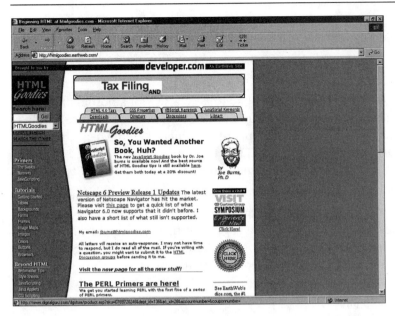

Figure 2.13
HTML Goodies.com Killer App: It teaches you to build a Web site.

Allow me to again relive my days as a disc jockey. The rule of thumb was every time the jock opened the mic to talk, he was to go into one topic and one topic alone. If the jock would talk about the weather, then his shoes, then the next songs coming up, then something else, the information would all become jumbled up in the listener's mind and the main push of the break, the weather, would have been forgotten. It's the same thing here. You should have only one killer app per site.

Instead of trying to be all things to all users, the previous sites stay true to their single killer app. Yes, Yahoo! has branched out into games, and stocks, and auctions, but they did it by creating separate sites. When you arrive at Yahoo.com, that site only has one purpose, to search. You have to leave that search engine page to get to the other elements.

Let's look into that. If Yahoo! would have attempted to be all things to all people from a single Web site then users would have done all searches from a single text box. It would have slowed the system, words would have become jumbled and the mistake of returning unusable links would be committed again and again. As it stands now, you go to a fully separate site to search stocks, a separate site to perform auctions, and so on.

HTML Goodies could easily have gone into selling software and reviewing books and any number of other areas. They have all been offered and all have been turned down. HTML Goodies has one killer app. It teaches you what you need to build a Web site.

Your Web site cannot be all things to all people. You won't attract a larger audience by being a fan page to seven different TV shows. You will garner a larger, and quite possibly more loyal audience if you pick one killer app and stick with it. It is also easier to create a site geared to one thought rather than multiple areas.

I had a gentleman tell me at a trade show that he had to keep a site for a hospital that had multiple areas under one heading. He said that it all had to be one site. I told him it didn't. My suggestion was to keep the main logo in the upper-left corner of all the pages, but to differentiate each section as a site in and of itself. The logo would serve to remind the user that this site was under the bigger umbrella of hospital, but still was a site unto itself.

For instance, let's say the domain was Hospital.com. Under that umbrella there are three divisions, pediatrics, respiratory, and surgery. The author could have chosen a single look for the site like a certain background or look to the pages, but then differentiated each area into a different site. Maybe pediatrics would be blue, respiratory is pink, and surgery is yellow. Furthermore, each section could be made a separate virtual area under the main heading. There could be

```
http://pediatrics.hospital.com

http://respiratory.hospital.com

http://surgery.hospital.com
```

Just like Yahoo!, the areas are similar enough that the user knows they all fall under the main umbrella, but different enough that each has its own site. Notice that each of the previous elements above would even bookmark as separate sites. That's very important. I would even go as far as to make sure that each site had a different TITLE text format so that if a user bookmarks two of them, the text won't be confusing.

Let's say you're one of the many people who write to me saying your boss has laid the job of putting up the company Web site on your shoulders. Finding whom your site is for is fairly easy. Who are your customers? Most likely, that's who your common visitor will be.

Now the question of the killer app comes to light. This is actually the hard one.

What Do You Want the Site to Do?

Will it sell product or will the site act as a simple Public Relations vehicle?

If the site will sell product then you need to create something that will support your killer app. You'll have to put your catalog online. Users will need to be able to find information about your product. You'll need to have a staff to take the orders and a system built to take orders online. It's a pretty big decision.

If your site is a Public Relations vehicle meant to give you a Web presence, you'll need to fill the site with a reason for the customer to come again and again. Take complaints online. Offer the company records online. Put the catalog online. Make sure the user can contact people to find out more. Update the site frequently.

Both killer apps can be very important to a company. I suggest you do one or the other. If you try to do both, unless you hire a full time staff, you'll never devote enough attention to either, especially if you're a secretary who has just been saddled with the responsibility of putting up a site.

To you bosses out there...stop doing that. Your administrative assistants and enlisted personnel have my permission to take this text to your superior and show them my plea from them to stop doing that.

If you absolutely must have two killer apps, my suggestion is to start two different sites. That's how strongly I believe in this concept.

So, what's your killer app? Remember that piece of paper you scribbled on just a moment ago? Use that again and write down your site's killer app.

Personal Sites

People love to put up personal sites. I have one. I think they are wonderful, but I ask you again. What is your killer app?

Design Goodies Survey

Goodies Survey Question: Do you ever go out onto the Web specifically to look for personal homepages?

Yes	70.5%
No	29.5%

N=487

The one quality that has never left the Web is the love of simple personal homepages. I think that's great. Go ahead, put up a homepage dedicated to you. You've earned it.

Let's say your name is Debbie Washington and you create "Debbie Washington's World of Wonder."

Okay, fine. Good title. What is your killer app?

What was the purpose of putting up the pages? If the answer is something like, "Well, every one else has one," or "I just wanted one," start again.

Here are a few killer apps I think might be appropriate for personal pages:

> I am about to graduate from college. My site is an interactive résumé containing all my previous work experience and links to those sites. I have a writing sample, my core beliefs, examples of my Web abilities, and reference email addresses so the entire hiring process can be done right from my site.

> I play a lot of computer games. I have put up a site so I can review the games I play. I also have a place where other game players can comment on my reviews or leave their own reviews.

> I am a poet and I use my personal Web site to post my poetry. I update it weekly so people will have a reason to return to the site to read more.

> My hobby is beekeeping. My site is dedicated to helping those who want to be beekeepers get up and running correctly. I offer my own advice, stories of success and failure, as well as links to other sites that might help.

> My site is dedicated to what I will wear today. People who come to the site can click a calendar and see a photo of what I wore that day

Does the last one seem kind of silly? If so, good. The site is whimsical. It's not going to change the world, but it sounds like something I could get hooked on. I'll take twenty seconds out of my day to quickly click and see what the person wore that day. I think that's fun.

I've seen sites dedicated to performing experiments on marshmallow Easter bunnies and a running total of a person's weight loss attempts. The weight never varied more than 10 pounds either way, but I went every day for at least a month. I even wrote and offered encouragement.

Note

I made these statements about personal Web sites while delivering this chapter as a lecture to a group of designers. One gentleman told me that I was right in terms of corporate sites, but not for personal sites. He believed that personal sites are for the person and design concerns should not even play into the mix. If you believe that, please let me talk you out of it. Just because the topic is you rather than a business does not mean that the surfers are any less important or any less willing to leave if you do something they don't like. You won't get any more forgiveness from a surfer just because you posted a personal page. Personal pages must take design into mind as much as any business page.

I once spent an entire evening in a site that simply allowed people to post their stories about snorkeling in Mexico. Each previously mentioned site might not be your cup of tea, but they all have one thing in common, they have one killer app. They are not trying to be all things to all people. Yes, some of the sites offer chat rooms, or bulletin boards, and links, but all those things are geared to one idea, the site's killer app.

Now it's your turn. Take that piece of paper and write down your future site's killer app. You should be able to do it in one or two simple sentences. When you have it, move along to question three.

Question Three: What Is Your Identification?

This is often overlooked when someone is putting together a personal site so I wanted to make sure you make a point of thinking about it now.

Please understand that I do not mean slogan. I mean identification. A slogan is much more a verbal thing then a static visual. I'm looking for a static visual here.

By your identification I mean, what will act as a representation of your site? I can break these identifiers down into four broad categories: logo, character, text, color.

Please understand I don't mean for you to have one of each, although you can. HTML Goodies uses all four. Just one of the four will do just fine if that's all you'd like to use.

Your identifier should be something that is unique to your site. It should be something that defines and identifies your site. If you were to make a small banner image to hand out to people, this identifier would be that banner. The identifier should represent your site to the point that if I see it somewhere else on the Web, I would know it represents your site. This is why I say that you needn't have all four. One will do the trick because one is really all you can use elsewhere on the Web. Let's look at the four in depth.

Logo As Identifier

This is easiest when a logo already exists for the company or organization for which you're making the site. The CBS homepage is a pretty good example of logo use (see Figure 2.14).

You can basically take that eye logo and put it anywhere and it will represent CBS. But the logo doesn't have to be a famous one that existed before the Web. Figure 2.15 illustrates a Web page a student of mine put together for phantomvoice.net.

The student created that logo in about 20 minutes in a shareware image editor. His site isn't famous yet, but when it is, that logo will act as his site's identifier. Those of you who think making a logo is out of your grasp, take another look at the PV logo. You can make something like that.

Figure 2.14
Count the number of times you see that CBS eye logo.

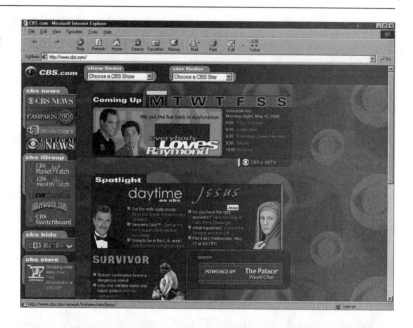

Figure 2.15
See the Circle-PV in the upper-left corner?

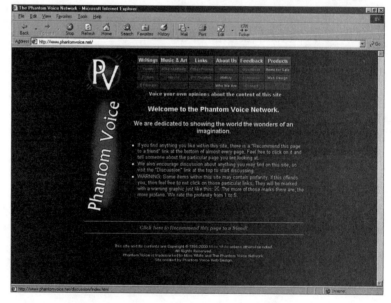

In fact, the identifier logo doesn't even have to be a logo per se. It can be a picture or an object. Figure 2.16 shows a Web site I built my father for Christmas 1998. It's a Web page devoted to his Air Force squadron.

Figure 2.16
603rd AC&Wpage at
`http://www.`
`i-55.com/~joe/`.

See that arch in the picture? That arch is found on every page and on every piece of paper associated with the squadron. That arch is their symbol and thus it has become their identifier. Any links back to the site will include that arch.

Now, if you have a business you're doing a page for, your logo is pretty well set. If you're not lucky enough to have a premade logo then try your hand at making one, or find someone to make one for you. Maybe you've seen an odd image somewhere that you feel would be a good logo identifier. Just don't pick something that already identifies something else. That's confusing to an audience. For example, maybe you like the CBS eye logo. Don't take it and print your name in the middle for your identifier. For one, it's illegal, and for two, it's confusing. People will continue to identify the logo with CBS, not your site.

I'll use the next story as a segue into the next little section of identifiers, characters. It's a good example of why once you pick a logo, or character, you should stick with it.

Characters As Identifiers

I used a goofy drawing I had done for me at an amusement park as my logo for HTML Goodies. Most people know it. It's the one on the front cover of this book.

After I had had the image posted for a couple of years, I had changed my hair, shaved off the beard, gotten better-looking glasses, lost 20 pounds, and became a better dancer. To stay with my current look, I went out and had another drawing made. I scanned it up and posted it in place of the old one.

Wow! People wrote in droves asking where my old drawing had gone. They told me flat out that they hated the new drawing. Some even said it didn't look like me even though they had never seen me. I felt like Coca-Cola did after presenting the New formula.

People had become accustomed to the character. They associated HTML Goodies with that character and when I took the character away, people got upset. They asked whether I was going to change the site. Some demanded I bring back the old character or they would stop coming.

This really happened. I'm not clever enough to make something like this up.

Here's the point. If you go with a logo, or a character, as your site's identifier, pick one you like first. Once people start coming and associating your site with that logo then you are stuck with it.

It's very hard to change identifiers in the middle of the game. People will identify your site with your identifier. If you keep changing it, people will begin to refer to your site as "the site formerly known as..." or they won't refer to you at all. That's not good.

I'm thinking of growing the beard back.

Okay, so maybe you don't want a logo, how about a character? The following are three of my favorite identifying characters from the Web.

Ask Jeeves

I can't think of a better name to call a butler (see Figure 2.17). In addition, the character goes to the site's killer app. What does Askjeeves.com do? It searches. It helps you. What does a butler do? He helps you. The character does more than act as an identifier, it acts as reinforcement for the killer app. This is just a perfect character choice.

My Simon

Simon will do your shopping for you (see Figure 2.18). The best part about Simon is that he dresses up in different costumes in order to denote different elements of the site. This goes to multiple sites all under one umbrella. You know you're in MySimon.com, but furthermore you know you're in a specific section of MySimon.com.

The Spider

That spider has been on the Webcrawler.com page since day one (see Figure 2.19). It's great that Webcrawler.com never tried to change their character identifier and replace the spider. I would really miss the little guy.

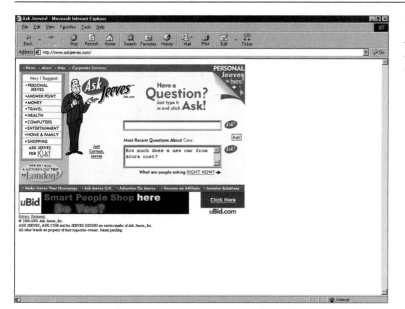

Figure 2.17
Ask Jeeves at
`http://www.askjeeves.`
`com/.`

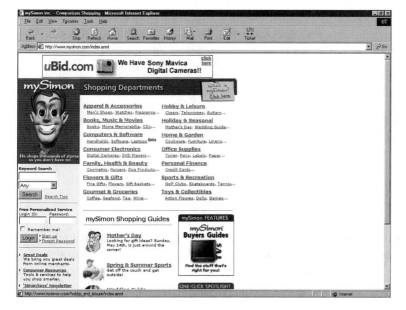

Figure 2.18
My Simon at
`http://www.mysimon.`
`com/.`

Figure 2.19
The Spider at
`http://www.webcrawler.`
`com.`

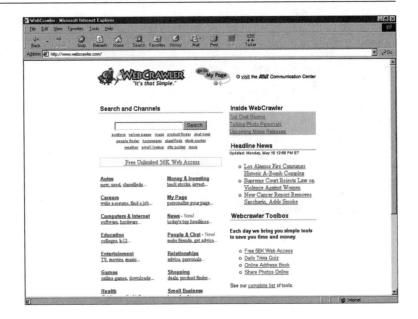

The thing about using a character as your identifier is that it really personalizes your site. AskJeeves.com is nothing more than a search engine, but because of the character you have the impression that there's a butler actually doing the work for you.

MySimon.com wants you to picture that little guy running from store to store, checking prices for you. The Webcrawler.com spider goes and gets the pages you request.

As I mentioned earlier, you can dress these characters up many different ways. Why not put Jeeves into a red and green jacket at Christmas time?

Why not put bunny ears on Simon at Easter?

Why not make the spider body into a pumpkin at Halloween?

The possibilities of using a character are endless.

I was asked to create a homepage for a school I worked for one time. Because I think most university homepages are dull and boring, I decided to create a character. This character would be named Dr. Walter Wendell Winchester or, as the students used to refer to him, "Old WWW."

Get it?

I found an art student who drew Old WWW in a graduation cap and gown left open so you could see his three-piece suit. He was heavy with a big nose and moustache and just looked that part of an older university dean.

I had 20 different pictures drawn of Old WWW throwing a football, singing a song, talking on the radio, mixing beakers, in a nursing uniform, and so on.

It's one of the few characters I wish had come to life, but never did. Hey, maybe you can use the idea. Feel free.

Had it come to life, the character would have represented the entire site not only as an identifier, but also as a specific type of identifier. He would be a dean so the character would obviously have represented a school or university. It would have all pointed to the killer app.

If you would like to use a character, my suggestion is to make your own. Don't use a character that already exists like Mickey Mouse or Bugs Bunny. For one, you'll get into copyright problems, but more to the point, those don't represent your site. Get something that represents just you.

Find someone with some artistic abilities and get them to draw out some sketches. If you know someone who is good with graphic programs, maybe they can make one for you.

Getting a character is not hard nor is it expensive, just be sure you're happy with the one you decide on. That little drawing will become your identifier and it'll be hard to change in the future. Only Prince gets to change his name again and again. You don't. One more note on characters. You have noticed that MySimon.com has changed the look of the character. They made him less a doll and more a human form. You may have also seen that Kentucky Fried Chicken updated the Colonel.

In both cases, it doesn't feel right. Yes, it's the same character but they are somehow incorrect because they have been updated. Tradition is gone and the character is now hip and cool. The problem is that hip and cool goes out of fashion very quickly.

My suggestion is that a character shouldn't be updated unless something about that character is so tragically out of date that it could cause harm to the product. What that means in a nutshell is to take a good long look at your character before you make that character your permanent identifier. Shoot for longevity before hip and cool.

Text As Identifiers

Take another moment and look back at the WebCrawler screen capture. Notice that the logo is so much more than just the spider. The text is part of the logo. That orange block font where the "W" and the "C" are capitalized and outlined in thick black represents Webcrawler.com as much as the spider.

That leads me into my third style of identifier. Text. The following sites are my favorites.

Amazon.com

Some may consider this header a logo, but I don't (see Figure 2.20). This identifier is text. Notice the "Amazon" is always bold and the "com" is not. The letters are in lowercase and that smile is a nice touch. What if you saw this and the "A" were capitalized? That wouldn't be right...right? There would be something wrong with that. That "A" is supposed to be lowercase. That's the thing about identifiers. Pick one you like up front. Even the smallest change can be unsettling to a user.

Figure 2.20

Amazon.com at
`http://www.amazon.com/`.

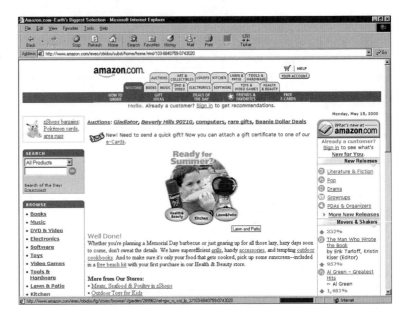

Straight Dope

There's nothing fancy here (see Figure 2.21). The identifier is straight block capital letters. It looks great—if you think you can't make an identifier because of a lack of artistic talent, take this one as your guide. All this guy did was type in all caps. You can operate at that level I would assume.

Street Artist

I like text identifiers a great deal. Figure 2.22 is a page I built for my wife's Web business StreetArtist.com. The identifier will be the text "StreetArtist.com." Notice only the "S" and the "A" are capitalized. The font face is called BlackChancery. The font follows through the site showing up just about everywhere. I want people to recognize that text and that font as her site no matter where they see it.

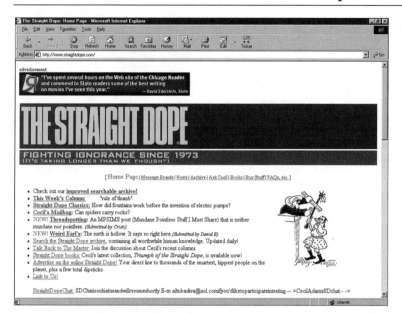

Figure 2.21
The Straight Dope at
`http://www.`
`straightdope.com/`.

Figure 2.22
Street Artist at
`http://www.`
`streetartist.com/`.

If you feel a text identifier is for you then go for it. Text identifiers are great because they are within the reach of just about everyone. If you can type, you can pretty much make a text identifier.

The only real rule of thumb in creating text identifiers is that the text must not only read the site name, it has to say what the site is all about. It should represent the site's killer app.

In the previous examples, the text for StreetArtist.com was elegant rather than block. The block was great for StraightDope.com because it looked like newspaper print.

Other text examples I've seen are digital letters used for a game room Web page, letters made from wicker for a wicker store, and text that appeared to be written in crayon by a three-year-old for a children's clothing store. It wouldn't have surprised me if the logo was literally written by a three-year-old and scanned.

Text is easy. That doesn't mean you should give it any less thought than you would a logo or a character. It is, after all, your identifier.

Color, Color, Color...

Now, let's talk about color. If you remember when I first listed the four identifiers, I wrote color last.

The reason is that color itself cannot act as an identifier. It certainly isn't an identifier that can leave your site and represent you elsewhere. I highly doubt someone will ever be able to create a simple red square and have everybody realize that red represents the site.

By color I am talking about your site in general. Will you use a specific color as an identifier when the person is in the site?

I am asked a great deal why I chose orange as the predominant color for the HTML Goodies site. Some have theorized it is because I am from Cleveland and am a big fan of the Browns. That's not it.

When I first started the site, I was lucky enough to get in with a company called Wolverine Web Productions, now known as Go Beyond Media.

The people at Wolverine Web Productions were real design thinkers and they made me pay attention to every detail of the site. I was told to pick a color that would help register the site in people's minds. When someone comes to the site, that's the color he will see and that will help to reinforce that that person is in the HTML Goodies site.

This is not a new idea. Associating color with a product has been done as long as advertising has been around. What if all of a sudden Coke started coming in blue cans? What if Pepsi started coming in red? What if Mountain Dew started coming in purple cans? What if McDonald's started making their arches orange?

It just wouldn't be right, would it? Color matters.

I chose orange not because of the Browns or because I thought it was a great color, but rather because it was a color I just never saw on the Web. I went surfing around to look at the colors that other sites were using. Every color of the rainbow popped up except orange.

We'll go with orange. It's now one of the HTML Goodies identifiers.

Think about your site. What will be your predominant color? What color will help to reinforce in the user's mind that they are in your site? Also—how does that color go to the killer app?

If you're using a logo, maybe you should pull a color from the logo. The StreetArtist.com page uses a deep red for the main color because the background image has hints of that color. It helps to bring out the flowers.

Just remember that when you pick a color, just like the text, that color must complement the site's killer app.

A site devoted to gothic literature wouldn't use pink. That just doesn't work. A site dedicated to good health wouldn't use black. Again, it just isn't right. Find that complementary color that not only complements the rest of the site, but also speaks to the site's killer app.

The only colors to think about avoiding are extreme bright colors. Maybe you have a site for a punk band and you want screaming bright colors. Well, you may want to think it through before you go with it. In fact, create a sample page for yourself and try to stare at it for five minutes.

I'll bet you can't and that's the main reason to avoid those bright colors.

So, let's get back to that piece of paper. Take your pen in hand and write down a few of the ideas you have about an identifier. You don't have to create it right now, just write down a few good ideas. Think them over. Try to picture how each would look as part of your site.

Maybe you should try one of each. Whatever you do, just be sure you're completely happy with the identifier you choose because, as I've tried to burn into your mind throughout this entire section, it's very hard to get an audience to change their thinking and accept a new identifier after they're already linked you with one.

Are you ready for the last two questions?

Questions Four and Five: Who Is Your Competition? and What Makes Your Site Different?

I always ask the final two questions together because you can't answer one without answering the other.

At this point in time you should have a piece of paper with some bits of information written down. You should have your audience somewhat defined, your killer app defined, and your identifier and predominant color written out. I understand these writings may not represent your final decisions, but at least you've pointed yourself down a path. You have an aim in mind.

I am now going to ask you to do one of the most humbling things you've ever done. I want you to go out onto the Web and search your competition. I want you to find other sites that are doing something similar to the ideas you've written out.

If you are building a Web page for a business, search your competition and other sites selling something similar to yours. If you are putting up a personal page, search for pages that have chosen the same topic as you have.

I say this is a humbling exercise because your searching very often brings you to pages that are very well done or are doing exactly what you want to do. It can get quite discouraging and can sometimes make the best of you want to scrap the whole idea.

Don't. You simply must do this. You must know what else is out there. You must understand who else is vying for the same audience you are after. Better yet, you have to know whom you intend on taking audience from.

Maybe you won't want to scrap the entire idea. That's good. Maybe you'll just think every other site sucks. I say that because I've seen it happen. Students get very defensive and do nothing but nay-say every site they see.

I hear over and over again, "this stinks," "this stinks," "this stinks."

You know what? No, it doesn't. Not everything stinks. In fact, the majority will be very good. Don't get defensive. Take each site as help or as assistance for you to create a better site for yourself.

I had a student once that just thought everything he visited just stunk. He said that no one would ever visit these sites.

"You did," I said.

Perplexed, the student nodded his head. I asked him how he found the site.

"Through a search engine," he said.

I sang, "ta da," and walked away.

He really put together a nice site at the end of the semester.

Set aside an entire evening and surf specifically for those whom do what you want to do. Keep a journal of the sites and be sure to write down their killer apps.

List the things you like about the sites. List the things you dislike about the sites. Make yourself a spreadsheet of information you can return to. Once you have visited every site the search engines can dish out, read over your writing. Here's the plan:

You're looking for a hole.

Start marking off the elements of the sites that you didn't feel were very well done. Start writing down things that you didn't feel were covered at all. Look for areas that you feel you can improve upon.

It is dangerous to not know your competition and blindly put up a site intended to grab an audience. I'll bet you piles of money that a blindly posted site would offer nothing new to an already satisfied audience. You'll wonder why no one is coming to your site. The reason is that you're giving them no real reason to come. You're not doing anything different, or better, than the sites that already exist.

Once you've searched through the other sites and studied what they are doing, you should have found a hole to fill. Keep looking. It's there. The hole exists. Find it. That hole is something that isn't being done or isn't being done well enough in your opinion.

It is your filling that hole that will bring people to your site and will keep them coming back. I'm not telling you to change your killer app off of this research, I am suggesting that you use what you have learned to better that killer app and give the already overwhelmed Web audience something new.

At this stage of the Web, just posting a page is not enough. You need to know what is out there and what is not out there. I guarantee you someone is already doing what you want to do. I also guarantee you they aren't doing it the way you want to do it. That's why your site will succeed where their pages don't.

All right, now you know the competition. It's time to answer the last question. Why should someone come to your site?

When I started HTML Goodies, there were already HTML help sites out there. Some of the biggest sites, at that time, had HTML help pages.

I surfed them all and found one glaring problem. They didn't teach me anything. The pages did little more than lay out the code and expect that you would magically know not only how to copy and paste the code but what to do with it once you pasted it into your documents. Forget about telling how the code works. That wasn't important. The level of instruction was "Here you go...good luck with it."

I had already written a few tutorials at this time so, I thought, why not offer the same coding but go one step further? I'll write the code into little four or five page pieces I'll call tutorials. Each will only deal with one piece of code.

You'll be able to copy and paste code just like the other sites except I'll go one step further and actually tell you how the code works. That way you'll be able to fix it once you play with it and mess it up.

In addition, I'll write these tutorials in a very conversational manner employing a question-and-answer format that actually sounds like the instructor is standing right there with you.

I'll take this code and make it accessible to just about anyone.

That was my thinking. I actually did just what I am telling you to do here. I looked at the competition, found problems in their methods and attempted to fix those problems inside of my own killer app.

I found the hole. I filled it.

After you surf through all of your competition, do just as I did. Go back to the piece of paper and write down exactly what makes your site different and why someone should come to your site.

What makes you different is the dirt that fills the hole.

Go No Further...

...until you've done just what I am suggesting. Write out answers to those five questions and keep those answers in front of you at every step of your Web site design.

I know it's not as much fun as coding and I know it reads a lot like a school assignment, but I can assure you that you'll thank me later when your coding and page creation has a focus from start to finish.

Chapter Two—Site Critiques

1. Shawn's Page/Author: Shawn (That Makes Sense)

`http://www.geocities.com/CollegePark/7027/`

Load Time: 22 Seconds, 57kps modem, cleared cache, 7/11/00 12:52PM.

My Screen Size: 1,024×768

Browsers Used: Internet Explorer 5 and Netscape Navigator 4.5

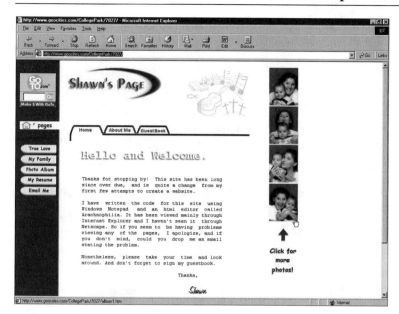

Figure 2.23
Shawn's page. (Color Plate C.4)

Concept: This is a personal homepage. I was drawn to it immediately because of the look and the strip of images down the right side. I enjoy looking at personal homepages the most because it is on a personal homepage where you can really see glimmers of talent. This is a page that has those glimmers. I hope Shawn thinks twice about possibly becoming more of a designer than he already is. He certainly has the talent.

Praise: First off, Shawn has done what I call "leaving the Web" on this homepage. Yes, there is the traditional blue stripe down the left side and the obligatory banner across the top, but Shawn then goes a step further and posts a couple of items that I wanted to point out.

First he had three tabs across the top, "Home," "About Me," and "Guestbook." While the links themselves aren't all that different, the method of making the links, tabs, is different.

I always make a point of telling students to go farther than just square pictures on a square screen making up a bigger square. Shawn has done that by using tabs rather than just three hypertext links. I know it's a little thing, but that little thing shows thinking past just piling Web elements on top of each other in a stacked format.

Second, note the bottom of the letter Shawn has written. It's signed. This, again, is "leaving the Web." It would have been so easy to just write the signature in the same text as the letter, but he didn't. Shawn signed a piece of paper, scanned it, and posted it. Again, a simple thing, but it sets the page apart.

I actually did just that on my first homepage. I went a step further, though, and made the white surrounding the signature transparent so the background image would show through.

Here's a word of warning. If you decide to post a signature, do not make it your traditional signature. It would be too easy for someone to grab it and forge using your name.

Praise: Shawn has made a point of carrying the same background across pages except for one. The left link that takes you to the Photo Album has a different background. Take a look at Figure 2.24.

Figure 2.24
Shawn's photo album.

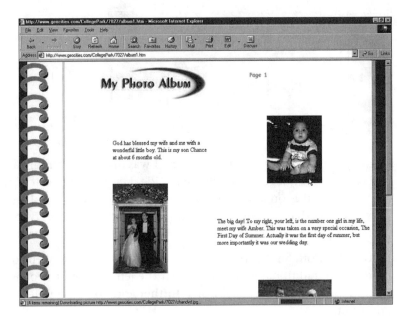

The background is now a spiral binder, which fits perfectly into the concept of a photo album. Yes, I know consistency across pages is good, and you might think this spiral harms that. Nope. Shawn carries the blue stripe down the left side with it. You can see it there before the rings start. The color is enough to keep the consistency across pages. Well done.

Concern: For all that's good about the page Shawn, you started on a negative. The letter you've written has a great opening paragraph stating that you've updated the site and are happy someone has stopped by. That's great, but then you go into what editor you used and that there might be problems and finally end on a down note using the word, "nonetheless." The whole paragraph was an apology for something that hasn't happened.

Suggestion: Stay positive! I couldn't care less about what text editor you used. What I want to know is, who is the kid you're holding? Where did you get those pictures taken? Were you on vacation? If so—where? Don't start on a negative. The site had too much positive about it to do that.

Concern: The links along the left side work. So do the links along top that look like tabs. Why did you separate them? Are some more important than others? I understand the Home link being set apart, but why not put all the links together?

Suggestion: Move all of the links together. I would move them all to tabs—then I would carry those tabs across all pages. You lose them after the homepage goes away.

Concern: Your résumé is well written, but it has your address and phone number on it.

Suggestion: Lose the address and phone and offer an email. There are too many weird people out there that would love to have just that kind of information.

Overall: Overall, I liked the page. I thought about putting up one more concern, but decided to put it here in the overall instead. The site is solid. What is there is good and there are some real glimmers of talent in the work. However, the site is still generic and common. It looks a lot like every other personal page out there. Now that you have this great start, try to find even more ways of setting your site apart. Look for methods of interaction.

I see you are a very religious family with small children.

Could this site be a meeting place where other young parents can discuss religion and raising a child? It's just a suggestion, but maybe it can get you thinking.

One of my favorite personal Web sites used an idea you should feel free to take. The author posted a picture of his infant son and the title read "Welcome to My Daddy's Home Page."

It made you want to cry.

2. All You Ever Wanted to Know About Chat/Author: Nowim

http://www.geocities.com/abi_lene/
Load Time: 34 Seconds, 57kps modem, cleared cache, 7/11/00 1:28PM.

My Screen Size: 1,024×768

Browsers Used: Internet Explorer 5 and Netscape Navigator 4.5

Figure 2.25
The Chat homepage. (Color Plate C.5)

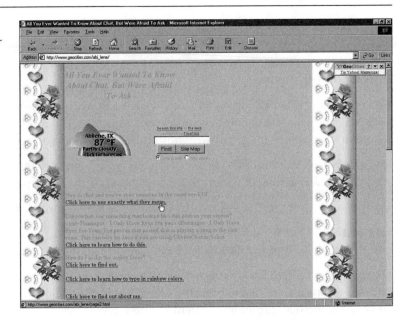

Concept: This site is dedicated to chat rooms. There aren't any chat rooms on the site, though. The site is more geared to what you can do inside of a chat room with the right tips and tricks. I don't know much about chat rooms so I will leave it up to you whether the information is valid. I am just interested in the design of the site.

Praise: Where this site excels is in its information. There are many links, each to a page that offers a great deal of information. I especially liked the first link that explained what a lot of the acronyms people throw around mean. It knew that "LOL" meant "Laughing Out Loud," but I didn't know that "DTLBBB" meant "Don't Let the Bed Bugs Bite." Huh.

Concern: Like I said before, the site has a lot of good information—it's just that it isn't presented in such a good manner. My first concern is the background. It's very pretty but I don't know what lace and roses has to do with a chat room.

Suggestion: If you posted this background simply because you like it then I would suggest looking for another one. It is confusing. It's akin to logging into a knitting site and seeing a background full of knights in full armor. It just doesn't fit.

Concern: The color of the background and the color of the text are very similar. I would suggest that on screens using only 256 colors, the text might completely disappear. I am running 16.7 million colors and I can lose the text now and again.

Suggestion: Try a darker text color.

Concern: I see you're from Abilene, Texas. I'm sure that's a nice place. I see the weather there is 87 degrees and partly cloudy. I am sitting in New Orleans only one state over from Texas and I'm not interested in the weather there. Imagine how uninterested someone in Ohio might be.

Suggestion: The weathercast adds nothing to the page's killer app. You should think about losing it.

Concern: Why are you giving me the opportunity to search the Web and leave your site before you even give me your first link? This, too, adds nothing to the site.

Suggestion: Think about losing the search function or putting it much farther down on the page. Your site is what is important.

Concern: Later in the list of links you offer .wav files and links to other .wav file sites. This does not go to the page's killer app. I can't use these in a chat room.

Suggestion: Think about possibly creating a whole other page for those links and make just one link to that page.

Overall: If you're into chat rooms, this page will give a great deal of very good information. I am always impressed by Web pages that offer just a litany of information like this one. I always wonder how long it must have taken for someone to compile all that information. To better the page I would suggest making it look more like a page that deals with chat rooms. The background and the light colors give a far different indication than what the actual page offers.

3. Internet Resources for Web Design/Author: Nancy Schmidt

http://www.ocm.cnyric.org/learntech/MyWebs/SchmidtWeb.htm

Load Time: 18 Seconds, 57kps modem, cleared cache, 7/11/00 2:56PM.

My Screen Size: 1,024×768

Browsers Used: Internet Explorer 5 and Netscape Navigator 4.5

Concept: This is a links page. It's a very popular format on the Web these days. That's the reason I chose to review this site here. The author, Nancy, has taken the time to set up a page dedicated to offering links for Web page design assistance. This format is popular in just about every field the Web covers. People who are interested in a topic take the time to search, catalog, and hopefully rate sites that all deal with one specific topic.

Figure 2.26
Want a Link? We got Links! (Color Plate C.6)

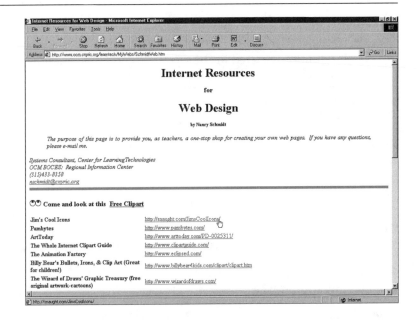

The concept is quite sound and, if done correctly, can be a tremendous help to someone who wants information. These links sites can cut a ton of time out of keyword searching and make life very easy on the user. I can probably rattle off ten sites that have made a good living doing just this. They never create any content past links and some ratings, but their hits are through the roof.

Praise: The main praise for the site is that you actually undertook such a task. The upkeep on the site must be great. I once attempted to keep a list of all those people that had a link back to the HTML Goodies site. Ugh! Links changed constantly. Sometimes the author would bother to tell you, mostly not. Information of the site would change, and new links had to be added all the time.

I like that you have made a point of keeping the site text-based. Links sites certainly do not require a great deal of graphic support. After all, it's the links that make the site, not the look.

Your presentation of the links is correct in my opinion. You gave both the name of the site and then the link represents the address. I like that look. Often the title is made into the link. I like your method better.

Concern: My main concern is that you only have 30 or so links. That's not a tremendous amount for a links page.

Suggestion: I would think that 30 to 60 links per topic might be more near the number you would need. You have four topic areas. If you had 30 links per topic that would be 120 links and I think that would be sufficient.

I would also suggest that some more topic areas be added so that more areas in Web design can be covered.

Concern: I understand that the links had to contain good content to be added to your list, but past that, is one not better than another?

Suggestion: Set up some sort of ratings system. It doesn't have to be grand, just something that suggests a hierarchy of sites. Maybe even something as simple as the higher the link is listed, the better it is. I've also seen stars and bars used to indicate a good site. Pick one and rank the links you choose to add.

Concern: Your site lists one section of top of another. That makes for a long page.

Suggestion: Maybe this page could simply be a series of four links. Those four links could then go to the four pages made up by the four topic areas. That way instead of scrolling, the users could click to the topic they wanted.

If you'd rather not make separate pages then at least offer internal links on the top of the page so that a user could click and jump right to the section of the page he wants.

Overall: When the Web first got started and those who could began putting up Web pages, the "My Favorite Links" page became very popular. People used it to show and define who they were. Of course, some saw that as their ticket to making it big on the Web and created huge listings of links categorized into section to help others. That's what you have done here, Nancy. It just needs to have more content and be a little better organized. The question is whether you want to go forward and really do what it would take for this to be a truly successful link site. People often underestimate the time involved in putting up a site that will attract a large audience. You have a good base here. I think your formats are good and I think you could really make this into a great site. The question is whether you want, or have the time, to do it at the level you'll have to reach to compete with other link sites.

Chapter 3

Begin the Design

Now that you have considered the five basic questions, you have a general concept of the big picture. You know who you're hoping will visit, how your site will be represented, and where you fit into the Web marketplace.

This chapter covers making decisions about overriding design concerns and what should be included in your Web site and on your Web pages. These decisions include big concerns like should you use frames or not? Should you use a background image or not? How can you make it so your pages fit well into any screen setting?

Remember that your site is for your users so you must make a point of making your pages fit their systems, not the other way around. Maybe you've entered a site that suggested the pages were best viewed using a specific screen setting and a specific browser. My guess is that the majority of you didn't bother to change your screen setting or browser. Your users won't, either. Why? They don't have to. There are too many sites out there that conform to them rather than expecting the users to conform to the site. Design should make it as easy on the user as possible. People almost always choose the path of least resistance. That's what you're shooting for.

Now it's time to make some decisions.

What Do You Want on This Site?

By now you have a plan. You have a killer app in mind and you have a general idea of what the site will do. Now, what will you want on the site to complete that task?

You're only thinking at this point, it's not costing you anything, you don't have to code anything, so anything goes.

Think in terms of pages first. You'll obviously have a homepage and I'll get much deeper into what that should contain later in this chapter. Past that, what subpages will go toward your killer app?

Would a picture page help? Would a page with links be helpful? How about a Guestbook page, would that be helpful?

If this is a site dealing with a business or organization, you'll probably need a separate page for each department or each area your business is into. You may need a separate page for each product line. Maybe you'll need a separate page for each product in and of itself. Would a page listing the owners of the company including their phone numbers and emails be helpful? How about creating a page for complaints? A page that explained company policy would be nice. A page where people could gather information about applying for a job might be in the mix, also.

Design Goodies Survey

The HTML Goodies survey asked users what they expected to find on a business page. Here are the pages that scored highest:

Contact Information	92%
Search Capabilities	89%
FAQs	86%
About/Information pages	82%
Available Downloads	72%
Interactivity	65%

N=483

People want to be able to find what they want quickly and be able to contact you equally as quickly.

Is your site going to be personal? Well, then you'll probably need a résumé or some other page listing accomplishments. You'll probably want a separate page for each of your hobbies, or interests or whatever you happen to be into. You'll need a page with some pictures. 're a writer, you'll need some pages for your stories or poems.

Design Goodies Survey

The HTML Goodies Survey asked users what they wanted to see on a personal site. Here are top answers:

Links Page 82%

Guestbooks 73%

Contact information 61%

Users who come to personal sites apparently want to know what you're into and have the ability to contact you. You may also find it interesting that the survey respondents expected to find other things on a personal page. These were elements such as outdated information (54%), Background Music (43%), and blinking text (38%). People expect to find a lower level of information and site upkeep on a personal page. Keep that in mind when you're working on your personal pages.

If you start finding that you are running into multiple levels of pages, start keeping your list that way.

Maybe you won't want every page linked right from the homepage. Maybe users will get to a specific page from the first tier of subpages. Maybe you'll have three subpages connected to your first page from the homepage. That's fine. Just list the pages that way. It might look something like:

Homepage

> Subpage

> Subpage

>> Subpage

>> Subpage

> Subpage

>> Subpage

> Subpage

I'd love to be able to give set rules at this point, but I can't. I don't know your topic and I don't know what you're attempting to do with the site. This one is up to you. What pages will you need?

It's a whole lot better to over list than to under list topics for pages. Write it all down. Every idea is a good idea at this point. Don't be afraid to have 100 pages. You can always cut it down to size later. Think about your own surfing. What pages did you like? Maybe you should go out surfing right now. What pages do you like?

Think not only about what pages you would like to have but also what order they should be in. When you list the pages, list them with, in your mind, the most important pages high in the list. If you're not sure what pages to list first, think of it this way. If your site were something where you could take your readers by the hand and guide them through, what page would you like to have them see first? Which should they see second? That should help to set your order.

Write it all down on that trusty piece of paper.

Your Shell—Your Template

Ah, now the fun part. I'll actually have you drawing out pages here in a moment, but first I want you to stop and think about what you want on each of those pages you have listed.

You've read, in the critiques, that I am a huge fan of consistency across pages. That consistency is going to be first set by the homepage. I'll get into that later in this chapter.

Right now, I'm interested in your artistic capabilities.

Don't worry. I haven't any artistic abilities, either. If you can draw a fairly straight line, you're advanced enough for this exercise.

Take a clean sheet of paper and begin to draw out blocks on the page representing the elements that will appear on the pages.

The concept here is to create a shell for your site. This shell acts as the commonality of your site. This shell is the stuff that helps define your site in your users' minds. This shell is the frame that goes around your site. Stay with me. I have some examples coming up.

Some of you may think telling you that your pages must follow a set shell surrounding only a small portion of the page that changes is being too rigid. If that's the case, you're missing the point.

Say I'm a surfer and I just rolled into your site. Your homepage has a green background. I have not been conditioned that your site is somewhat represented by that green. I go to the first subpage. Blue. The next is purple. The next is orange. None of the pages carries any consistency, there are no similar images, and each page appears to stand on its own.

How am I to know that I am still within your site? How will I be able to conceive that your site has any semblance of cohesiveness? Did you build a site or just throw pages together? You want some level of consistency across pages.

Some sites are quite rigid with their shell.

For example, the ABCNews.com page (see Figure 3.1) has a shell that it carries across all pages. It's the top and left side areas. The links down the left side is always there. The top portion always carries the logo and a banner ad. What changes is the text section within the shell. Click on any page. It looks like this page except for the text in the white section. That's real consistency across pages.

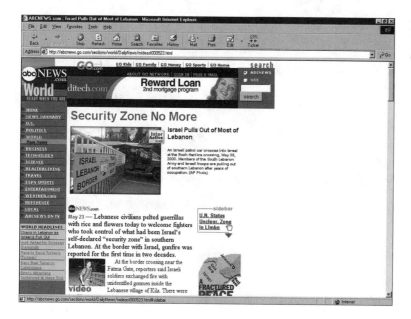

Figure 3.1
The ABCNews.com page always looks the same.

There are a couple of real benefits to using such a rigid shell.

First, it really does set consistency. I think I said that previously. Also, the images that make up the shell load very quickly as the user moves through the site because those same images are carried across every page.

Please understand that your shell or template need not be anywhere near that overt.

The author of the Van Halen News Desk shown in Figure 3.2 has been an HTML Goodies visitor since the beginning and I visit this site every day simply because I want the latest news. He's following the concept of a shell, but he's doing it through colors. There are two different colored bars down each side of the browser window. Those two bars plus the small centered site logo are his shell. Only those two elements are carried across the pages.

Figure 3.2
VHND.com: The colors are the shell.

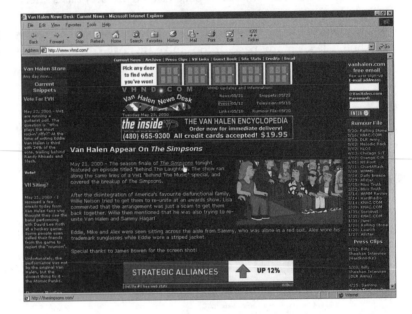

When you first pop into the site, you get a feel for it. When you move from page to page, that feel continues.

What do you want on the pages, a background image or just a color? Do you want your identifier on every page? Will there be an email link on every page? If so—where will it sit? Up high or down low? Do you want a rigid shell, or will you allow colors and form to set the site apart?

Either way—start drawing! I'm not looking for high art here; I simply want a simple block drawing of what the pages will hopefully look like. Figure 3.3 is an example of what I'm talking about. It is a block drawing of the ABCNews.com page.

If you will use only a background color and a logo to create the shell of your Web site, draw that out.

have finished some block drawings, pick the one you like and stick to it.

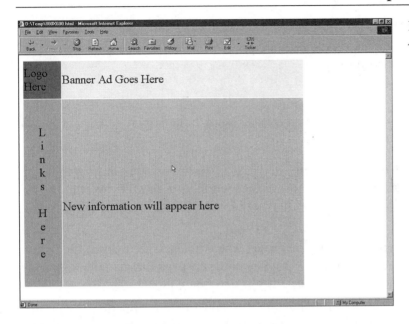

Figure 3.3
A basic block drawing.

Placement Equals Importance

This is a fairly easy concept but one you must grasp. Think about how you, the human being, look at any piece of written media. This includes newspapers, magazines, comic books, matchbook covers, and a myriad of other printed material.

Please understand that I am speaking in general terms here. There are languages that teach their readers to read right to left or vertically. In those cases, the pattern the eye follows may be different. I am speaking of the most common format.

Your eyes follow the printed material in a set pattern you've been following ever since you could understand what you were looking at.

The flow across the page is top to bottom while at the same time left to right. This holds true for Web pages.

So what? Why should you care? Well, you should care because that eyeball flow across the page helps to set importance. As a general rule of thumb, you can state:

> Elements found in the upper-left corner are perceived as being more important than elements found in the lower-right corner.

You can even break it down further stating that

> Elements placed higher on the page are perceived as more important than elements placed lower on the page.

And...

> Elements placed to the left are perceived as being more important than elements placed to the right.

Call it Feng Shui if you'd like, but placement on a page matters. Think about the pages you've looked at in the past. Where have most of the identifiers been? They were in the upper-left corner, right? Where did you find most of the navigation, the links? They were either down the left side or across the top, yes?

Now, let me ask you this? Have you run across pages where the links were down the right side? I'll bet you have. It seemed odd, yes? Have you been to a page that had the logo down at the bottom of the left navigation bar? It was odd again, I'll bet.

Please understand I am not telling you that you must follow this similar pattern. Quite the contrary, I've seen many sites that break with tradition and put their links down the right side simply to break with tradition. They did it to shock the user, to make the user think a little. It's a risky proposition, but maybe one you feel would be worth trying.

It may be that the elements you have on your page cannot fall into this nice top and left pattern. In Chapter 7, "Images and the Visual," I'll show you a couple of sites that through sheer image size draw attention away from the top of the page. I know many sites that use a single animation to draw the eye out of the comfortable top to bottom, left to right format.

Remember that there are no bad choices in Web design as long as the choice aids your killer app. I'm simply letting you know that there is a traditional format that you can bet your users feel most comfortable seeing. Maybe the format was created rather than being truly ingrained, but think for a moment.

When you see an identifier in the upper-left corner, do you expect it to be an active image? Where do you expect it to take you? The homepage I'll bet. When you log in to a page and see an ad banner sitting up above everything else, centered, pushing the page down a fourth of the screen, it's a little uncomfortable, yes? Why? Because the ad banner's placement is suggesting it is the most important thing on the page. It holds the top spot. It is sitting in the highest and most left position. Oh, it may be centered, but because it's pushing the page down and leaving blank space in the left corner, it's occupying it nonetheless.

That's an uncomfortable look to a page. The page is pushing the ad over its content. My guess is that you'd feel a great deal more comfortable if the ad banner were nested in the upper-right side sitting next to the identifier. That would at least show the identifier as being the most important thing on the page.

Are you following me? It isn't just what you place on your pages it's also where you place the elements that push importance.

When you stop to draw out the elements you are going to place on your page, think not only in terms of elements, but also in terms of importance.

If you see a vertical list of links, what link to do you expect to see on top of the bunch? My guess is the most important link. The homepage. Is that what you were thinking?

I'll bet it was.

To Frame or Not to Frame

That pretty much is the question in a lot of people's minds. Students seem to agonize over it. Sharp-witted Web designers have, by now, probably noticed that everything I am suggesting can be handled simply by using a frame set.

The most common frame set formats splits the page into two sections employing either the top or the left-side frame window as a navigational bar. Users click on the links in the navigation bar and the other, larger frame window, receives the page. Figure 3.4 is an example of what I mean.

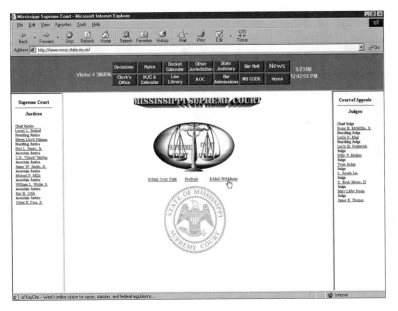

Figure 3.4
The Mississippi Supreme Court's new frames page.

I found this by searching for sites that are happy to proclaim their use of frames. On this site, you can click on a lot of links and only the center section changes. You never lose the shell.

Success! The users never leave the site, they always know they are in the site, and there is consistency because the users never lose the navigation bar. You can have a ton of links and only the one window changes. It's a win-win all around, right?

Maybe, maybe not.

I am not an overt fan of using frames. The abilities and the upside I mentioned previously don't outweigh the problems I see popping up again and again when someone uses frames.

To begin with, the frame windows alter their height and width depending on the size of the browser screen they are loading into. The problem is that the pages that load into the browser window often cannot resize themselves fully and all of a sudden that beautiful frame set that you built now has a series of scrollbars.

Howard University's (http://www.howard.edu/) homepage is one example of this (see Figure 3.5).

Figure 3.5
Not only a vertical scroll, but a horizontal one as well.

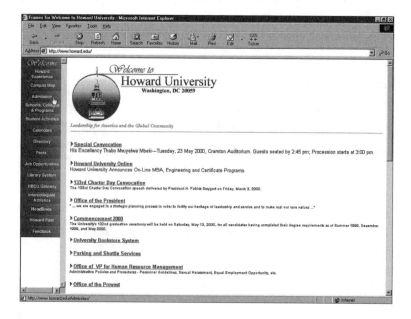

The images on the left side are in a frame set for all the same reasons I mentioned previously. The images stay put while the large section changes. The problem is whoever set the site up didn't take into account the width of the images as opposed to the width of the frame window. They got a scrollbar.

When using a frame set, the designer must always overcompensate for the images in the navigation frame or this kind of thing happens. Those of you who have worked with frames have found that setting the frame window width in percentages produces the prettiest frame sets across differing browser screen sizes. The percentages amend themselves to the screen. The problem is that smaller screen sizes produce the scrollbars. Why? It's because the images don't get any smaller but the space set aside for them does.

For example, let's say your browser is displaying on a screen that is set to 800×600. That means you have about 730 pixels of space in the actual browser screen. Remember that your browser screen does not go all the way to the end of your monitor.

You have an image in the left frame that is 220 pixels wide. In an 800×600 screen setting, you could set the frame set to make the right frame window 34% wide. That's around 248 pixels wide. That should be enough, right?

Well, now let's display that same page in a computer screen set to 640×480. That would leave about 600 pixels of browser screen to play with. That same 34% set for the left is now only 204 pixels wide.

Oops. You got a scrollbar because the image is not too wide for the frame set percentage.

I think I've said this already, but I'll say it again. Users don't much mind clicking. Scrolling bugs them. Horizontal scrolling really bugs them.

So, what's a framer to do? The usual answer is to go with a fixed frame window width. Set the width in pixels. This works to eliminate the scrollbars, but can also make a site seem extremely crunched on larger monitors.

What to do, what to do?

Test. Test. And don't use percentages.

If you go with frames, you need to make a point of testing your site in different browsers and different screen settings. Test. Test. Test. You should find the problems before they pop up.

Oh, and don't try putting a line on the page asking the user to let you know if her or she finds any problems. That's being lazy. You're there for the user, not the other way around.

Figure 3.6 illustrates a frame set that was put together fairly successfully.

This is a great example of hiding frame sets and allowing enough space for the items in the frame sets so there are no scrollbars. Yes, there's a scrollbar on the far right, but in a frame setting that is common—that's the page that users expect to see. If you can avoid that scrollbar, great, but if you can't, it's the one acceptable scroll in a frame set system. It's that scroll that appears between the two frame sets that drive me, and most users, up the wall.

Figure 3.6

DRCNet Online shows three frames, but only one scrollbar.

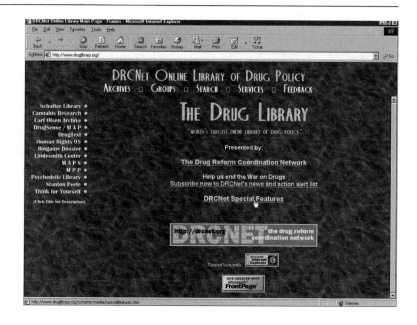

This page is very clean and very well put together. If you intend to use frames to create your shell then you need to make a serious point of viewing your pages in multiple browsers over multiple screen settings just to make sure the frames do not produce scrollbars.

Wait! I just said that earlier. Hmmmm. It must be important.

I have other reasons for not using frames other than just the scrollbars. Frame sets are more taxing on the server. A page loads with only one request of the server. A frame set must make at least three requests of the server to load fully (the frame code page and the two pages that load into those two frame windows). More frames mean more requests of the server, more load time, more frustration on the user's part.

Frame sets require the designer to create more pages than he would with single pages.

Bookmarking is a pain with frame sets. Often people set up their frame set pages so that the domain name never leaves the location bar. It always reads `http://www.something.com`. I agree that that's a real clean look, but it makes for a single page being bookmarked every time. Yes, I know that Internet Explorer 4.0 and above has a system that bookmarks frames correctly, but is that enough, one browser and only a few versions?

I knew a designer who wanted frames that loaded a new frames page every time the user clicked so that if someone wanted to bookmark, the user would get exactly what was on the screen at the time of the bookmark. It was clever, but what a lot of work. He agreed it was a lot of work, but he wanted the frame set look and was willing to put forth the effort to do it right.

More power to him!

Look, frame set pages and sites are extremely popular on the Web. People who like frames swear by them. If that's you then by all means, use a frame set. Just make a real point of testing your site on multiple platforms and multiple screen settings. If you can get the frame set to work properly then you will enjoy all of the benefits described previously.

This is just another choice you're going to have to make while planning your site.

The Top 10 Things You Probably Want, but Probably Shouldn't Have on Your Web Pages

Are you sure you want these on your pages?

When I teach Web design to a class, one of the most enjoyable classes is the one where I discuss things that probably should never appear on Web pages, but seem to always do.

Over the course of a few years of teaching Web design, I have noticed a few Web page elements popping up again and again in these class discussions. I've taken these trends and compiled them into a list I like to call "The Top 10 Things You Probably Want, but Probably Shouldn't Have on Your Web Pages."

For an element to appear on this list, it must give the appearance of adding to the Web page, but doesn't. It must give the appearance of helping the user, but doesn't. It must give the impression that is it part of the killer app, but isn't. In short, the element must look very important, but really isn't.

For the first time in print, here are those Top 10 elements starting with the worst offenders. Most people offer top ten lists starting with 10. I'm going the other way. I want to get to number one right up front.

1. Under Construction Images

Why do people have these on their site? The use of the images is very popular. Every day I see new and improved animated gifs depicting a shovel or a backhoe digging away. I don't get it.

Your Web page should always be under construction. Period. You don't need an image telling people you're working.

When I see an Under Construction image, I'm a little offended that the site designer didn't feel my presence was worth finishing the page. I am not quite important enough for him to actually finalize the work. That's bad. Figure 3.7 helps to drive my point home.

Figure 3.7

At `http://www.cs.utah.edu/~gk/atwork/` *they share my feelings.*

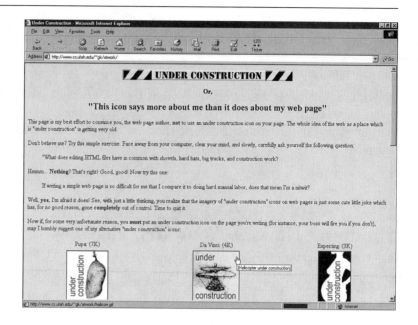

I know what the author wants the Under Construction image to do. He wants the user to see the page, be unimpressed, but let it all slide because of the image. Right?

If I haven't swayed you, how about over 65% of people polled by HTML Goodies reporting they dislike Under Construction images. They hate them even more on business sites.

If you want to denote construction, at the bottom of each page post a date showing the last time the page was updated. That keeps you on your toes far more than an Under Construction image. If there is a date, you are more inclined to update and get that date current.

2. Counters

Let me ask you a quick question…whom is the counter for? If you answer, "my users," you're lying. It's for you! Counters have always been for the people who post them. To suggest a user has ever visited a page because of the counter is just silly.

This is a point I've argued with Web designers too many times to count so I decided to ask a few questions about counters in the HTML Goodies survey. The answers suggested users don't much pay attention to counters, nor do they even believe them. Almost 90% of those polled said they feel counters were either not credible or highly not credible (how's that for poor English?). I myself find it very hard to believe counters that sit on two-page, poorly designed sites proclaiming millions of visitors.

Design Goodies Survey

HTML Goodies Survey Question: The appearance of a counter on a Web site represents:

Nothing   72%

It is a personal site   26%

It is a professional site   2%

N=492

Counters don't move users.

Be honest. The counter is for you. If something on the site is specifically for you, then lose it. If you want to know the amount of visitors to your site, do it through the server's access logs. If you can't get data from there, find another server or live without the counter. It's not helping anyone but you. It's especially not helping you if you set it to start counting at ten million.

3. Blinking Text

There's a reason why Internet Explorer never allowed blinking text in their browsers. Users dislike it. The HTML Goodies survey found 74% of people said they disliked blinking text. Twelve percent said it didn't matter to them. Only 14% of people polled liked blinking text.

If you want to pull attention to a portion of the page, do it with color, do it with an animated image, do it by moving that item closer to the top-left portion of the browser screen.

Just don't do it with blinking text. Please. I'm begging you.

4. Cute and Nondescript Titles

Many people who are new to designing for the Web don't take the time to think over the text they put in their page's title bar. Did you know that the text in the title bar is the text the browsers use if someone bookmarks the page? Some search engines use it as the text for the link back to the page.

In the Goodies Survey, 70% of those polled said they took note of what text appears in the title bar. Furthermore, almost 80% said they keep the text suggested by the title when bookmarking a site if the text isn't too long.

I'm as guilty of doing this as anyone. The very first HTML tables tutorial I wrote had the title "How to make a table without wood." How stupid is that? I still see it today being used on search engines. Ugh! I wish I had never written it.

Think about what text will appear in your page's title bar. It's far more important than you think. Make it a description of your page. Make it so that if a person bookmarks the site, he will keep the text.

5. Download Now!

I'm a little baffled when I see sites that have the traditional Netscape, Internet Explorer, or Opera images at the bottom of the homepage suggesting users quickly go and download the latest version of the browser. Why? Why would you suggest that someone leave your site immediately and get the latest browser? If they do, do you really think they'll come back right away?

I think people put these images on their pages mainly because of two reasons—fierce loyalty to one browser or the other, or their site has some new, high-level programming widget that requires the latest browser.

Here's some information you might find interesting. There are still a ton of version 3.0 browsers out there even though at the time of my writing this book IE5.5 and Navigator 6 were out.

Why? Because the browsers work. Those level-three browsers do just fine for people. I didn't throw away my computer simply because a faster processor came out. In the world of the Web, people really need to be shown a valid reason for them to upgrade a browser and the latest DHTML effect won't be enough.

Users know there are new browsers available. Don't add two more images to your page to remind them. It slows the completion of the page and only 34% of those polled said they upgraded their browser after being prompted by a Web page. Whereas that may sound like a lot, remember that once someone has upgraded, they won't upgrade again right away. The number doesn't suggest that 34% upgrade every time. They only say they've upgraded once.

Keep your page's load time down. Forget asking people to download a new version browser unless your page specifically requires the browser and someone cannot view your page without the browser. And...if that's the case, why would you write page like that?

6. "Get Out of Frames" Link

Ah, the saving grace link of the people who really want to use frames but don't want to upset any of the other surfers.

If you like frames and you designed your page with frames, use them. I've gone into sites that offer that link on every page and I always wonder why the author used frames at all when he keeps asking me if I want out.

If your purpose for using the link is for people who are using text-oriented browsers, then you need to either use a JavaScript that tests for that and send those people to a text version right off, or you need to change out the site so that you don't use frames.

When I see those links, I want to ask the author why they went with frames in the first place. He certainly can see problems resulting from their use of frames, so why go with them? Why start out assuming problems will come?

Don't be wishy-washy. If you use frames, use frames. Don't keep reminding me that frames are not so good and that I might want to click to get out of them.

7. Awards

Before you write me and say that I have awards on the HTML Goodies site, hear me out.

I don't mean for you to never post awards. On the contrary, I love my awards. I display them proudly even though I know the vast majority of them are basically fake awards images sent out to other sites hoping to get a link back from the award. (What, you didn't know that?)

If you are going to post your awards, don't force your users to view them. Put your awards on a separate page and place a link to the awards page. That way the users are at least made aware you have won some awards and if they choose to, they can click to see the awards.

If you put your awards at the bottom of your homepage, the award does little more than act as another image that slows down the completion of your page. You don't want that. You want the pages to load and show up fast, fast. The award images are not helping anyone through your site's killer app, and may also act as an element that users click to leave your site.

That's not good, either.

8. Chat Rooms

Oh, I'll catch heck for putting this on the list because everyone wants a chat room. No matter the topic or the site killer app, public-domain chat room sites are offering designers the ability to set up chat rooms simply by filling out a form.

Now, remember that the title of this section is "probably" don't want on your Web pages. If your killer app screams for a chat room, you may want to override these statements and put one on the site. I am just asking you to stop, think for a moment, and truly decide if putting a chat room on your site will do any good.

Design Goodies Survey

HTML Goodies Survey Question: When you enter a site that offers a chat room, will you go into the chat room?

Highly Unlikely	61%
Unlikely	20%
Neutral	14%
Likely	4%
Highly Likely	1%
N=483	

Chat rooms appeal to a small slice of your audience. Is it worth the trouble to create something that simply does not appeal to the audience?

Less than 30% of the respondents to the HTML Goodies survey said they visit chat rooms. Of that percentage, less than 3% said they do it frequently.

Think about your site's killer app. Does it need a chat room? Unless the answer is a screaming yes, don't do it.

9. Flash Intro/Skip Intro

I'm not a fan of this because you are stopping me no matter who I am. It would be a great deal better if you had a page that asked if I wanted to enter a Flash site or a non-Flash site. Make that Flash (or Shock or Java, or whatever) question page display first so I can choose. Don't just assume I want the Flash page and on that page give me a link to the non-Flash site, a link to download flash, and a link to bypass the intro. Again, you look wishy-washy. Make a decision.

Ask me which I would like and take me there. Don't assume I want Flash and will go and get the plug-in just for you. I probably won't.

Before I installed the plug-in I would get blank pages and error messages galore. You don't want that. I'm not a big fan of stopping people just before entering a site, but Flash is becoming so popular that people are designing in droves using Flash. Furthermore, over 70% of those responding to the HTML Goodies survey said they do click to go to the Flash-enhanced site when asked to make a decision. People don't see it as a bad thing.

Let me choose. Don't force it on me and make me deal with errors and suggestions for downloading.

Design Goodies Survey

HTML Goodies Survey Question: When a Web page pops up a box suggesting you download a plug-in, what do you do?

Click Cancel   77%

Get the Plug-In   23%

N=488

Most people won't get the plug-in even if you offer it.

You'd be surprised at how many Web surfers are scared to death when a Web site suggests downloading a piece of software. They leave the site and never come back. Again...you don't want that.

Logo Page—Click to Enter

Why? Why oh why oh why? Why would you do this? I know you've seen it. I'll bet some of you have even done it.

You're surfing along and enter a site. The site posts a page that contains only a logo and then asks you to click to enter.

That's it? Click to enter? You made me stop, look at your logo, and all I get to do is click to enter? What on Earth good is that?

Oh, sure, some advertising pundit will tell me that the logo page enforces brand recognition and helps the viewer to recognize their place and blah, blah, blah. Some other designer will tell me that the logo is a firewall page that looks at the browser and the screen setting and blah, blah, blah. Set recognition by placement on the page. All of those firewall elements can be done behind the scenes using JavaScript.

What makes me most angry about the logo page is what it does. Why would you stop me? I want to come into your site and you're making me stop at the door and knock?

Some might be pointing up the page a few lines saying that I thought it was okay to have a Flash or not Flash page. That's right. That choice page is helping me. It's solving problems before I get into the site. This logo page is not. It is simply stopping me.

When I have to knock on the door of the local grocery store to gain entrance, that's when I'll accept this as a viable programming tool.

10. This One Is a Tie: "This Site Best Viewed with...Screen Setting" and "This Site Best Viewed with...Browser"

Design Goodies Survey

HTML Goodies Survey Question: You enter a site that suggests the pages are best viewed at a screen setting different than yours. Do you change your screen setting to accommodate the site?

No   93%

Yes   7%

N=488

You've probably never done it, why suggest that others do it?

You want to write your pages so that the user is asked to do as little as possible. You should write your pages so that they conform to the user rather than expecting the user to conform to you.

Design Goodies Survey

HTML Goodies Survey Question: You enter a page that suggests viewing the site in a different browser than you are using. Do you change browsers to view the page?

No   92%

Yes   8%

N=488

Write your pages so they can be viewed across browsers. No one effect is worth cutting your audience in half.

Be honest with me. Have you ever shut down your browser and opened another simply because the page suggested it? Probably not. Then don't ask your users to do something you've never done.

The users will not make changes to accommodate you. You must make pages that accommodate them.

Which leads me into my next rather important little section.

So Goes the Homepage...So Goes the Rest of the Site

As you've probably picked up from the critiques, I think a great deal of focus should be placed on the homepage. I don't say that because people visit that page most often, I say that because the homepage is the page they visit first.

The homepage is a welcome mat. It must set the standard for the remainder of the site. It has to explain the site, denote the identifier, set the colors, direct the viewer, and welcome the viewer.

Do you know the one thing it doesn't have to do? It does not have to give any information.

One of the problems I see a great deal with first-time designers is that they feel their homepage has to get everything out there right away. I've seen homepages that scroll 20 screens just because the author felt all of that information must be on the homepage, out there first for the viewer to grab and consume.

Don't do that. Remember that you are building a Web site, not a Web page. People expect to move through pages. That's how things are done on the WWW. Users click to get information.

Think about it. Would you rather click or scroll? The vast majority of Web users would rather click.

Design Goodies Survey

HTML Goodies Survey Question: You enter a site that has what would be equal to ten pages of typed information. Would you rather scroll through the information all on one page or have it broken up over multiple pages you click through.

All text on one page	29%
Break the text over pages	71%

N=482

Over two-thirds of the audience would rather you let them click.

Think of your site as a spider web with the homepage being the centerpiece of the site. The homepage itself is used to direct people to the information they want to see. Don't feel that you must get everything inside your site onto your homepage. The majority of Web users go deeper into a site than just looking at the homepage. Almost 80% of people polled suggested they would view at least a few pages before deciding if they liked the site or not.

The people of the Web do not judge a book by its cover. Use that information to your advantage. Build a Web site. Don't just build a page.

I'm quite serious when I say that. I made mention earlier that the homepage not only acts as a navigation instrument of the Web site, but it also acts to set the standard for the rest of the site.

Again, this is a Web site, not a Web page. (I must stop saying that so often.) The site itself has to have some semblance of cohesion. If I come to your site and I am greeted by a homepage with a green background, I am immediately going to be conditioned that a green background relates to your site. If I click and your first subpage has a purple background, I'm a little confused. If I click again and I'm looking at a background that's rainbow-striped, I'm really blown away. I have to look at the location bar just to make sure you didn't take me off site for some reason.

Putting together a Web site full of differing backgrounds and differing navigation formats, and differing identifiers confuses your users.

You need to make a point of picking a format, an identifier, a color scheme, a format for making links, and so on, and stick with it.

It is on your homepage that you set the standards you will follow throughout the remainder of the site.

So goes the homepage, so goes the rest of the site.

Design Goodies Survey

HTML Goodies Survey Question: Do you prefer all of the pages within a site to have the same look?

Yes	51%
No	16%
Doesn't matter	33%

Only 16% said "no." Over half said "yes." Those who claimed it doesn't matter can be assumed to like familiarity across pages. I say that because if they wouldn't, they would have said no.

Size Matters

Begin with examining your homepage, and thus the rest of your site in terms of the big picture. You need to decide on some parameters first. I'll try to help you make those decisions with some insight from the Web.

One: The most popular screen setting on the Web is 800×600 pixels. Unless your users have forked out the money for the bigger monitor, the stock monitor probably showed up with their system and that monitor is most likely set to 800×600.

Yes, there are larger settings and yes, there are smaller settings, but this is the most popular.

Have you ever run into those statements on a homepage that reads something like "This site best viewed at 1,024×768, 16.7 million color on the Netscape Navigator 4.5 browser"?

I'll bet you have. Those statements are all over the Web. Now, let me ask you another question. Have you ever changed your screen settings?

Two: Neither will your visitors.

When you begin to design your site, you'll need to play to what the visitors have available to them. Don't expect them to conform to you. They won't. I would suggest that a third of the people out there surfing wouldn't even know how to change their monitor settings.

Help them view your site correctly. Design for what they have, not for what you want. It's actually pretty easy.

Force the Parameters

Has this ever happened to you? You design a fantastic page that displays perfectly in Internet Explorer. Then, because this is what good designers do, you check it in Netscape navigator just to make sure it looks good there, too.

AAAAAAAAAAUUUUUGH! What happened?!?!

Nothing happened. It's still the same page, same coding, and same text. The problem was that you were allowing the boundaries of the browser to set parameters and Netscape Navigator and Internet Explorer are simply not the same animal. You need to make a point of forcing your page's parameters.

There are multiple methods of forcing parameters. Each has good points and each has some downfalls. Let's take a look at the most common formats first.

Tables, Tables, Tables

This is the method I see most often used to force a page's height. Not to sell it too early in the process, but this is the format I use to set the size for the HTML Goodies pages.

You can set the parameters of a page to fit perfectly into an 800×600 screen setting by simply surrounding the code of the page with a single table cell set to fit nicely into the parameters.

Note

Even though the screen settings are set to 800×600, the browser window (the space where the pages display) is not. Remember that you've got the navigation buttons, the location bar, and goodness knows whatever else up there. You need to take that into consideration when setting the parameters of your homepage.

If you want to ensure the page fits completely within the browser window, you'll need to set the table cell to a width of approximately 750. You really don't need to worry about the height as the page will tend to scroll. If you do worry about height, then you're undertaking a design that sits within a true box parameter. I've seen it done well. Maybe it's the format for you.

The code would look like this:

```
<HTML>
<HEAD>
<TITLE>Page Title here</TITLE>
</HEAD>
<BODY>
<TABLE BORDER="0">
<TR>
<TD WIDTH="750">
Entire page code in here
</TD></TR>
</TABLE>
</BODY>
</HTML>
```

Figure 3.8 shows what that code produces in an 800×600 monitor setting. I have set the table cell background to a darker color for you to see the actual cell walls.

When a page is long and scrolls, the bottom of the browser screen is referred to as the "gatefold," just like the gatefold inside of an album. Remember those? If not, think of it like the gatefold of a newspaper. That's the part where the paper...well...folds.

Anything past the gatefold is off of the screen when the user arrives, so if you do want to allow your page to scroll, you need to be careful not to put any crucial information down there—links, for instance.

By using the table format above, your page resizes beautifully to larger screen settings. Figure 3.8 is an example of the same 770-width table in a 1,024×768 screen setting.

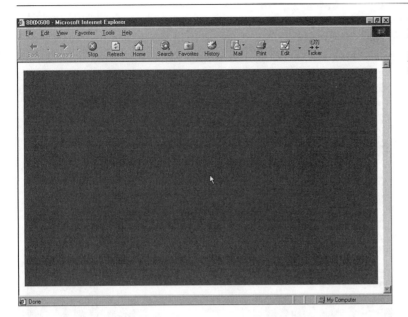

Figure 3.8
The box represents the parameters of the page elements.

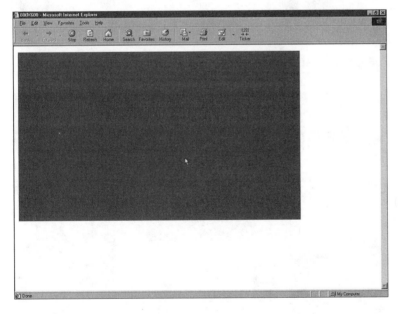

Figure 3.9
The whitespace is increased but your page isn't allowed to spread out and become oblong.

Of course, your Web page won't be a block of color like the previous one, so here are a couple of examples of sites that used the table format to get their sites to fit comfortably into the 800×600 format yet still look good in the larger screen settings. The Rotten Tomatoes Movie review site is a great example of using a table to set the width so that at any screen size setting, 800×600 or above, the layout and design don't move. The table cell holds the parameters steady (see Figure 3.10).

Figure 3.10
Rotten Tomatoes
`http://www.`
`rottentomatoes.com/`
has its table set to "760"
with no height setting.

Rotten Tomatoes at 1,024×768 is shown in Figure 3.11.

Figure 3.11
The table is centered for
the larger screen settings.

Figure 3.12 is one more, USA Today (`http://www.usatoday.com`).

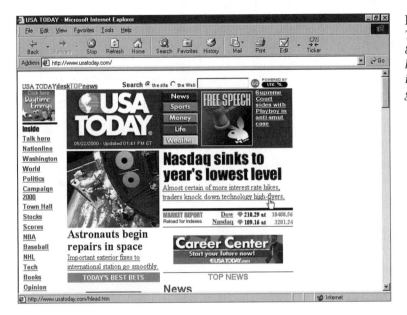

Figure 3.12
The page frames nicely in 800×600. The main headlines and most important information are above the gatefold.

Figure 3.13 shows what the USA Today site looks like in 1,024×768.

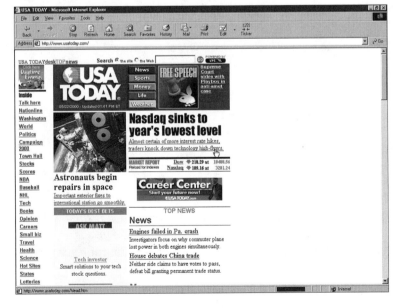

Figure 3.13
The table is allowed to remain hard left this time leaving a great deal of whitespace on the right side.

Going with the USA Today table format, playing to the 640×480 screen settings does create the ability to leave a great deal of whitespace on the right side.

My research has shown that those who use larger monitors aren't always pleased with the big empty spaces. In fact, almost 30% report not liking the effect. That's a pretty big chunk. I think Rotten Tomatoes does themselves pretty well by centering the table. You'll notice that USA Today didn't do that.

The table on the USA Today site is only 570 pixels wide. That leaves a TON of whitespace. Why would the designers do that?

They are taking into consideration those who have their screens set to 640×480. You may find that to be a little too small of a width, but give it a try. Maybe you can make a page that looks as good and is sure to fit on screen as low as 640 pixels wide. I've found it very hard to construct a page that fits nicely into 570 and still offer a solid homepage. USA Today has done it and done it well. Maybe you can get the same success.

I said previously that people dislike a lot of scrolling on homepages. They would much rather click than scroll through a lot of information. I was discussing vertical scrolling at that point.

Here's where you start to get into a smaller, smaller, smaller conundrum. People aren't that fond of a lot of vertical scrolling, but they HATE any horizontal scrolling.

Design Goodies Survey

HTML Goodies Survey Question: You enter a page where elements run off the right side of the screen causing you to scroll to the right. What do you think of this effect?

Like the effect	2%
Dislike the effect	87%
Doesn't matter	7%
Never seen the effect	4%
N=494	

Design or scrolling, design or scrolling, design or scrolling...

Okay, now what? Do you design for the smallest screen sizes—it does go even smaller for users of WebTV—or do you design for the most popular screen setting? Do you attempt to include everyone or do you shoot for the majority of the users making the minority with very small screen settings scroll to the right?

The overt thinking amongst designers is to design for 800×600 and above. My suggestion is to try the 570. If you can get a good page, use it. If not, go for the 800×600 settings first.

The use of a table cell is by far the most used format of setting parameters. The reason is the HTML table flags are understood universally in all browsers.

Another format of setting parameters is done through the use of a JavaScript. It used to be that using JavaScript was a little scary because not all of the browsers understood all of the commands. That era has pretty much passed and JavaScript, at least simple JavaScript v1.0 commands, can be used almost anytime you want.

Create a Page for Every Setting

This process involves the previous table format, but takes it one step further. Instead of designing one size that hopefully fits all, you create a different site for each different screen setting. Yes, it's a little more labor intensive, but you really knock out just about any downfall the table format offers.

What you do is create a site for each screen setting available. That means you need to redesign each of the pages and probably resize each of the images to make the pages fit nicely.

I say you'll need to design three sites because you'll have to make sure that the homepage that displays in the 800×600 setting only links to other pages that display the same. A great homepage that then links to nothing but poorly constructed pages does not go over well.

Again, I suggest using the table format for each an every page no matter what the screen setting format. It just makes good sense to do that because there is still a major difference between Netscape Navigator and Internet Explorer and designing for one or the other leaves you in trouble. Use the table.

Once you have designed the three sites, you will make your true homepage, the page that everyone comes to, nothing more than a JavaScript.

The JavaScript looks at the user's screen settings for you and loads the appropriate homepage for the screen setting. It's really a very slick process. Plus, it happens instantly. You need not create a firewall page.

A firewall page is a page that exists only to send the user to another page. Say your homepage is index.html. What you would do is make that index.html a firewall page. The page contains only the JavaScript below that redirects users to a page built specifically for their screen setting.

The index.html page never displays. It is only there to look at the user's screen setting and then send the user to the correct page for his screen setting.

The code that sits on the JavaScript homepage looks like this:

```
<HTML>
<TITLE>Screen Size Test Page</TITLE>
<BODY>
<SCRIPT LANGUAGE="javascript">

if (screen.width => 1024)
{parent.location.href='1024page.html'}

if (screen.width == 800)
{parent.location.href='800page.html'}

if (screen.width == 640)
{parent.location.href='640page.html'}

if (screen.width < 640)
{parent.location.href='text.html'}
</SCRIPT>
</BODY>
</HTML>
```

Notice what is happening. When the user arrives, the script looks at the user's screen set-ting width only. Height is pretty much immaterial at this point. You should mostly be interested in width because vertical scroll won't kill you, but horizontal scroll is death.

The script first asks if the setting is equal to or greater than 1,024 pixels. If it is, then a page titled "1024page.html" loads.

If the screen width is not equal to or larger than 1,024, it moves down the script and it check if the setting is equal to 800. If so, the page "800page.html" is called upon.

It happens again if the page is not 800 wide. Next it checks for 640. Up comes the "640page.html" if it is.

Finally, if the page is less than 640 then a simple text-based page named "text.html" loads.

The process is pretty easy to run. It's getting all those pages set up to run that takes the time. In case you're wondering, the screen sizes above 1,024 are as follows: 1,152, 1,280, and 1,600. The extra code to cover these sizes would be pasted into the script above the code for the 1,024 setting and would look like this:

```
if (screen.width == 1600)
{parent.location.href='1600page.html'}

if (screen.width == 1280)
{parent.location.href='1280page.html'}

if (screen.width == 1152)
{parent.location.href='1152page.html'}
```

Again, this process is fairly labor intensive, but it eliminates some of the downfalls of trying to design a table format that fits all screen settings.

I have a working copy of this script in a tutorial on the HTML Goodies site at `http://www.htmlgoodies.com/beyond/post_by_screen.html`.

The thinking here is instead of creating one page to fit all screen sizes, you create a page for all screen sizes and send the user to it using the firewall page.

Next up, maybe you can resize the user's browser window.

Resize the Window

I haven't seen this very often, but I have seen it. Usually this format is used when the physical size of the browser window is required for an effect, and any whitespace would kill the look. Here's the code:

```
<SCRIPT>
window.resizeTo(400, 200);
</SCRIPT>
```

The two numbers refer to pixels relating to the browser window. The first number is the width and the second sets the height.

Paste the code between the <HEAD> flags. Now, when the user arrives, his browser resizes to what you put into the preceding code.

Figure 3.14 shows what the code would look like.

Again, I don't see this very much and you really should have a solid reason for using it. I think the effect is very new to people so even a warning before resizing may be in order.

It wouldn't be good if someone continually attempted to restore his or her browser to the maximized size and you kept trying to make it smaller again.

Figure 3.14
A resized window against my desktop.

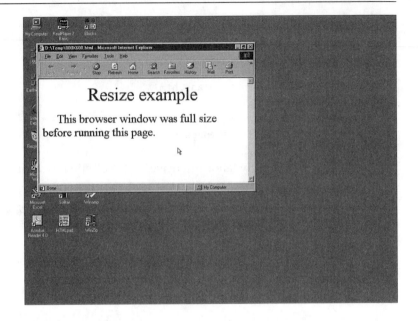

The pages I saw using this effect were very small in size. The entire page was maybe 400×400 pixels. If that small of a page displayed on a full browser screen, it would be lost. By altering the screen size, the page was framed pretty well.

That said, this is a rather abrupt change. If you decide to use it, you may want to run it past a few of your friends first to get their reaction.

How About Just Text and Few Images

I would be remiss if I didn't include this as part of the formatting of the parameters of the page, no parameter settings at all.

I had a student ask me one time if her page was good enough. She saw others with well-designed pages and saw hers as something less because she didn't have any whiz-bang programming in there.

Her pages were dedicated to people who had died. Each page was a simple white background with a 200×200 pixel picture of the person that passed in the upper-left corner. The text on the page was about the person, his life, and what he left behind.

There was no formatting. The words just flowed down around the image and off the page waiting for someone to scroll to read them. Each page ended with a simple Back hypertext link to return the reader to the homepage.

Perfect.

These pages would display wonderfully no matter what screen setting they came up on. Sure, the lines would break at different places on different screen settings, but so what? The design isn't the main push—it's the content. The browser can determine how it is presented because the look isn't the important thing. The text, and thus the content, is the important thing.

I say this because if you are intentionally designing a simplistic site then maybe you don't need to set the parameters. Remember that as an option.

Web site design must always focus on the site's killer app.

In this student's case, the killer app was the writing. Setting a parameter would have standardized the pages, but would it have added to them? Probably not.

Think about what you want your site to do and how you want it to look. Choose one of the previous formats and get ready to begin designing your site.

Site Critiques

1. Giggles/Author: Laura Arellano-Weddleton

`http://www.everycreature.com/Giggles/Pink.html`
Load Time: 13 Seconds, 57kps modem, cleared cache, 5/23/00 8:35AM.

My Screen Size: 1,024×768

Browsers Used: Internet Explorer 5 and Netscape Navigator 4.5

Concept: This is another personal homepage that is constructed solely to provide information about the author, Laura. I liked the look of all the pages once I got into the site. The author has found a theme of color and texture and has stuck with it. The topics are a complete mish-mash, but on a personal page, that's okay. You'll find anything from Laura's poetry to her love of rats. Yes. Rats.

Praise: Let me mention again, the fact that the author has chosen and kept a color scheme throughout the site. Figure 3.16 shows the homepage. It'll give you an idea of the scheme.

The wipe of colored texture with the script writing follows through. The backgrounds are always white. That might be a little too bright, but it's consistent. Keep in mind the author is only 13, and you'll see why I am giving her overall praise for the work. If you're doing this at 13, I'd like to see your work at 16. It will be leaps and bounds ahead of this and you'll still be very young in the game.

Figure 3.15
The Giggles welcome page.
(Color Plate C.7)

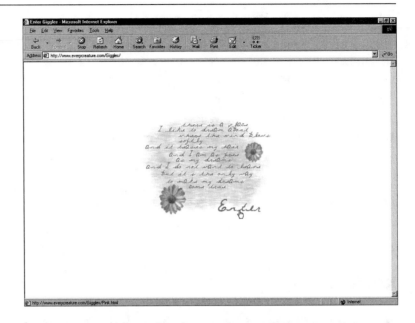

Figure 3.16
The Giggles homepage.

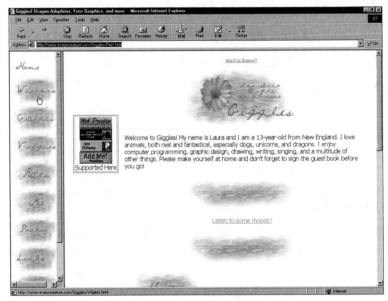

Concern: There are few things I dislike more than a welcome page that doesn't do anything. Notice how in Figure 3.15 the image that acts as your welcome page has a very nice poem and keeps to your format, but why make me stop on one page and then go on? In addition, the image was a splash, which took a long time to download.

Suggestion: Either lose the welcome page altogether, or change the image into a jpeg for speed sake. The Web is about speed and ease of use. That welcome page harms both of those elements on your site.

Concern: Frames don't blow me away to begin with because of all the problems they can cause across browsers and differing screen settings. You've chosen a frames format and some of those concerns have popped up. You have created a page in the left frame that is taller and wider than the frame allows for thus you have two scrollbars, a horizontal and a vertical. That simply has to be fixed.

Suggestion: Either make the left frame wider or make the page that displays within the frame smaller. Either way, get rid of those scrollbars. The purpose for having that navigation frame is so that you give a sense of consistency to the site. The links stay and the other page changes to remind you that you are still in the same site. It's a good effect until a scrollbar divides the two frames.

Concern: You've done what a lot of first-time designers do; you've made banner ads and off-site items more important than your own page. The small link images down the left side of the right frame are well displayed, but they do nothing for your site. Meanwhile, the links to your Guestbook, updates, and music pages are almost or totally off the screen.

Suggestion: Your site is what is important here. Put what is relevant to your site highest. The external links can be below the gatefold (bottom of the browser window).

Overall: For your age and limited abilities, you've got a rock-solid start here, Laura. If you make just the previous changes, you'll clean it up nicely. The only other suggestion I would make is to really look at the pages that appear in the right frame. They all scroll a great deal but also have a lot of whitespace. Can those pages be made more compact? Less scrolling? No scrolling? Just wondering.

2. David Neubauer: Magician/Author: David Neubauer

http://www.dnmagic.com/

Load Time: 21 Seconds, 57kps modem, cleared cache, 5/23/00 9:02AM.

My Screen Size: 1,024×768

Browsers Used: Internet Explorer 5 and Netscape Navigator 4.5

Concept: How about a magician at your next party? Dave is looking for work. This is a page dedicated to Dave Neubauer and his vocation. He's using it as a cyber-business card to find work. You can read references, see photos, and book him right from the page over email.

Figure 3.17
The homepage. (Color Plate C.8)

Praise: The biggest success, Dave, is that you went ahead and bought your own domain. It is my opinion that if you intend to use the Web for business purposes, you really need to be a domain unto yourself. You may want to check with your server, though. I ran into a goofy problem. I put in your address and got a DNS error, twice. The third time I hit enter it came up. Check into that. I like the background and the image it displays is perfect. It spells out that you are a magician straightaway.

There's just one thing driving me crazy...

Concern: Dave, where are your links? The homepage is two and a half screens long on my big monitor, more on smaller screen settings, and your links are way at the bottom (see Figure 3.18).

To get to your email, photos, reviews, or schedule, I have to scroll past your review from the Entertainment Media Awards and the long text about your getting married. Both pieces are well written, but they hold less interest than the links that will help me get to know you.

Suggestion: Get the links up high, right under the title if you can.

Concern: Is the animated image that reads "magician" needed? I know it's cool, but it's five times the size of a static image and slows the loading of the page. Your picture came in before the spinning text did.

Suggestion: No spinning text? Maybe go with a static image—better yet, text.

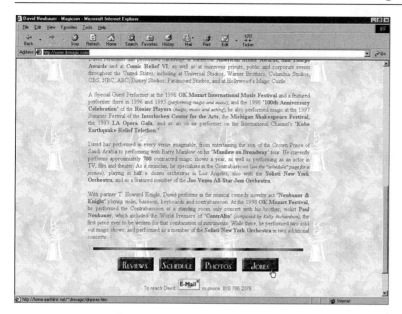

Figure 3.18
Scrolling along with Dave.

Concern: You have a stacked page here. One element is on top of another, on top of another. Can you create any kind of left-to-right eye-movement? Maybe have your image hard left and the four buttons that act as links listing down the right side. That would break up the list effect the page has now.

Overall: I'm not getting into subpages as much on these earlier critiques because I really haven't gotten into how they should look or what should be contained on them, but I wanted to say that your subpages were well done. I especially liked your photos page (see Figure 3.19).

You carried the background, the title, and the text format across pages. It was obvious I was still within the same site when I clicked around.

The best praise I have for your photos page is that you only offered three. That was just enough. I got to see what you looked like, there was a caption under the images, and the page loaded very quickly. Too often people set up photo pages that carry 20 or more jpeg images when I get the concept of the page after the first two. Yours was done well.

The other subpages carried the same formatting and I liked them as well. You have constructed a nice site here. I think it can be more functional and better suited for the audience. It'll take just a few changes here and there.

Figure 3.19
Just enough photos.

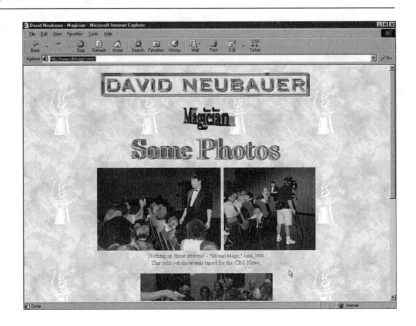

3. Keith Black: Realtor/Author: Keith Black

`http://www.1ststop4homes.com/`

Load Time: 1 minute 37 Seconds, 57kps modem, cleared cache, 5/23/00 9:26AM.

My Screen Size: 1,024×768

Browsers Used: Internet Explorer 5 and Netscape Navigator 4.5

Concept: This is a site dedicated to Keith Black and his work as a realtor.

Praise: The site offers an absolute wealth of information both about Keith, realty in general and selling and buying a home. Keith has put a great deal of work into the site, that's a given. You won't run into any under construction signs here. I think the site could offer that information a whole lot better and be more helpful to the user if Keith would make a few changes.

Concern: The load time for the page was waaaaaay toooooo looooong. Anything over 15 seconds is leave time. I looked at your code to see what exactly was stopping the page from coming in. Did you know you have three applets on just the homepage? Those things are big, too. In Figure 3.20, I attempted to catch the biggest of the applets. That's the one at the very top that is a swinging watering can that fills up your name. The entire process takes around 15 second to complete...every single time I come into the page. In addition,

108

you have two applets at the very bottom of the right frame that didn't help me at all. One proclaims who wrote the site and the other scrolls some credits. The thing is, once I arrived at the bottom of the right-side frame, the scroll is over so all I had was the background with no scroll. I had to reload the page to see what the thing did.

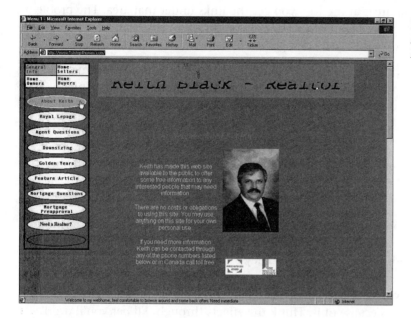

Figure 3.20
Keith's Page. (Color Plate C.9)

Suggestion: I agree the applets are slick. They are a neat effect, but they are not bigger than the site itself. Think seriously about losing all three simply for load time sake. A text banner and text at the bottom of the page for help credits and design credits will suffice. They are not the push of the page. The realtor information is the big push on the page.

Concern: The red lettering against the deep green background is doing what's known as "moiré." As you look at the red text, it appears to move around on top of the green. It's hypnotic, but not good for the user.

Suggestion: Go with a deeper red.

Concern: What is important to this page? It is the fact that anyone can use anything on the page or is it the ability to contact you and see your listings? I would suggest it's the listings and your contact info. That's not the way you have it on the page.

Suggestion: Get your address, you phone, your email, your listings up high. Get that information next to your picture. The permission stuff can come secondary.

Concern: It took me a good minute or better to figure out how that navigation system on the left worked. I see it's in four sections and then under each section are links. Note how in Figure 3.20 that as I put my mouse over each link within the oval, the section the link appears in lights up. I thought it was an applet at first, but it's really a huge JavaScript.

If you click one of the four areas at the top, you get the links under that area. The problem I ran into was, once I left the General Info section, I couldn't get back to it. No matter how much I clicked, it wouldn't return. That's not good.

Suggestion: Lose the script. It doesn't work correctly and is pretty darn confusing. Go with a hierarchy of links down the left frame window. I know it's not as whiz-bang as you'd like but it'll work and that's what matters.

Overall: I went to every subpage in the General Information section. I was pleased to see that you followed the same background all the way through and used the same applet at the top of each page. The text changed, but it was the same applet that had already been put into cache so it loaded very quickly. The text in the subpages was white and thicker than the homepage. That was great. I could read it all.

This page has the same problem a lot of pages have. The author has placed programming above the load and usefulness of his page. The applets aren't important to the page. The JavaScript style links are not useful to the page. They look great, but they're doing more harm than good. Keith, your killer app is to teach people about selling and buying a house and maybe sell them one yourself. No one came for the fancy programming. The problem is that they just might leave because of it. Think the effects through. I'll bet you'll drop most of them.

Chapter 4

Your Site and Your Server

Hopefully, you've given your site some serious thought and have gone out onto the Web to see what others are doing. At this point you should be well enough along to make some more specific decisions about not only what will be on your site, but also where your site will be located.

The server side of a Web site is rather important both to how your site is perceived and to your design. I'm talk about both the server where the site will be housed, and how you will set up the site on the server. Both are important, not only to you, but also to how the user navigates the site.

Now, you need to examine the relationship between your site and your server.

So...what do you want from your ISP?

That all depends on what you intend to do with your Web site. It also depends on what you might want to do with your Web site in the future. You may not want to post a Guestbook right now, but what about down the road a few months? Yes, I know you can always upgrade to a new server later on, but that's not overly good for your users. If you keep moving, they may not find you so easily again.

Do yourself a favor. Pick a good ISP up front. I am most interested in your making your best pick up front because moving your site from server to server is just not a good idea.

What if you have to change servers? That's a problem.

You'll need to not only move all your files from one server to another, but what of any links to you that might already be out there? What about the submissions you made to the search engines? All those links point back to your old site.

You could attempt to ask everyone that had a link to your old site to change it, but that would take forever. You'll have to hang onto the site you're leaving just to have redirect links. You've seen them. Those are the pages that proudly proclaim that, "Our Site Has Moved" and then ask you to wait a second or click on the new link.

By the way, surfers don't like that. It shows a lower level of professionalism.

Yes, you could perform a redirect that doesn't have that page using a meta-refresh command set to zero seconds so that the user is automatically sent to the new site. Then the problem you run into is that there are a lot of browsers out there that don't understand the command and will not redirect. That's why people still post the page that suggests you wait a couple of seconds or click the link.

Yes, sometimes it's out of your hands and you have to change servers with your site. I had to change HTML Goodies once when I went from the school server to a domain of my own. It caused a real headache with all the external links that were on the net pointing at the old address, even with server redirects done by the previous Webmaster. The problem was that people had linked to specific tutorials on the old site, but when I went to a full domain format, the server redirect from the old server only sent people to the new HTML Goodies homepage. I really upset some users.

Have I driven this point into the ground? The choice is yours. You may choose whatever server you wand. You just need to make darn sure that it's a server you will be happy with in the long run. Users will not follow you around forever.

First Concern: Where Are You Going to Put the Site?

As I see it, you have three broad choices regarding where you will house your site:

1. A free access Internet service provider (ISP)
2. A pay-for ISP
3. A domain of your own

A Free Access ISP

The question I'm often asked is if anyone really cares if a Web site is housed on a free ISP or not. The short answer is that it depends on how the free ISP deals with keeping itself free. Do they blast the user with ad banners and little pop-up windows or do they have ad banners on the page? Are there ads at all?

Survey after survey related to ad banners show that people don't like them and would rather they not be so prevalent on the Web. A recent report by DoubleClick.com suggests less than one percent of all ad banners displayed on the Web are actually clicked on.

I spoke to a representative at DoubleClick and he said they felt that was a high number in relation to the number of ads being displayed. Thus, don't look for ad banners to leave any time soon.

I've purchased advertising for numerous sites. I remember one time where an ad banner received just under a two-percent click rate. The sales person was jubilant. It was almost double what he was used to.

Design Goodies Survey

HTML Goodies Survey Question: Have you ever clicked on an ad banner?

Rarely	56.15%
Never	23.17%
Sometimes	19.2%
Many Times	1.46%
N=479	

Obviously, ads don't move your users. In fact, too many ads will upset them. Is free housing worth frustrating or driving away users?

Web sites housed on free sites such as Geocities.com and Tripod.com are seen in a lesser light than a Web site on a pay-for ISP or a site that has its own domain name. As you might have guessed, it's not the Web site itself that garners the poor response from users. The reason is mainly the amount of advertising that a free ISP user has to display.

I use Geocities.com and Tripod.com as examples of sites that can upset users because both of the sites allow free access to users through a series of pop-up windows that contain ads. As of late, Geocities.com has wisely made their pop-up advertisements much smaller and Tripod has started to use embedded ads. That's good, but users still report a great dislike for the ads popping up each time they change the page. Tripod is still running the tried and true new window containing a full-size ad banner.

Programming has improved, but I vividly remember when, if you used a frame format on your Geocites.com site, an ad banner would pop up for every frame window. There could be twenty frames and twenty little ads from one click. Ugh.

I write a weekly newsletter and every time I mention ad banners and free sites, people write to be in great mass telling me of this site or that site that offers free access in order to get you online. Each, they claim, is better than the last.

I went surfing around a few of these sites and found some to be better than others but it's not my place to tell you where to house your site. Besides, by the time you read this, any site I suggest could very well be out of business or 20 new sites offering better service might have popped up.

If you're looking for a free service to house your site, go to any of the major search engines and enter "free ISP" without the quotes and get ready to read. My Yahoo! Search turned up well over 100 hits.

Go to the sites, read over their policies, and be very, very sure before you sign up for any of the services.

A free service will not offer you a great deal more than space, but I do think there are a few things you should look for:

- Look for speed. If you are thinking about a specific free ISP, go to many of the sites already housed on the site and surf. Was your experience an enjoyable one? Did the pages come in quickly and without a lot of extra elements placed there by the free ISP? If so, that's a positive.

- Look for space. What you are buying, or not buying in this case, is space. How much do you get? All other elements being equal, choose the most amount of space.

- Can you write your own pages and post them or must you use the site's templates and Web text editor? Again, all other elements being equal, choose the server that allows you to post pages you write offline. That will simply give you better control over your site.

- Do you get an email address? Most often you won't, but sometimes you do. Take that into consideration.

You'll read those words time and time again in this chapter. Be very, very sure of the service you choose.

I say that because if you make a quick rash decision on a server simply because of cost, you may find out later that you don't have access to a lot of services that you might want. These services might include Telnet, the ability to place Common Gateway Interfaces (CGI) which will help you create fancy Guestbooks or counters, and File Transfer Protocol (FTP) in case you would ever like to offer files for people to download. You may not understand or even want these services now, but maybe down the line you will. Very few, if any, free services offer these abilities. You get what you pay for.

Free sites come and go. If you are interested in making a serious go of this Web site then think seriously about paying for the space with a reputable ISP that's been in business for a few years.

However, this is your site. Maybe you're just looking for some space where you can play around and try out new elements. Maybe this will only be a site for you and a few friends. Many people believe the WWW should be free at all points. If that's your thinking then maybe the free ISP is for you. Just think it through in a true and realistic manner before you sign up, create the site, and register it with every search engine under the sun.

A Pay-For ISP

Maybe the free access route isn't for you and you'd like to go with a server that wants a basic $10 to $20 or so per month for Internet access. I actually have three of these accounts. Don't ask why, the answers get really silly.

Again, just like the free access ISPs, there are a slew of these sites out there at both the national and the local level.

The national sites are pretty big names, Aol.com, Compuserve.com, TSN.com, BellSouth.net, and so on. Again, I found a list of them, 262 to be exact, simply by going onto a major search engine and putting in "Internet Service Provider." This time I used the quotes because I wanted to search for those words specifically.

Read the descriptions and then read the policies of a few that strike your fancy. Again, you're looking for a service that offers as many abilities as possible. The less the server allows you to do, the more you'll be restricted as your knowledge base grows.

Here's a list of some of the elements you should be looking for in a pay-for ISP:

1. I would suggest that you find a server that allows free dial-up service. You don't want to have to pay to attach to a local ISP only to put your files on a national ISP. Paying for two services doesn't make much sense.

2. You'll want FTP access so you can upload your files. All the software should come with the package you buy.

3. You want at least five megabytes of space. That's the very low end.

4. The site should come with at least three email addresses.

5. A few nice extras should be free guestbook programming, and/or the ability to upload CGIs.

6. If you have access to upload CGIs, make sure you also have telnet access.

7. Access to the site access logs would be nice so you can keep track of the number of visitors without having to post counters.

8. Does the ISP offer a telephone number you can call for help? I believe that all things being equal, choose the site that offers a telephone number with a real person on the other end over a site that has you write an email if you run into trouble.

Compare the features of those that you found interesting. Remember, these ISPs are vying for your business and they are always trying to outdo one another. Allow them to play in your favor.

If a national ISP isn't your cup of tea, try to find a local ISP. Forget the Web at this point, open the yellow pages and look under "Internet" or buy a Sunday newspaper. That's the same advice I give everyone who asks and they have all been successful finding a server.

I personally like a local server. The reason is because I can actually go to the server site and look at their facilities. I can meet the people who will be servicing my system. I can actually talk to a tech that is doing more than manning a phone; he or she is close enough to the system to fix a problem before I hang up.

Just like national ISPs, the local ISPs are in competition with one another and they want your business. Contact three or four providers. Ask to come in and see their systems. Ask to talk to or email some of their clients including some of their local business clients. Any ISP worth its salt will have no trouble with these requests. In fact, many will probably jump at the opportunity to show off their hardware. Server technicians tend to be very proud of their own work. I've received some of the best tours from these people.

Take the time and choose wisely.

A Domain of Your Own

It used to be that becoming *www.something.com* was rough doings. Today it's as easy as buying any other ISP account.

First, you need to get the name. At the time I was writing this book, sites were popping up all over the Web that had received permission to sell you a domain name. Deals were flying and domain names were being sold for up to ten-year spans of time.

The three sites you'll want to visit first are NetworkSolutions.com, DomainDirect.com, and Register.com. At each site you'll be allowed to put in a possible domain name and check to see if anyone already owns the name. You should make a list of possible names first before you get your heart set on any one particular name.

Go to these sites with your list of possible domain names and find the one you like. Will you be a "com" or a "net"? How about a "biz" or a "museum"? Hmmm. Maybe you're an "org."

What in the world do all these extensions mean? Do you need them all? Maybe yes...maybe no. Here's a quick look at each:

.com stands for commerce. This is the most common domain suffix. It is so common in fact that one of the top methods of searching people use on the Web is to add .com to a name or work and see if anything comes up. You need to buy your domain with this extension. This will allow you to sell advertising and product should you ever decide to do so.

.net stands for network and should represent a network, but it doesn't. In most users' minds, .net is pretty much .com. You can do everything with a .net that you can do with a .com.

.org stands for organization. You cannot post advertising or sell on an .org. You can, however, accept donations.

.tv, .ws, .cc, and a slew of others are just now coming into the fold. The choice to buy them is up to you. I personally never have.

Here are a few things to keep in mind when you go about buying a domain name:

- You want a domain name that is short, easy to speak, and hard to hear incorrectly.
- Do not use numbers if you can avoid it. If you must use a number, buy the domain name with the number both spelled out and as a number. For example: 2dogs.com and twodogs.com. Have the ISP that will house your domain set it up so that no matter which one the user puts in, the same page pops up. The ISP can do that. It's fairly easy, I'm led to believe.
- Avoid hyphens. They are often misunderstood when people first hear a Web address.
- Do not include words such as "the" or "a" if you can avoid it.
- You may also want to make a point of buying the .net, and .org domain names as well. You may never use them, but by buying them, you stop someone else from having them and possible taking some of your traffic.
- If your domain has a word that can easily be misspelled, buy the domain with the misspelling. You can always set those misspelled domains to take the user to the correct domain.

One of the very good things about buying your own domain is that you can move the site around from server to server and not mess up any of the links back to you out there on the Web. The domain name follows you everywhere. The HTML Goodies pages have been housed on three different servers since I changed to a full domain name. Users never knew that changes occurred because the address always stayed the same. Only the server changed. This may be enough of a reason to go with a domain name in itself.

Which servers can give you a domain? Well, pretty much any server can do it, it's if they offer the service or not. You have to ask.

Are There Free Domain Services?

Yes.

I get letters all the time telling me of the multitude of free domain servers out there. These are sites that will basically do every step for you including securing the domain name of your choice. Even though these services will get names for you, it's still a good idea to check to see if your preferred domain name is available. It'll cut way down on time.

If you'd like to see a list of free domain servers, head to a major search engine and enter the words "free domain" without the quotes. I had ten pop up on the first try.

Again, read over their services and policies. Choose the one that you feel will offer the best deal.

You're going to run into the same concerns you will have choosing one of the free ISPs noted previously. Yes, you'll have a domain name but you won't have a great deal of control over it.

I've been made aware of two major downfalls of using a free domain ISP. The first is that they can tend to be a little slow if the server people put too many accounts onto one server. The second is that if your site grows a great deal, the free server may not allow you to keep the site on their machine. HTML Goodies receives over one million hits a week. No free domain server will accept that size of a site for free.

If you expect your domain to grow to great proportions, 10,000 visitors a month or better, a free domain ISP may not be the way to go.

Paying for a domain server is a little easier and, as you might have guessed, you can get a lot more access and abilities with a site you pay for.

Let me suggest again that you look at a local ISP for this service. The local ISP can set up what's known as a virtual domain name so that your site sits on one of their servers, but acts as its own domain. Users will never know what server you're actually on. I ran HTML Goodies this way for years.

The cost structure for buying a virtual domain varies widely, but basically you'll pay a one-time setup fee to get the domain name on the server and then a monthly cost of some sort.

Some servers charge a flat monthly rate. Others charge per the number of hits you accumulate in addition to a lower monthly rate. One of my deals asked for a dollar for every thousand hits of the server. When Goodies began to get to half a million hits per month, I went with a flat rate provider. That was the first of my domain moves.

You need to contact multiple ISPs and gather the rate structure of each and what services you receive in return. I would make a point of asking if your site will receive any additional attention because it is a domain and you're paying more than the normal account rate.

Pick the ISP that you feel offers the best deal.

Buy or Rent Your Own Server

There is one more option you should know about, but I'll tell you up front, it's pricey. It's possible to buy what's known as a "co-inhabit." That's a deal where you either buy or rent your own server. That server is then attached to the Internet through an ISP.

I've done this myself. I own a machine that I have never seen. It's housed in Hollywood, California, at an ISP there.

The benefits are that you're the only domain on the machine and you have seemingly unlimited space to play around with. Your site will run quickly and only service your needs. You also don't have to worry about the number of hits or visitors driving up your price. You can have any access you'd like as long as someone at the ISP can set it up for you.

The downside is that you must take on the cost of the server purchase or rent and then a monthly fee for taking care of the server. My co-inhabit runs me around $700 per month. Of course, costs may have changed greatly since I wrote this page.

Cybersquatters Are Out There

If you purchase your own domain, here's one more concern. If you become successful, there will always be someone out there attempting to make money off of that success. Those people will buy up domain names that are similar to yours hoping to cash in either by selling the domain names back to you or by setting a site to grab the runoff from your site.

These people are called cybersquatters. If you purchase a domain, think seriously about buying the extension equals to the name. For instance, you buy Zonkers.com. Maybe you should also buy Zonkers.net and Zonkers.org and so on. You should cybersquat yourself before others do it for you.

Just because you purchase a second domain name doesn't mean you have to set up a system for it. You can just flat out own it and do nothing with it. It's just that others cannot own it. I have purchased a ton of domain names that come close to my wife's site StreetArtist.com. I was interested in killing both the cybersquat and having sites available if my wife decided to expand in the future.

So, the choice is yours. Take the time to decide what type of server is appropriate to your future site and then make an informed decision regarding your ISP. Please don't make the mistake of saying you'll start small and build up if the site gets popular. You could tear the site down moving it around. Think as big as you can afford.

The decisions you make this early in the game are unbelievably important to the overall success of your site.

Don't take your ISP decision lightly.

On the Server

Some of the greatest lessons I've learned regarding Web design were taught to me through horribly embarrassing moments. Allow me to illustrate my next point with one of the most painful memories.

While I was a graduate student, I kept numerous different sites. The two that pertain to this story were the official site for the Central States Communication Association, a prominent university-level communication research group, and the official David Lee Roth homepage.

How's that for a diametrically opposed pair of sites?

I, stupidly, kept both sites out of the same account. To further show myself to be an idiot, I kept both sites out of the same directory.

One day I received an email from one of the officers of the Communication Association telling me that David Lee Roth had no business being associated with Central States.

I was infuriated. How dare he tell me what additional sites I can and cannot keep? I felt that as long as I kept the sites separate, he had no basis for telling me not to keep the David Lee Roth site. To further prove my brain-dead state, I wrote this down in a letter and sent if off. This was my first lesson in never writing an angry email letter.

He replied asking if I had been to the Communication Association's site lately. It had been a day or two, so I went. There, in full color, where the Communication Association's banner marquee should have been was a glaring picture of Dave's face covered in war paint.

Whoa. That's not good.

I had named the original Communication Association banner marquee "banner.gif." Then, without checking first, I created the David Lee Roth image, named it "banner.gif" and uploaded it to my site. The second image overwrote the first image and the fun started from there.

I offered to resign and they luckily didn't let me, and we all had a big laugh over the entire event. At least that's how I like to remember it. There really wasn't a tremendous amount of laughter.

So, what's the point? The point is that now that you have a server to house your files, you'll need to make some decisions regarding how those files will be organized on your server.

Do This! Equal Your Computer and Your Server

No matter what format you go with, you must make a point of creating the same format on your home computer as you create on your server. If you have a series of subdirectories on your server but keep your files at home in one giant directory, then you're going to have problems.

Make the two equal.

Do This! Learn to Work with Subdirectories

How you will break up your site depends on how large your site actually will be. I'm talking in terms of number of pages and number of images more than physical size of the elements. Will you have a lot of pages and a lot of images or will you have just a few?

If you have just a few, then maybe keeping them all within the same directory, both on the server and on your home computer, isn't such a bad idea. You can pretty easily keep an eye on 20 to 30 files if that's all you're going to have.

This format has its benefits in that in the HTML code, you only need to call for the images by their names alone. Like so:

```
<IMG SRC="joeimage.gif">
```

Because the pages and the images are all within the same directory, there's no need for a path.

However, if you intend on keeping a lot of pages and images, or you intend to run different sites from the same account, then you will want to try a more broken-up format. A series of subdirectories will make your life a great deal easier.

Believe me, I know my suggesting this scares some people. I've known many authors who have done everything in their power to not create subdirectories on their server. They've gone as far as giving images with absurd random names so they can't possibly overwrite them by mistake.

Some who run multiple pages out of their single account would go as far as starting each page and image name with a different identifier to keep the two sites separate. The list would look something like this:

```
Dave_banner.gif

Dave_index.html

CSCA_banner.gif

CSCA_index.html
```

You know what? If the thought of setting up subdirectories scares you, maybe this is the best method. That's what I did after the Web debacle described earlier. It took forever to update the pages and the image names when all I really had to do was create two subdirectories and put each site's files in each of those two directories. However, if you start doing it this way, maybe you'll have better luck.

I would still take the time to try working with subdirectories, though. Once you get it, you'll wonder what you were so nervous about.

Live and learn.

A Web designer friend of mine turned me onto setting up sites with multiple subdirectories and I've done it this way ever since. The format is quite sound and will help you tremendously when looking for files or updating pages.

The simplest format is to create only one subdirectory in your Web account and name it "images."

Once you do that, you can separate the elements of your site into to two groupings, pages and images. The pages will go into the Web account like they normally would and the images will go into the images subdirectory.

You'll have to account for this in your HTML code, of course. Images can no longer be called upon simply by their name alone. You'll need to add that subdirectory path. It's not hard by any means. You just have to remember to do it. Inline image commands would look like this:

```
<IMG SRC="/images/banner.gif">

<IMG SRC="/images/dave.gif">
```

Once you master the art of that image subdirectory, try setting up more. Make one for just your ad banners. Make another one for applets. If you have multiple sections to your Web site, put each section into its own subdirectory.

It's up to you if you want to put another images subdirectory under that new section sub-directory. I never do. I keep all my images in just the one directory.

Here's an example. Figure 4.1 shows what my FTP client looks like when I am logged into HTML Goodies. Notice all the subdirectories on the right, the server side, and how I have those same directories on the left, my computer side.

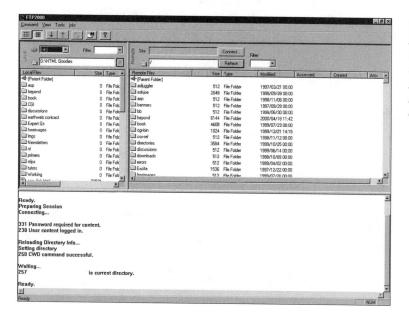

Figure 4.1
Look at how the HTML Goodies site is broken into a series of subdirectories. I keep many of the same subdirectory names on my own computer.

Now, the real glory of this format is that it allows you to easily see what files you have on your site. The images directory only contains images. The HTML file directories only con-tain HTML files. It's extremely clean and very easy to follow. If you have all your files dumped into one large directory, even if you make a point of adding identifiers to each element's name, the names get hard to read, especially if you give some of the images the same name as some of the pages. I do that all the time.

So, at this point, think about your site. Into what sections will you be breaking it up? You may only be putting together a small personal site. That's not a problem. You will at least break up the files into HTML documents and images. I've seen some people go as far as even breaking their images into GIF and JPEG subdirectories. I broke images up into thumbnails and full size images on one project.

It's all a matter of your own personal taste and how you want to break up your site. Just remember that whatever subdirectory you create, you'll need to call on the elements inside that subdirectory using that path in the HTML flag, just like the image code examples previously mentioned.

Site Critiques—Section Four

I am always amazed at the work that amateur Web designers can put together in their spare time. I have made a point of not reviewing any professionally built Web sites in this book. I wanted you, the reader, to see some of the great coding that you can learn and put together even when you just build sites on the weekends for fun. The first critique in this small series of three is such a site.

1. The Connecticut Guild of Puppetry/Author: Chris Grande

`http://www.ctpuppetry.org`

Load Time: 24 Seconds, 57kps modem, cleared cache, 6/02/00 10:34AM.

My Screen Size: 1,024×768

Browsers Used: Internet Explorer 5 and Netscape Navigator 4.5

Figure 4.2
A clever page dedicated to puppetry in Connecticut. (Color Plate C.10)

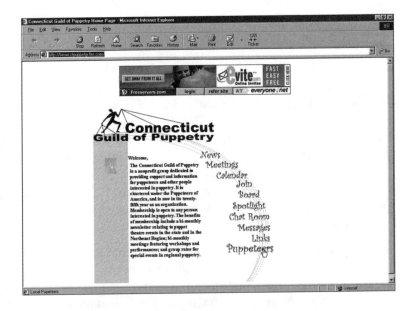

Concept: The page explains quite clearly what it intended to do. "The Connecticut Guild of Puppetry is a nonprofit group dedicated to providing support and information for puppeteers and other people interested in puppetry." The site is dedicated to all things puppetry and stays true to that killer app. If you're interested in this niche art form and you live in Connecticut, this is your page.

Praise: HTML is blocky. There's no getting around it. The language does not allow for easily smooth flowing lines. Arcs and curves are hard to pull off.

As you can see, this author has been successful is getting a very smooth arc of ribbon to cascade down the right side of the screen. The author used a technique that is getting a lot more play on the Web these days. It would be quite easy to simply create a large image with the words cascading as they are and then turn the image into an image map, but the author also has rollovers on the links, more on that in a moment. In order to get the roll over effect, each of the links must be a single image. So, rather than make a giant image map, the author has built a larger image out many smaller ones. The page actually looks like this without the images loaded. You can see the building process in Figure 4.3.

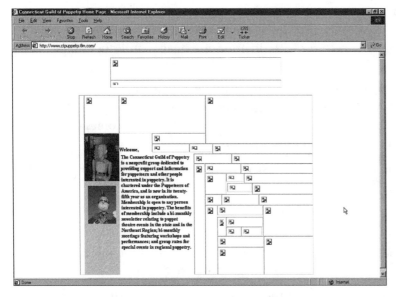

Figure 4.3
This is what it's like to play with blocks in HTML.

The images on the right are posted by an applet so I really can't get rid of them, but take a look at the format of the smaller images on the right. You can see how the larger image was built.

Now, to give you a better idea of how the curve was created, Figure 4.4 shows the same screen capture with the links made visible.

Figure 4.4
Links made visible.

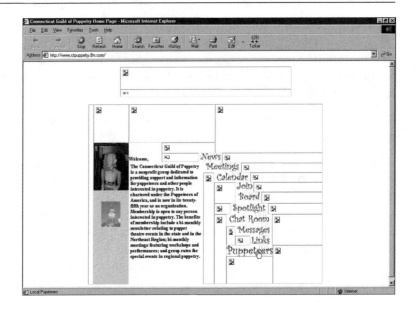

I'd like to say that there is some quick trick to creating something like this, but I'll bet it's nothing more than a lot of trial and error with differing-size images until they all fit like Lincoln Logs. It's a fantastic effect.

Look again at Figure 4.4. Notice my pointer on the last link, "puppeteers." The word is slightly larger than the other link text. That is the result of a well-thought-out rollover. When the mouse passes over top, the word gets slightly larger. It almost comes out at the user. That's a solid use of a rollover to aid in navigation.

You can now see why the author wanted to make each link an individual image. Without it, he couldn't make the individual links rollovers.

Let's go in to one of the subpages. When I click "News," the page shown in Figure 4.5 comes up.

This subpage is a pretty good example of the format used across all of the subpages in the site. I wanted to point out a couple of things I thought were well done.

First off, look at the small navigation bar on the left. On the homepage, the author set the text firmly in your mind. You know the text down the left side represents navigation, not because it's down the left side, but more because of the font. The homepage set that font, and that run of words, as the navigation for the site. Now as you move through the site, you are aware that that text and that list of words are navigation. Because of that fact, the navigation on the subpages does not have to be as prevalent as the navigation on the homepage.

Concern: Allow me to start with this subpage. Everything on the page seems to go toward the killer app of the site except that site search function. What should I search, old news? If so, what exactly am I searching for?

Suggestion: I like the idea of a search engine for searching old news, but its placement is wrong. I would put it further down the page. Maybe even put it in place of the counter...which took a long time to load.

Concern: On each subpage, you have the same navigation going down the left side, but one of the links simply reloads the page. Users aren't big fans of clicking links that don't do anything.

Suggestion: Eliminate or highlight the name of the page currently being viewed for the user. For example, on the News page, instead of keeping news a link, make it simple bold text so it denotes the user is on that page. You might even think about eliminating the News links altogether since you have the title across the top. Either way, don't leave up a link that will do nothing but reload the page when the user clicks.

Concern: On the homepage, you have an applet running that has three images come in and then fade away. It was the last thing to load on the page. Ask yourself if it is truly a required element.

Suggestion: If it is needed—keep it. If not, lose it.

Concern: You have a large block of text that you've set to a small font size then you bold-ed the small-size text. That bold tends to muddy small text making it look blocky and somewhat unprofessional. It's almost as if you were contradicting yourself. First, you want it small then you don't and bold it.

Suggestion: Either lose the small or the bold, one or the other.

Concern: This is such a wonderful site, please, oh please, get off the free server. That top, center ad banner just kills the entire effect.

Suggestion: Find the $20 a month to get on a server that doesn't post ad banners in exchange for space. Ask if any members would chip in to buy space—pay for it by yourself, anything. Just get off of that free server. The money you're saving is nowhere near worth the scar that ad is putting on your beautiful site.

Are you a nonprofit organization? If so, many ISPs will cut you a big price break. I know of stories where servers have donated space for free as a tax break for the ISP. Think about asking a few servers for that deal.

Note: The site took the advice and can now be found at `http://www.ctpuppetry.org`.

Overall: I really liked the site and was very proud of the work you did. I'm pleased that an amateur can build a site like this. It gives hope to those who are just getting started in Web design and wonder if they will ever put together a really striking site. Well done.

2. WEBmaintenance/Author: Jan Wilhelm Lohne

`http://www.webmaintenance.org/`

Load Time: 8 Seconds, 57kps modem, cleared cache, 6/02/00 11:27AM.

My Screen Size: 1,024×768

Browsers Used: Internet Explorer 5 and Netscape Navigator 4.5

Concept: I was moved to look at this site simply because of its name. I expected the site would offer some HTML instruction or design suggestions. The site denotes its reason for being this way: "WEBmaintenance.org is made for one goal only: To promote quality on the net. Not by itself, but as a great tool for communication among the important factor—the people."

After moving through the site, I'm not overly sure what the author means by that. I think the site is meant to be a forum for people to discuss what make the Web good and what makes the Web not so good. That type of forum makes sense. The trouble is the author has, himself, put together a site that has some problems making the WEBmaintenance arena one that is hard to get around in.

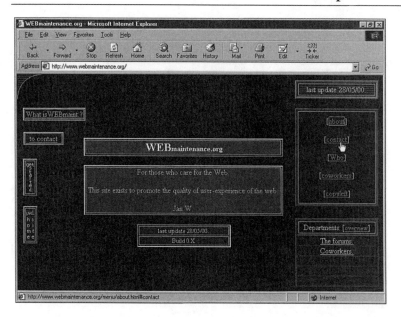

Figure 4.6
The WEBmaintenance homepage. (Color Plate C.11)

Praise: As you can see from the screen capture, the site resized the window for me making my browser conform to the page rather than the other way around. I actually like that look. I don't mind a site resizing for me. If it makes my surfing and viewing a little easier then the effect is fine with me.

Black backgrounds are all the rage lately and this site has a black background, but the author went one step further and set aside his text blocks with different background–colored tables. I like that look. It's easy on the eye and I can read all the text.

You may not have grasped it at first, but this page is in a frame layout. There's a big frame window on the left and three windows down the right side. The page is built to never leave the format and to load into the many frame windows available.

That's where the problems come in…

Concern: The problem with setting yourself up as an authority, which this site has, is that when you make a mistake it is amplified tenfold. When I make a coding mistake on HTML Goodies, I hear about the mistake in the nastiest of email letters. I am supposed to be the expert thus I should not make a mistake. It's the same thing here. Each of the links on the left produced something that looks like Figure 4.7.

Suggestion: Make sure every link at least goes to a working page. Do not go live with a site that is not complete.

Figure 4.7
AAAAAAAUUUUUGH!
404 error!

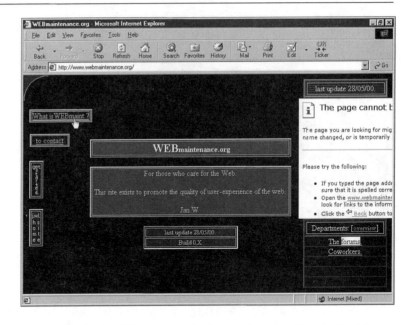

Concern: I cannot read the links on the left. You've made the text so small and piled it vertically. It took me a good 30 seconds to figure out that the one link reads "Get Started." That should be a little more obvious. In addition, why did you write the top link as "What is WEBmaint?" Why would you not write out the entire title of your site? The abbreviation is actually a bit confusing.

Suggestion: Go with a more traditional format for links. A vertical list within its own colored background table cell would go a long way.

Concern: Under "Departments" you have two lines of text that are both white and underlined. The lines scream of being links, but they're not. That's misleading and can upset users.

Suggestion: If the link is "to come…," don't put it up until it has arrived.

Concern: You have "last updated" dates on the site twice.

Suggestion: One will do just fine. The one in the top right is best to keep.

Overall: I have to ask a simple question, "What does this site do?" What is its purpose? Why is it up for the world to see? Maybe the answer is within the pages that didn't come up when I clicked.

You have a very good design concept here. I was impressed with the resizing of the window down to a seamless frame look that would stay fixed. I liked that a lot. Past that original look, the site doesn't do much. Stop, take stock of what you're attempting to accomplish, and come at this site again. You really do have something good here. Work toward making it great.

3. The Anime Enclave/Authors: David Wren & Seung L. Park

`http://home.maine.rr.com/dwren`

Load Time: 41 Seconds, 57kps modem, cleared cache, 6/02/00 11:57AM.

My Screen Size: 1,024×768

Browsers Used: Internet Explorer 5 and Netscape Navigator 4.5

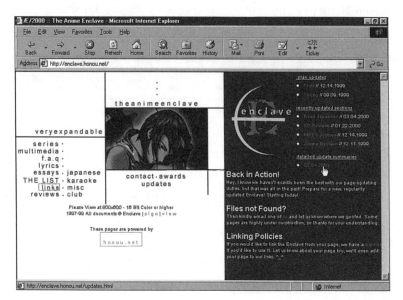

Figure 4.8
Welcome to the Enclave.
(Color Plate C.12)

Concept: The Anime Enclave is a site dedicated to all things Anime, a form of Japanese cartoon art. The site offers just about every aspect of the art form, but also gets off into other elements of Japanese culture like the language and karaoke.

Praise: I have been involved with the design of a lot of sites and it isn't often that I see a design that really sets me off. When I logged in, I really liked the look of the page. It almost looks like two sites in one, yet on the same page, almost like a book was opened and laid before me. You may not see the design as anything spectacular and coding wise—it isn't—but it's different. The author split the page down the middle and unapologetically created what is equal to two homepages. I don't know Anime, but I'll bet this design is a "tip of the hat" to something dealing with Anime. The author might have seen this format before and carried it over into his design. If not, well done. I like it a lot. You might notice I captured the site at 800×600 this time because I wanted to see how it would size down. As you can see, it sized beautifully.

131

The format for layout and design is similar to the first site reviewed in this section. The many links surrounding the image on the left side are multiple images making up links. However, the author did not go as far as to make the images rollovers. He should have, because the text links on the right do produce a rollover.

The logo, the one on the right side, is great. Plus, even though it is in the middle of the page, it is still correctly placed because it sits in the upper-left corner of the darker background. Well done.

Concern: Why do you lose your homepage format on the subpages? Figure 4.9 shows the page that displays when you click on the FAQ section.

Figure 4.9
Users enjoy a FAQ section. Maybe your site can use one?

Each subpage loses the split format and goes to this full-page look with a small blue line down the side. In addition, you lose the logo and go with a very futuristic text that reads "The Anime Enclave."

Suggestion: I would keep the homepage look at all costs. It is so different from anything I've seen and by changing your pages as people go deeper into the site, you're not staying true to the design. Remember, so goes the homepage, so goes the site.

Concern: Why are you asking users to find problems for you? You tell people that mistakes lie ahead and ask if they would email when they hit one. It's little more than an under construction sign in a request format.

Suggestion: The users might write, but they shouldn't have to because the site should be good as gold and all the links work fine when the user arrives. You are the authors. It's up to you to find and repair these problems.

Concern: On a couple of the subpages, you have text that carries no underline, yet makes up a link. The pages under plan updates is a good example. Yes, when I go to other subpages, like the series page, the same text appears, yet none of the text makes up links. I ran my pointer over each one hoping to get a link.

Suggestion: Make straight text different from links text through color or some other means. I noticed on the Multimedia page that you used larger block letters to represent links. That was good—the links were obvious.

Overall: I hate to keep harping on the homepage, but I can't stop. That's the page that's different from almost everything else I've seen. Then, once I get into your subpages, the site becomes very much like any other site I've seen. Stay with the homepage format throughout the site. You certainly have the content and have stayed true to your killer app; now you need to stay true to your homepage. It's a winner.

Chapter 5

Text and Color

Text?

Why start here? Shouldn't I be talking about images and scrolling text and backgrounds and animation and JavaScript and DHTML and Flash and anything other than boring old text?

Nope.

When I first started laying out the chapters for this book, I wanted to put them in such an order so that as a reader went through the chapters, that reader would follow along building the most important part of a Web site first. It's my opinion that text and navigation are the foundation of any Web site.

I would go as far as to say that if you get the text and the navigation right, you're 70% done with your site. The text and the navigation of the page are its meat and potatoes. Give these elements the time they deserve. Don't get taken away by the latest image formats or the coolest animation. Images are support. They are helpers to the text that will be the bulk of your site.

In fact, if you stopped reading this book after the next chapter, links, you could actually be done. There are a ton of sites out there that don't even include images (horrors!).

The text and links serve the killer app and people come to the site because its content is what is important.

I'll say that again. Content is what is important.

That content comes through in your text. No amount of graphical support or whiz-bang programming helps a site that goes on and on for pages and says nothing. Get the text and the navigation right and you can stop.

Of course, you probably won't want to. Images are pretty cool.

Okay? Good. Text and links are important, but let's start with the text.

Italic Meets Bold Meets Font Meets Blink

Here's a question that proves to you that I have a firm grasp of the obvious. What is the most important thing about the text you put on your Web page?

The answer is: The user can read it.

At this point, many of you have rolled your eyes, said "duh," and asked yourself why you blew money on this book.

Well, maybe your work always takes into account the text and whether it's visible or not, but many sites don't. I can't tell you how many pages I've been to where I couldn't read the text if I wanted to. I've even gone as far as looking at source code to find out what something actually read.

Figure 5.1 is a page sent in by an HTML Goodies reader for critique.

Figure 5.1
Can you read the text over top the pointer?

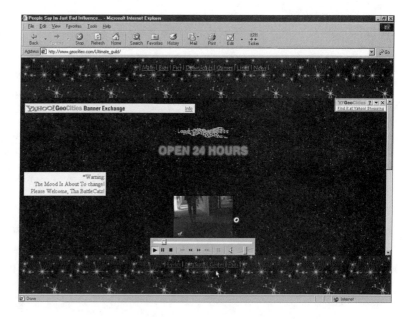

This is actually a pretty nice site. You'll find it at
`http://www.geocities.com/Ultimate_guild/index2.html`.

The concern I have is that the star background has some big stars right behind the text toward the bottom. The background is mainly black and the text toward the bottom is dark blue. Those elements combined make for difficult reading. The text reads "JavaScript Codes," by the way.

Okay, take another look. See the cat image about a third of the way down the page? What's the text over top of that? It's "Land of Darkness." The reason you can't see it is because the color the author chose for the text and the cat image's main color are in the same family. Both are a yellow orange.

Figure 5.2 shows another one that's not quite as blatant.

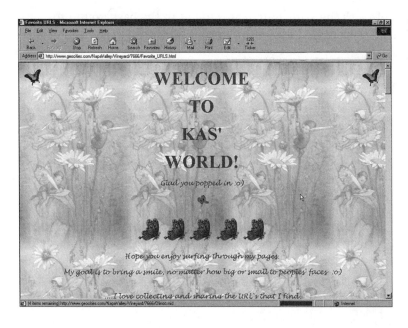

Figure 5.2
Very busy background, script text.

Can you read the text at Kas' World
(`http://www.geocities.com/NapaValley/Vineyard/7666/Favorite_URLS.html`)?

I bet you can read the very large text. That's easy. The concern here is the smaller text. It is in a script font against a very, very busy background.

The eye wants to look at the background because it's so pretty and busy. In addition, the background moves vertically. See that? It's the same image again and again. The text moves horizontally. That's a real conflict.

Design Goodies Survey

HTML Goodies Survey Question: If the text on a site is hard to read, what do you do?

Leave the page   74%

Try to read it   24%

N=497

You may love that background and love that text font, but if it's going to drive away two-thirds of an audience, make some other choices.

The star field in the previous example didn't draw the eye away because it was a random pattern that didn't create a line for the eye to follow. This does.

Furthermore, the text is purple—it's the same purple as is found in the background so when those two colors meet, the eye is taken away and moved vertically.

Can you read the text? Sure, but you have to work at it.

Okay, one last page (see Figure 5.3).

Figure 5.3
Group of divisions flew into the wrong place.

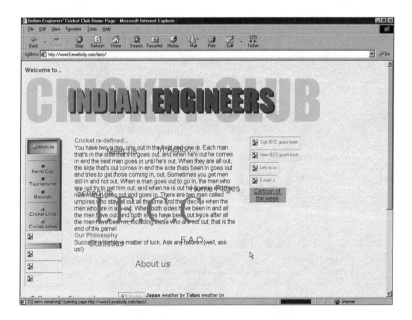

At the Indian Engineer's Cricket Club homepage (http://www3.ewebcity.com/iecc/), someone wanted a neat DHTML effect. It is a neat effect. The circle of words spins, and it's visually pleasing except for the fact that it's sitting right on top of a big block of text that explains the site.

Have I made my point? The texts found in the previous examples are not readable. If you kept at it, yes, you could read the text. It's just that the authors certainly didn't make it easy on you. It appears as if graphical and programming support were outweighing the message of the site. In each case, it appears as if the author put pizzazz before content.

I lied. Figure 5.4 shows one more site.

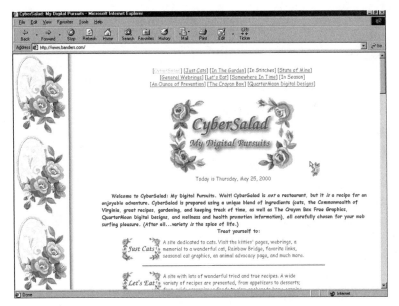

Figure 5.4
What is important on this page?

This site is titled "CyberSalad" (http://www.banders.com/). No, I don't think it's the greatest page ever and below the gatefold I would make a few suggestions, but do you know what I like most about it?

I can read it.

I can read it without any interruption of the text or without having to squint because of a blockage. The author used images, a lot of images (load time over a minute), but those images are support for the text that appears on the page. The colors are complementary. She could have easily used black text, but chose instead a deep red. The font is Comic Sans MS. It's not a far cry from the default New Times Roman font, but it does soften the page a bit. The letters are still large enough to read easily and don't become a mass of color when made bold. These were good text choices.

I titled this section of the book "Italic Meets Bold Meets Font Meets Blink" because that's what I call a lot of pages created by first-time designers.

When I teach HTML, I start with text and text alteration. I don't know if you've ever counted them up, but there are actually 40 different HTML tags that affect text (see Table 5.1).

Table 5.1   HTML Tags and Their Functions

Tag	Function
<ABBR>	Abbreviation
<ACRONYM>	Acronym
<ADDRESS>	Address
<B>	Bold
<BASEFONT>	Basefont
<BDO>	Explains the direction of the text
<BIG>	Bumps the text size up one
<BLINK>	Blinks
<BLOCKQUOTE>	Sets text aside in a block
<CITE>	Sets text to italic
<CODE>	Shows text as code—block format
<COMMENT>	Comments out text
<DEL>	Delete
<DFN>	Definition—italic
<DIV>	Division—used to surround text in a block
<EM>	Emphasis—like bold
<FONT COLOR>	Changes font color
<FONT FACE>	Changes font
<FONT SIZE>	Changes size
<H#>	Heading
<I>	Italic
<INS>	Insert
<KBD>	Keyboard effect
<LISTING>	Small text as listing
<MULTICOL>	Sets text to multiple columns
<NOBR>	Sets text to not break at end of screen
<PLAINTEXT>	Uses default text font
<PRE>	Sets text to format in source
<Q>	Quote (will soon replace <BLOCKQUOTE>)

Table 5.1   HTML Tags and Their Functions continued

Tag	Function
<S>	Strike-through
<SAMP>	Sample
<SPAN>	Surrounds text—carries other alterations
<STRONG>	Like bold
<SUB>	Subscript as in H_2O
<SUP>	Superscript as in O^2
<TT>	Typewriter text
<U>	Underlined
<VAR>	Variable—like italic
<WBR>	Sets a break point for no break text
<XMP>	Sets text to format like source code

You can see all of these HTML Flags in action at
`http://www.htmlgoodies.com/tutors/textcodes.html`.

With that many methods of changing text around, the types and sizes of text you can create seem almost endless. If you then factor in all the neat stuff you can do with Cascading Style Sheets (CSS) then you've got thousand of formats lying there before you.

That means you have to use them, right?

Wrong.

Let's look at the real world. When was the last time you read a book? Ah, you're reading a book now. I mean the last time you read a novel. Did you remember any super text fonts in amongst the text? No? Where was the altered text? It was at the beginning of the chapter, the heading, right?

Now, some of you might say that you're not creating a novel here and you're not, but you're also not creating something that should confuse the heck out of the reader.

I seem to be asking questions all through the book, so here's another one.

Question: What is the purpose of using text alteration?

Answer: To draw the eye.

If you have a site that deals with medieval literature, you may go with a font that gives the impression of the time. As long as you make such an involved font large enough to be read easily, that's good. The eye was drawn to the page and the text font pointed toward the page's killer app.

Design Goodies Survey

HTML Goodies Survey Question: Should a Web page maintain a consistent font all the way through or do you mind changing fonts?

Stay consistent	63%
Use different fonts	18%
Doesn't matter	19%

N=494

Pick one and stick with it.

Now, let's say you make the first letter of the first word of each sentence bigger. Now you've created a marker to draw the eye. This is still somewhat okay as the marker denotes a new sentence.

Then, you decide to make some words underlined because you feel they are important. You've drawn the eye again.

Lastly, you want something that's really important to blink.

You now have four elements just in the text of the page that you're using to draw the eye. Which one wins? None of them wins. They are sure to cancel each other out. Yes, the blink may grab attention first, but that only further confuses the reader.

For example, a person stops into the site. They came there for a reason. They have to think there's something in your site they want to see or read. That's good. Now that they have arrived, you're not allowing them to read correctly.

Design Goodies Survey

HTML Goodies Survey Question: What do you feel adds emphasis to text best:

Bold	80%
Italic	8%
Underline	6%
All of the above	6%

N=494

Even readers point out that filling text with multiple text decoration doesn't impress them.

When you read, how do you do it? I bet you go left to right and top to bottom, yes? Well, if you have all the "italic meets bold meets font meets blink" you can cram into your text, then you've stopped the user from reading as they would like to read. You made their eye first jump somewhere it shouldn't have jumped. They are reading your text out of order because you made them read your text out of order. It's not the reader's fault they didn't get your message. You're the one that made them do things differently than they're used to. You did it through text alteration.

This past semester, I went through my traditional "italic meets bold meets font meets blink" tirade much like the one you just read and a student raised her hand and said something like, "But I have to do that. There are so many pages on the net, I have to do something to make people remember my site."

That seems logical, yes? It isn't. My response was, "What do you want to be remembered for?" Should your readers remember that you had a page that was so overprogrammed that it was hard to read, or should they remember that you had some great content?

The hardest part of this discussion to get across to any new programmer is that using correct text formats is kind of like working for the sewer system. The only time you'll be recognized is when something goes wrong. No one calls the sewer company just to tell them they're doing a stunning job of water removal. They call when the toilets are backing up and spraying stuff all over the walls.

No one is going to write to you and say that your text was great and that they could read it perfectly. They might write to tell you they had a heck of a time reading what you wrote. Or worse, they won't write at all. They'll just leave.

Design Goodies Survey

HTML Goodies Survey Question: What do you think of the use of all caps to draw attention?

Dislike it	81%
Like it	5%
Doesn't Matter	14%

N=488

This is another one to avoid like the plague.

So, what is an author to do? First, understand that text is there to convey the content of the page. You don't need a lot of text by any means. You just need enough text to explain the site and further explain the subpoints of the site.

People read the text you have on your site. Let me say that again. People read the text you have on your site. When a user arrives at a Web page, he does not require prodding. He reads without you making him read.

Your job as a programmer and Web designer is to make that reading as easy as possible.

Follow a Traditional Format

The traditional format of text is left justified. The majority of those polled by HTML Goodies reported they would like to see text left justified. The next most popular format for text, 17%, was for equal margins of both the left and right.

If you look at the traditional print media, newspaper, magazine, and so on, they follow that traditional format. Now, you as a designer may say, "Forget it! I want my page to be completely different from anything out there."

I won't stop you, I can't. Just know that when a person arrives into your site, they have to immediately be retrained to read your text. They have to stop, think about how you have the text, and then begin reading. Users may enjoy that and then again they may not. Just think about that before you center or right-align everything.

I saw a site one time that had every even line right-aligned and every odd line left-aligned. It was nearly impossible to read. I'm sure the designer looked at it when he had finished and just thought it was the greatest accomplishment of his text-writing life but

It was almost impossible to read.

Italic Is Mainly for Quotes and Titles

Italic font is not script font. Italic font should not be used over the entire page. It makes the text hard to read and on smaller screen settings, impossible to read. Use italic font to set aside quotes, titles, and to draw the eye. For emphasis, bold is the way to go.

Bold Font Muds Smaller Text

When you mud text, you make it so that the loops, like in a P or a B, almost close up. Setting text to a font size of minus two and then bolding it basically muds it to the point that it cannot be read. Be careful bolding small text.

Also—if you find yourself having to make text smaller and smaller in order to get it all to fit correctly, stop. Either find a way to say what you're trying to say with fewer words or rethink your design. The smaller you go, the more people you confound.

Underlined Text Disrupts Paragraphs

This comes into play a lot more when I get into the discussion of creating hypertext links. For now, realize that if you do underline text for emphasis, you run the risk of two problems. First people might mistake the text for a hypertext link. Hypertext is traditionally underlined. Second, if the text is within a paragraph, the underline disrupts the nice block look of the paragraph.

Choose a Font That Can Be Read

Respondents to the HTML Goodies survey reported that the font an author chooses has no bearing on their opinion of the page. What does help the reader form an opinion is if the font can be read or not. When choosing a font, choose one first that can be read easily. That means staying away from heavy script or overly fancy and involved fonts. Keep the text at a size level so that the letters P and B are easily told apart.

It all comes down to the question can the user easily read the font you've chosen? If so, then mission accomplished.

Use a Margin

I don't know why, but lately I am seeing a lot of Web pages that have taken the time to program out the left, right, and top margins. The text just butts right up against the browser window walls. Obviously, authors like the look but readers sure don't. Almost 70% of those polled said they didn't like a lack of margins.

The very nice thing about keeping to this rule is that the browsers themselves put the margins in for you. Woohoo! You don't have to do anything. The margins are just done for you. What a break.

Don't Be Afraid of Paragraphs

If you have a good deal of text, make a point of breaking the text into many smaller paragraphs instead of using one large block of text. The use of multiple paragraphs helps the reader follow along and gives him a sense of accomplishment.

Really! People like going to a new paragraph because it gives the impression of forward movement. The reader feels as if he is making progress.

Don't Be Afraid of New Pages

I've said this before and I'll say it again. Your users don't mind clicking. It's scrolling they dislike. If your pages scroll over two or more browser screens, think about possibly breaking the text over two pages. Again, clicking to continue reading gives a sense or forward momentum. Why do you think they call a good novel a page turner?

Just don't get too crazy with this. Make sure that each page has a solid amount of text. If you have people click after every 50-word paragraph, you may upset some people, especially if you have ad banners on your site. The users might start to think you are only making them click to see new ad banners. That upsets a lot of users.

Think About Indenting the First Line of New Paragraphs

This isn't a hard and fast rule, but the HTML Goodies survey results suggest people like the effect. A total of 45% of those responded that they wanted to see the indent. Thirty-five percent said it didn't matter so you wouldn't be putting them off.

It's traditional and easy to do. I get a five-space indent by simply putting in five blank spaces using ampersand commands:

```
     
```

I have the previous line set to a hotkey in my HTML assistant program and just pop one in at the beginning of each paragraph. Sure, there are other methods to getting the indent, but I grew up doing it this way and it works across all browsers, all versions.

Proofread It

Over half of the respondents to the HTML Goodies survey said they lose respect for a site if they find a lot of typos and grammar mistakes. I am as guilty as anyone of running into this problem.

I tend to quickly write a tutorial thinking about the content first and the grammar second. That allows me to gloss right over mistakes. Then, in the rush to get the page to the Web, I often make the mistake of not proofreading very well.

When a typo shows up on the HTML Goodies site, I am told en masse. It's embarrassing and people seem to really enjoy telling me I made the mistake.

Don't allow yourself to get that type of email message. Check your work carefully before allowing it to go live.

Unless You Have a Very Good Reason, Text Is All One Color

A full 65% of those polled reported not liking text in multiple colors. Yes, that means that 35% reported they do like text in multiple colors. For that reason, I suggest that unless you have a very good reason, keep your text a single color.

I don't mean that all text must be black. I mean to simply keep the color consistent. A black background calls out for a light color text. A white background calls out for a darker colored text. It could be deep red, or deep purple, but yellow? Nope. Yellow text just doesn't work against a white background.

Colors and What Color They Are

There are very few black and white issues in the world of Web design. What works for one site can kill another. However, in terms of using color, there is a correct set of colors and an incorrect set of colors.

It is my opinion that any time you set a color on your Web site, you use one of the 216 nondithering colors. A list of the colors and their hex codes is in living color online at `http://htmlgoodies.earthweb.com/non_dithering_colors.html`.

These 216 colors are the correct colors because they make up a palette supported by all, yes all, computer operating systems. That means that the same nondithering hex code used on any computer looks exactly the same. The color is smooth and reproduces perfectly.

You see, computer monitors today can be set to display 16.7 million colors, but that doesn't mean that you should use any one of the 16.7 million. Many of your users don't have a monitor that can read 16.7 million colors. Really. Not everyone has the latest and the greatest. You have to make a point of playing to all users, not just those you consider with it.

You may be put off because the colors require you to use a hex code rather than a word color. I know it's easier to simply call for brick if you want a deep red, but it's not always good for your users. The color brick is not produced by a hex code within the 216 non-dithering colors. The means that if your page displays on a monitor that does not support the hex code represented by brick, the color becomes grainy and dotted as the screen attempts to reproduce the color. That dotted, grainy look is what's known as dithering.

These 216 colors display on everyone's monitor. So, when you make a decision to use a color, use one of the 216 nondithering colors. Period.

Now that I've made that statement about nondithering colors, I might end up making it again before the book is over, so let's talk about text and color.

Text color is completely and fully linked to background color or to the background image. However, I only want to talk about background colors in this chapter.

Often Web designers set the background and then make the text fit to it. I know that because I often see text colors that no one would ever have chosen without first having chosen a background. Remember the order of importance for your Web site.

Your text is more important than your background.

First, you have to choose a text color then choose a background color. Too many times a student tells me that he really likes this wild swooping image background that contains every shade of green as it swirls around a skull set to deep purple.

The student gets so caught up in the background that he spends an hour testing different text colors to find a text they can read. The color is inevitably some bright primary like red or yellow.

When all is said and done, I can't read the text anyway. Do you know why? It's because no text color sits nicely over top of a green rainbow swirling around a purple skull. The background took importance and it killed the text.

So, here are some basic rules of choosing text color.

The Text Is More Important Than the Background

Always. It has to be. If not, you run into problems as I described previously.

Text Color Must Differ, Yet Complement Background Color

Have you ever run into a page where the user simply loved purple, or yellow, or pink? The background is pink, the text is a little darker pink and you can't read any of it.

Make a point of getting the text color completely out of the same family as the background color. Darker green does not separate well enough from light green. Pink is too close to red. Purple is too close to blue.

Rule of thumb: If a color is used to make up another color, don't use them as text and background. Green and yellow is a good example.

Furthermore, simply choosing a different color is not enough. The text and the background, although different, must complement each other. You've heard the quote that opposites attract? Well, opposites also complement.

The most successful background/color combinations are colors that are fairly far apart on the color spectrum.

Try these on for size:

- Black text on white background
- White text on black background

Color Plates

The sum of Web design is based on the user's personal experience when visiting a site. This experience is created almost exclusively from visual effects on the page (every site has a visual component; not every site has an audio one). Therefore, to enhance your skills in Web site critique, I have provided full-color figures of the Web sites critiqued throughout the book.

Every color plate in this section corresponds with the initial figure in every site critique. Use these to practice critiquing the effect of color and flow across the sites. The corresponding chapter figure number is included in parentheses next to each plate.

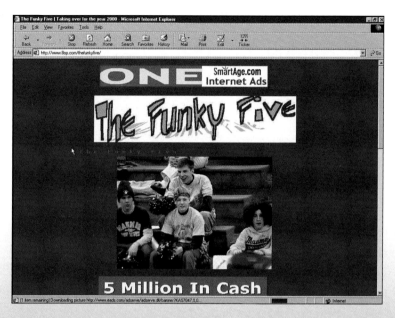

Color Plate C.1 (Figure 1.1)

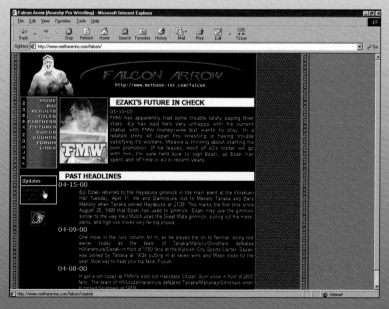

Color Plate C.2 (Figure 1.3)

Color Plate C.3 (Figure 1.6)

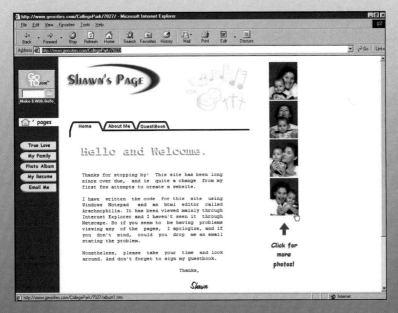

Color Plate C.4 (Figure 2.23)

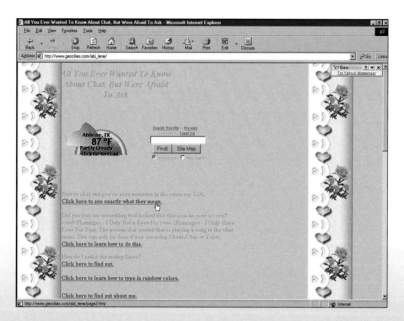

Color Plate C.5 (Figure 2.25)

Color Plate C.6 (Figure 2.26)

Color Plate C.7 (Figure 3.15)

Color Plate C.8 (Figure 3.17)

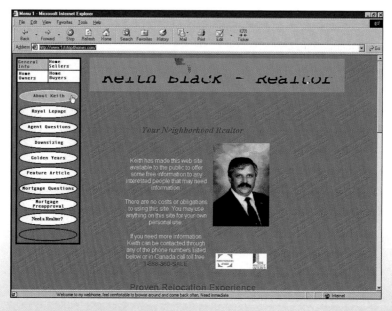

Color Plate C.9 (Figure 3.20)

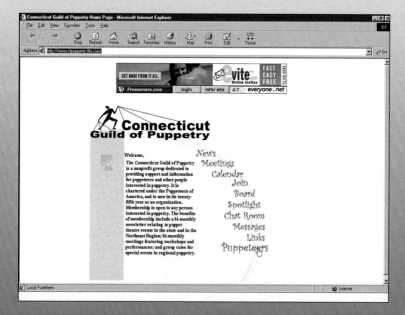

Color Plate C.10 (Figure 4.2)

Color Plate C.11 (Figure 4.6)

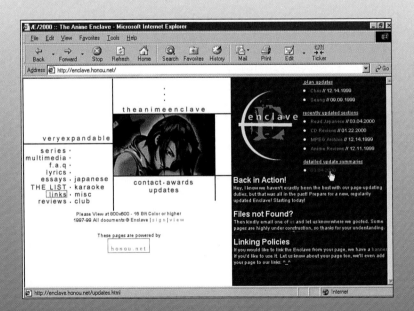

Color Plate C.12 (Figure 4.8)

Color Plate C.13 (Figure 5.5)

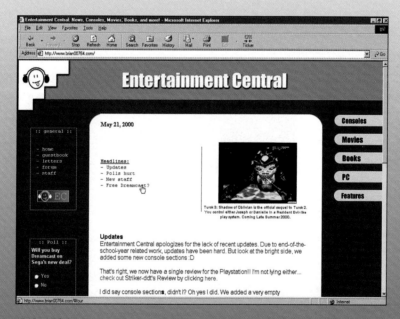

Color Plate C.14 (Figure 5.7)

Color Plate C.15 (Figure 5.10)

Color Plate C.16 (Figure 6.18)

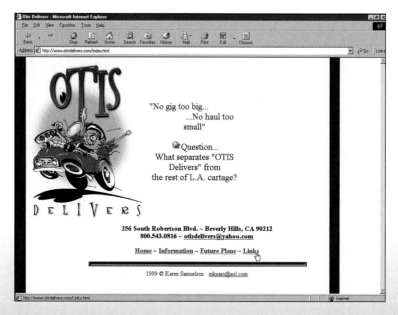

Color Plate C.17 (Figure 6.20)

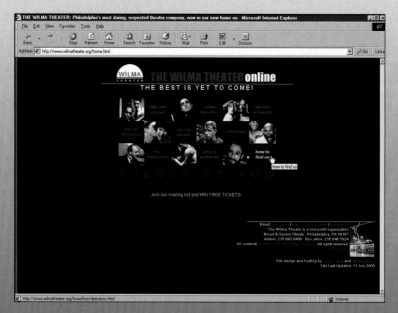

Color Plate C.18 (Figure 6.22)

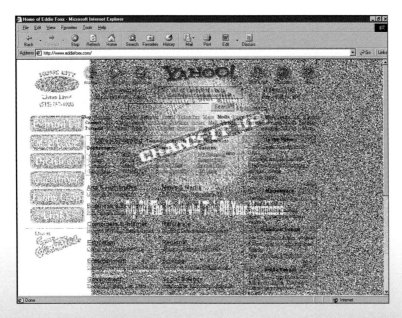

Color Plate C.19 (Figure 7.19)

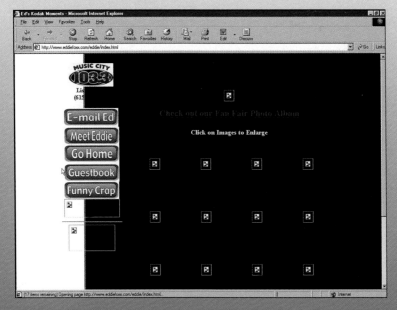

Color Plate C.20 (Figure 7.22)

Color Plate C.21 (Figure 7.25)

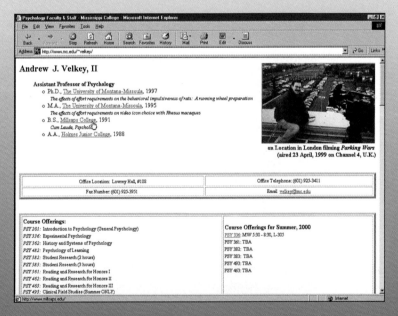

Color Plate C.22 (Figure 8.17)

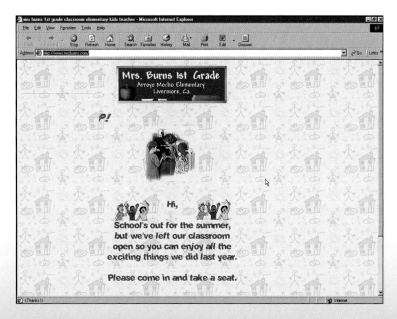

Color Plate C.23 (Figure 8.18)

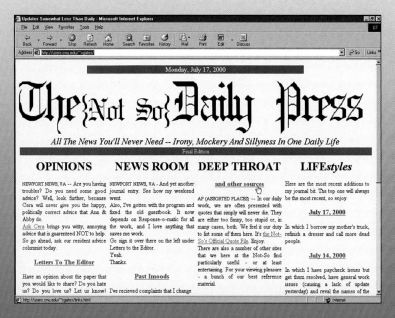

Color Plate C.24 (Figure 8.21)

Color Plate C.25 (Figure 9.16)

Color Plate C.26 (Figure 9.20)

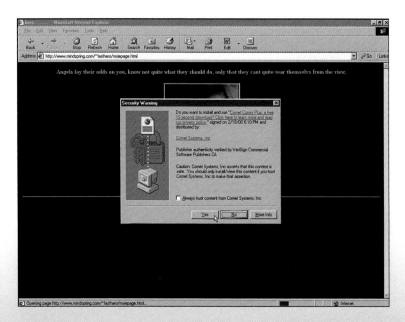

Color Plate C.27 (Figure 9.22)

Color Plate C.28 (Figure 10.4)

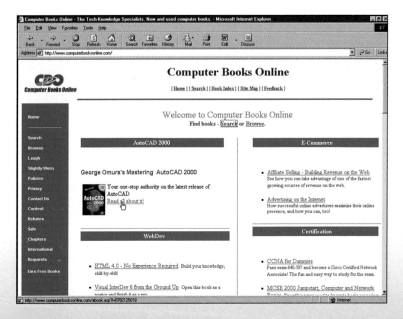

Color Plate C.29 (Figure 10.7)

Color Plate C.30 (Figure 10.10)

- Black text on yellow background
- White text on blue background
- Blue text on white background

There's no need to always go with primary colors, either. The white can always be an off white. The yellow can always be a more orange yellow. Just make a point of keeping the color separated by picking at opposite ends of the spectrum.

Text Shouldn't Move

The technical term for this effect is moiré. I've heard it called by other names not as nice.

After you've taken the time to choose your text colors, stop and stare at the page. Does the text appear to move around? If you slowly move your head back and forth, does the text seem to rock or elongate? Does the text give the impression it is sitting well up and off the background rather than being on it?

If your answer to any of these questions is yes then you've got moiré going on and you need to choose some different colors.

If you have moiré, my guess is that you've chosen some very bright or primary colors. That's when moiré happens most often. Remember that bright and primary color can have a very dulling effect after the user stares at them for a while. Even white can get dull.

You may have noticed above that I said black on white and white on black. However I didn't give the opposite of black on yellow. The reason is that yellow text on a black background really moves around.

Here are a few others to try to avoid:

- Yellow text on orange background (or the other way around)
- White text on yellow background (or the other way around)
- Blue text on black background (or the other way around)

Avoid Any Combination of Red and Green

Notice that I didn't mention red or green. I don't think they're good colors for text and background, but there's another reason.

When it comes to text and background color, you want to avoid using red and green together in any form. I know it kind of kills the Christmas spirit, but for people who are colorblind, they aren't able to differentiate where the text stops and the background starts.

Besides, red and green make a lousy color combination.

What Does Your Color Mean?

We talked previously about a text font denoting the site's killer app. A medieval site might use old English font or a kid's site might use letter drawn in crayon, but what about the color choice? Doesn't it say something for the page?

For example, two football teams meet on the field to do battle. The one team is in black and gold. The other is in pink and a lovely auburn brown. Without knowing anything about the teams, which looks like the winner? I would think the one in black and gold. Why? They look tougher. The colors are dark and thus promote strength.

Keep that in mind while choosing a text and background color combination. For example:

- Dark colors evoke feelings of strength. This includes black, gray, silver, and deep gold.
- Pastel hues have a calming effect.
- Primary colors tend to have a strong impact but dull quickly.
- The colors red, yellow, and orange have been shown to stimulate.
- The color yellow has been shown to make you hungry. Why do you think the arches are golden?
- Green has a calming effect.
- Black and white used together have very little effect. They are generic.

Lastly...

Color choice is not hard. In fact, it's one of the more enjoyable parts of putting together a Web site. Color helps your pages come alive.

Just keep in mind that there are correct colors to choose from and there are less effective colors to choose from. Stay with only the 216 nondithering colors and you'll never run into a problem with your pages rendering poorly on older models.

I can't tell you what colors to choose for your site. It's not my place. The best advice I can give regarding your color choices is this:

Your mother taught you how to dress. You certainly wouldn't go out of the house wearing yellow pants, a green shirt, pink tie, and gold hat. That would look awful, right? Yes. Then, don't use that color scheme on your Web site, either.

Your mother taught you better than that.

Site Critiques

1. Title: Math Man/Author: Mark Reed

`http://www.hasdonline.com/teachers/reed/`

Load Time: 18 Seconds, 57kps modem, cleared cache, 10/07/00 7:22AM.

My Screen Size: 800×600, 1,024×768

Browsers Used: Internet Explorer 5.5 and Netscape Navigator 4.5

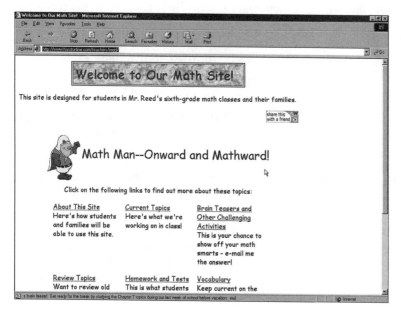

Figure 5.5
Math Man! Defender of all things numbers! (Color Plate C.13)

Concept: This is a site dedicated to all things math and geared toward the students and parents from Mark's sixth-grade math class. There are brainteasers, homework assignments, review topics, tests, and all other manner of things that make students say, "Do I have to know this?" Here's one from this week's site:

> Every third visitor to a new florist receives a rose. Every tenth visitor receives a plant. Every twenty-fifth visitor receives a bouquet. What number visitor is the first to receive all three gifts?

Praise: I've gone into this before, but I probably end up hitting it more than 100 times before I finish writing these critiques. One of the first things you must do as a site designer is decide who makes up your audience. Mark has hit it here. This site is not geared at the students. It's geared at the parents. Upon first look, there are cartoons and the letters are done in Comic Sans, but when all is said and done, this is a site to parents. The kids may do the work, but the parents are the ones who are using the site. In the section regarding how to use the site, Mark has a small paragraph talking to students. He then has this:

> "This site is also designed for parents and family members of the students. It will show them what we're studying in class, let them know what vocabulary their students should know, and tell them the weekly homework and tests schedule. This will allow them to help their student prepare and do his or her best."

Smart. The students are listed first—but this site is really for the parents. Mark knows this and is rather sly about it so the kids don't catch wind of the fact that their parents can keep up with their math homework.

I want to also point out the identifier. He is Math Man! Mark has chosen a character identifier. I love that the character had a fist in the air and a potbelly. That's what you would expect Math Man to look like.

Concern: I'm grouping my first two concerns together and stating them first as they have nothing to do with the design of the page. First off, you moved the site from the original server to the new location. When I went to the original free server, `http://www.crosswinds.net/~math6/`, and I got the familiar, "We've Moved" message. That's a bit bothersome, but furthermore, the page has a scroll in the status bar and a pop-up window trying to sell me something, darn free servers. What it doesn't have is a redirect. I must click to go. And! Because I come to the free server first, even if you do set a redirect to go immediately to the new site, I still get that dreaded pop-up window.

Suggestion: This illustrates the concern one must take for choosing a server right off. This site will grow away from the free server after a while, but for now, you're going to cause a few minor headaches with that "click for the new site" page.

Concern: You made a banner for the page in a clever way. It's a single cell with a stone background. Very clever. I like it, but it's way too big for the rest of the page.

Suggestion: I would suggest that only "Welcome to our Math Site" sit within that cell. The remaining text goes underneath in the whitespace. I would also lose the underline.

Concern: The color of the banner text is not complementary. I have no doubt you chose the background first and then spent the day playing with colors until you found one that could be read. The background is so busy and the text is so dark that it doesn't quite complement.

Suggestion: Brighter. Try to find a brighter color. I would pick a color out of the super-hero's costume to help tie the banner to the rest of the page.

Concern: You have a tremendous amount of whitespace. Just looking at the homepage, I can see a couple of places where you could tighten up and pull elements together.

Suggestion: To begin with, place the "Tell a Friend" image toward the bottom. Its placement suggests it is more important than the content of the site. Second, I think you could lessen the size of the text underneath the link headings. Just those two suggestions kill a good bit of unnecessary whitespace. You might want to think about nestling Math Man next to the banner above, also. The site has good left-to-right movement, but could allow for more.

Concern: Every so often I make a statement that people read and go nuts because I am not quite following my own advice. This is one. Your white background wears on the eyes. It's very bright. If there were a stripe of some other color to break up the background, it might not seem so bright, but wow, is it bright!

Suggestion: Try to find a light background that is slightly darker than the glaring white. I get letters all the time on Goodies that the pages are way too bright. Try this hex for the background: FFFFCC. See what you think.

Concern: The subpages all have a similar design concern to the homepage (see Figure 5.6).

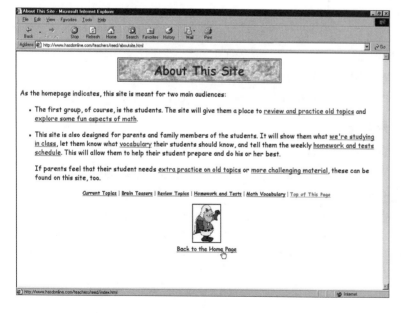

Figure 5.6
Math Man! Squished and in a box!

I like that you've kept the look across pages. That's great. I also see that you made a point of offering back navigation. That's often overlooked and a good point for your site.

My concerns are that back navigation image of Math Man. To begin with, you have him in a box. That box was created by activating the image. My research has shown that people are not big fans of that. Also, why did you resize Math Man? He's smaller on the subpages and looks a little scrunched. You set him to a smaller size through the user of height and width commands. The problem is that he didn't resize nicely. Much of his detail is gone.

Suggestion: Lose the box by adding the attribute `BORDER="0"` in the image flag itself. Either resize Math Man in an image editor so you can keep all of the detail or don't resize him on the page. One or the other will work.

Overall: Fun site. I love the little Math Man image. I see you use him on the subpages as your back navigation. That's smart. It holds the site together. Just make a point of losing the blue border around the active image.

Keep updating this site on a timely basis and you'll have a winner here. It'll only be a winner with a small audience of parents and students, but it'll be a winner nonetheless.

Oh, by the way—the answer to the first question. The 150th customer would win all three prizes. Why? Because 150 represents the first number that 3, 10, and 25 divide into without remainder.

2. Entertainment Central/Author: JedEye a.k.a. Brian Mattucci

`http://www.brian00764.com/`

Load Time: 12 Seconds, 57kps modem, cleared cache, 5/24/00 11:36AM.

My Screen Size: 1,024×768, 800×600, 640×480

Browsers Used: Internet Explorer 5 and Netscape Navigator 4.5

Concept: This is another review site. The author of the site collects information mainly about gaming, SEGA specifically.

Praise: The site has far fewer images than you would expect. It loads very quickly and the shell is carried across pages. The little round face sporting the headphones is always there in the upper-left corner to greet you. No one had to tell me that's the site identifier. I knew it simply from the image's placement in the upper-left corner.

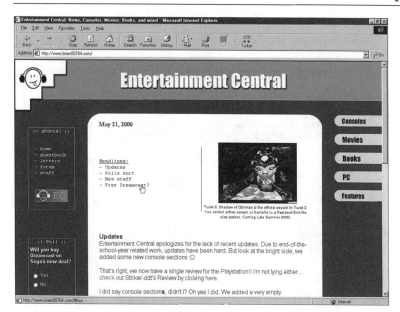

Figure 5.7
Entertainment Central Open and Ready for Business. (Color Plate C.14)

The site is one giant table. But the table is so well constructed that you cannot grasp the breaks between cells. Allow me to point out a small, but very well done portion of the coding. Table cells are square. They have sharp corners. Notice how the middle section has rounded edges when the top and side blue bars meet. The author simply used his table to butt a small, arced image up against the vertical and horizontal bars. The effect is a wonderful rounding of squared-off table cells. It was a little extra work for a small effect, but I think it was well worth it. Just that arc smoothed the page.

The stairsteps are the same idea of splitting images and allowing them to butt right up against each other to move across table cells. Well done.

Another thing to notice is that the site is the important thing. This is a personal page. An amateur wrote this page. There is no ad banner even though it seems like the author built with one in mind. I'm glad to see the site standing as the site alone.

Nice colors. What more can I say?

Finally, when you click on the left-side links, the main page scrolls for you rather than a new page coming up. It's a little extra coding, but if you are going to have a long page, these internal page jumps work wonders to help the user.

Concern: You have a table set to 100% width acting as the parameters of the page. I'm sure you used the `WIDTH="100%"` attribute because you wanted the table to resize with smaller or larger screen settings. I viewed your page at 800×600 and it did pretty well. Some of the text truncated (jumped to the next line), but other than that it looked pretty good. In Figure 5.8, my pointer is on one of the truncations.

Figure 5.8
Entertainment Central at 800×600.

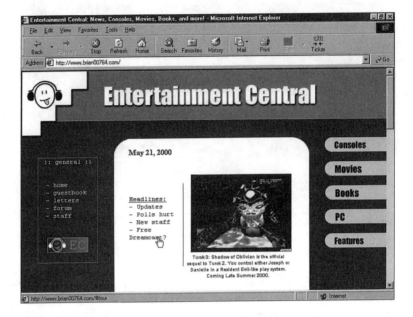

I also looked at the site in 640×480 and the table did not resize fully. The user simply got to see the left side of the page (see Figure 5.9).

Suggestion: I actually don't have one. The 100% worked pretty well. I just needed to point it out.

Concern: I write this concern even though I am guilty of doing the same thing. Your links are on the right. Yes, there are some links on the left, but the main image links are on the right. I've done it myself simply because it was different than what others are doing.

Suggestion: Ask users if they like that effect or keep an eye on your traffic numbers to see if those links are getting hit a lot less than the links on the right.

Overall: I don't have a lot of poor things to say about the site. The author has built a good-looking site that stays true to its killer app and doesn't attempt to be what it is not.

Usually I'm not a fan of putting up a poll, but on this site is works. Keep it.

I might suggest the counter should go away, but you've got it so far down on the page and the loading is in such an order that it never got in the way.

Good site.

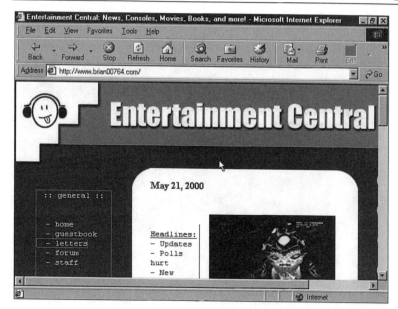

Figure 5.9
Entertainment Central at 640×480.

3. Doc Melson's Place/Author: Doc Melson

www.docmelson.com

Load Time: 41 Seconds, 57kps modem, cleared cache, 5/24/00 12:17PM.

My Screen Size: 1,024×768

Browsers Used: Internet Explorer 5 and Netscape Navigator 4.5

Concept: This site is, just as it says, dedicated to the U.S. Army's Fifth Division who served in Vietnam. The site is very moving and full of compassion and concern for those who served. I spent a good deal of time in the site reading the large blocks of test left by the author.

Praise: Like the last site, this one stays very true to the killer app. There's a lot of image support that goes with the site and the author has kept that image support across pages, but it is the text that really draws you in. Each page has a box that surrounds the text. The author is smart enough to break that text up. If it starts to get too long, you click to go to another page after he gets to around 300 words or so.

I enjoyed my time in this site. I'm sure had I lived through the space in time the author describes, this site would have moved me even more. This is truly a dedicated site told through the eyes of someone who lived it.

Figure 5.10
Dedicated to the U.S. Army's Fifth Division who served in Vietnam. (Color Plate C.15)

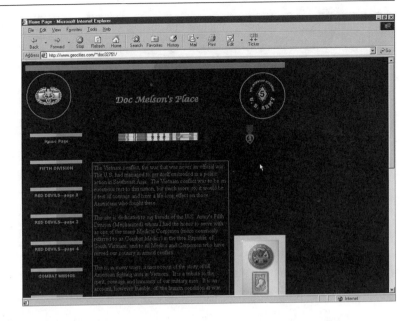

Concern: You have a great deal of images on the pages that I don't know anything about. I attempted to click on each one to learn more.

Suggestion: At least have an ALT command in the IMG tab that describes the image and what it represents. I would go as far as suggesting creating a page that lists each medal or bar and have each image linked to it. That way I can find out what each one represents.

Concern: This isn't really a concern. It's more of a thought process. Black backgrounds are very popular these days. You've chosen black for your background. I don't know the reason or even if there is a reason past it looking good on the page. The problem with black backgrounds is it means you have to change the text color. That change in text color makes it awful hard for someone to print.

Suggestion: If you can use a different background color than black then give it a try. If not, know that people might have trouble printing.

Concern: You have two award images at the bottom of the page.

Suggestion: Those images should be on their own page and not slowing the completion of the page. Make a link to that page so if others want to see the awards, they can.

Concern: You may not feel this is a concern, but I wanted to point it out. On the top of the Combat Medic pages you have an animated cartoon of a medic walking. The image stuck out in my mind because it just didn't seem to fit. The site itself is very reverent and the animated cartoon seemed to take away from that.

In addition, the animation has a halo, a white ring around it that is very noticeable against the black background (the same can be said for the animated red devil on the other pages). Those halos seem to make the image look shoddy and not overly professional like the rest of the site.

Suggestion: I don't know the thought process or if a whimsical image like the one in Figure 5.11 fits in with the site, but I would think about replacing it with something that fits in more with the site.

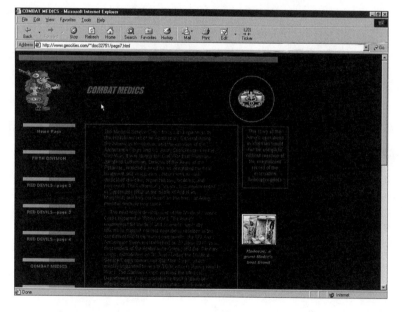

Figure 5.11
Animated Combat Medic.

Concern: Down the left side you have links that seem to double themselves. For example, you have "Red Devils Page 2" then "Red Devils – Page 3," and then again with page four.

Suggestion: You could greatly lessen the number of links, thus possibly lessening the length of your pages by combining those links into one. Maybe "Red Devils – Page 1, 2, 3, 4" as one link, each sending to a different page.

The pages are links to one another once I get in to page one, so I even wonder if all three links are needed. Maybe only a link to page one is truly required.

Overall: You took an idea close to your person and created a Web site that equaled it. There's no doubt about it—this site was built with a lot of respect for the idea it represents. I can see that you took every aspect of the site into account and created a package rather than simply text and images. Each element goes toward the killer app of the site. Nothing seems left to chance. Take a look at some of the previous suggestions and see if any of them would help make the site better. If not, you can be happy with what you have here.

Chapter 6

Links, Links, Links

The Web is called a Web because it's…well…a Web. Now that I've stated my firm grasp of the obvious, allow me to expand a bit. Before there was a World Wide Web, yes, there was a time, one of the most popular methods of disseminating information on the Internet was Gopher Lists.

Named for the University of Wisconsin's Golden Gophers, Gopher lists allowed a topic with multiple subheadings. Under each of those headings could then be many more subheadings. It went on and on.

Newsgroups were big, too. A topic headed a long list of posts and replies. People thought this form of interaction was great. I thought it was great.

Then came the World Wide Web.

When I first used the Web it was 1994 and I thought it was the dumbest thing ever created. "Give me my Gopher," I yelled. That turned some heads in the computer lab, let me tell you.

When the Web first came out there were no images. It was a text-based deal just like the other formats previously mentioned. You used a program called Lynx to surf around looking for words that where brighter than all the other words. Those were the links that you would click, by hitting the Enter key, to go to another page. You would jump from link to link using the arrow keys. When you found a link you liked, you'd strike the Enter key. Bingo. There would be a new page with more highlighted words.

I first started to understand how big the Web was going to be when, upon my third visit, someone asked why I was going backward through my page. "To get back to the main page," I said. You see you had to do that with Gopher and newsgroup postings. There was a starting point. If you went five steps down, you had to come five steps up. It is very logical and very linear.

Not now. Now the links on the Web page stand alone. There really isn't any starting or ending point. You cannot reach a level where you won't go any higher or a level where you can't get any lower. Sure, you could get to the homepage of a site, but that isn't a ceiling by any means. You just click and go somewhere else. It is as if the playing field has been leveled. All is equal, all is important. The Web allows what was once a linear movement to become nonlinear movement. Text becomes hypertext. It wasn't until long after my third trip to the Web that it hit me just how important links are to a Web page.

They are, without a doubt, the lifeblood of a page and are truly what first set the Web apart from the other Internet information dissemination formats. Sure, the ability to post images basically puts the other forms to bed, but it is the ability to create hypertext links that first set the Web apart. This was the first shot in the war for format dominance on the Internet. It has been a romp from then on. The Web easily emerged as the more used section of the Internet.

Gopher lists have pretty much gone the way of the dinosaur at this point in the life of the Internet. I did a search on the words "Gopher List" in a major search engine and a lot of pages came back. Most were dated 1996 or before. The links were pointing to addresses that looked something like:

`http://gopher.xxx.xxx` or `gopher://xxx.xxx`

I found many pages that called themselves Gopher lists but were simply HTML pages following the same Gopher format having lists leading to smaller lists. In fact, even the birthplace of Gopher lists, the University of Wisconsin, has posted a note that it does not provide information via gopher lists anymore. The funny thing is, the note is listed on their Gopher server:

`gopher://gopher.adp.wisc.edu/0ITEMTEXT`

I can't guarantee the page will even be there if you try it out.

Links are so easy to make, too. That's what kills me. Just a few very simple blips of code and you've got a link to any page you want. There is no class system or hierarchy of sites on the Web. The smallest of personal sites can link to the largest of corporate monsters.

Copyright law states that you can make a link to any other page you want. My mother's page about flower arranging can make links from her page to IBM, GM, Xerox, and that's okay. I think that's just great.

Understand that copyright also states that if you make a link, you do it with the graces of the person or company that owns the site you linked up with. They do have the right to tell you to take your link down. In short, you can link, but you're still responsible for the information to post to your site. If you libel the site you're linking to, they do have the ability to demand you take the link down, or worse yet, take legal action. It doesn't happen often, but it does happen. I once demanded a pornography site take down a link stating that the site was put together using HTML Goodies. Ugh. Beyond that one rarely enforced glitch, link away.

I have read the Web Content Accessibility Guidelines found at `http://www.w3.org/TR/WAI-WEBCONTENT/` so many times I about know them by heart. The page offers many great ideas but I think lucky number 13 is by far the best tip:

> Provide Clear Navigation Mechanisms

You just cannot state it any more clearly than that. Do not haphazardly place links. Put some thought into it. Get the text and the links right and you're almost home in creating a great design.

Links are great, but there are methods of using them to better advantage.

What Do I Click to Get Out of Here?

I know everyone has been to a page that displayed very nicely and looked pretty good, but then posed a problem.

Where can I go? Where are the links? Should I scroll? What do I do?

Take Anjaleck's Home Page, `http://home.talkcity.com/SpiritCir/anjaleck/index.html`, for example (see Figure 6.1). Yes, the background tiles, but that's easily fixable. The concern I have is that there are only two links on the page when I arrive...and they both do the same thing. One is an email link, and then on the same line is an image that asks you to send email.

Contrary to what you might think, I like the page. Fix the background and it works pretty well. I can read the text. The site is about poetry and I got a poem down the left side right away. The format is set to display on smaller screens through a table cell.

The problem is, I can't really do anything when I arrive. Let's scroll down Anjaleck's Home Page a bit (see Figure 6.2) and you finally find the links.

Figure 6.1
Am I allowed to do anything other than write to you from this page?

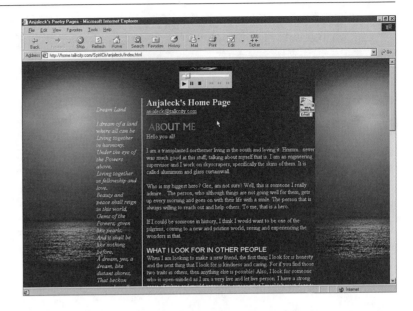

Figure 6.2
There are the links!

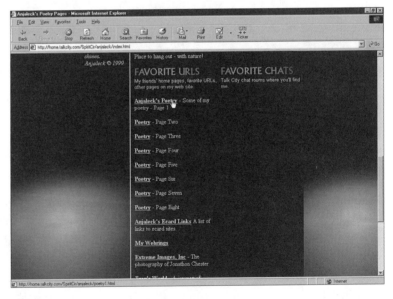

Okay! Now we're talking. Now I have links. I can see the other pages on the site and can get a general idea of how it branches out. There are actually more links following what you see here. I discuss how many links might be too many in a moment.

Design Goodies Survey

HTML Goodies Survey Question: You enter a page and do not see any links. Do you:

Scroll to find links   83%

Leave the page   17%

N=480

Yes, people scroll to find links, but remember what was said earlier. People don't like to scroll in general.

This page has the ability to be great. Here's a quick fix. Replace the poem down the left side with the links. If you want to keep the poem, put it to the right moving down the page.

The general rule of thumb in terms of links is

> Get them up high.

Get your links on the page so that the user sees them as soon as he enters the Web site. Yes, people have reported that they scroll to find links, but remember that users do not like to scroll. I guarantee that if you make a point of putting all of your links down low on your pages, people get tired of always having to scroll to navigate and leave the site.

Links are important. Remember that I put this book together in order of what elements I feel are most important. I have links listed third behind the killer app and the text of the site. My whole previous reminiscent diatribe told how important links are to a Web page. Don't hide them. Get them up high and get them on the page where they carry a sense of importance.

So, Where Do You Put the Links?

I've said this before, and I'll say it again. Think about how the eye moves across the Web page, top to bottom while at the same time left to right. People believe that the first elements they run into on a Web page are the most important. There's a reason why many companies always have their identifier in the upper-left corner. They are saying, through their design, that the logo is important.

Let's take this information a step further. You've going to put links on the page, right? Well, where do you put them? In the realm of a Web page, links are pretty important. That means they should be pushed toward the left and hopefully up high.

Those polled by HTML Goodies said they wanted to see link to the left most often (55%). The second highest response was that people wanted to see links at the top of a Web page (17%). Only 22% reported wanting links at the bottom of a page and only 6% reported wanting the links on the right.

Good. Now you have a general idea that links should be up high and possibly pushed to the left.

Allow me to go a little deeper into this link placement question. I also asked the HTML Goodies users how they would like to see links displayed. This time the response was overwhelming. Over 80% wanted to see links listed vertically, one on top of the other. The rest reported they liked their links listed horizontally or that it didn't matter.

Examine both formats and you can make the decision as to which you like. First, here are some links listed vertically. Figure 6.3 is a page by Trey Randolph named Trey3K.

Figure 6.3
Links are up and to the left.

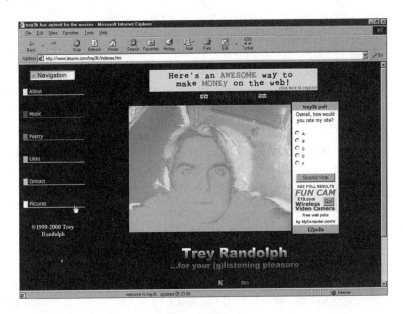

Now let's look at some links listed horizontally. Figure 6.4 is a page for the Sheet Metal Workers Local 38 by Chris Lomedico.

Which do you like better? It really is your call depending on what you want your homepage to look like. It is my opinion that people would be happy with either format as long as the links are up high and can be easily picked out as soon as the page loads.

Either way works well. You just need to decide which works best for your site's killer app.

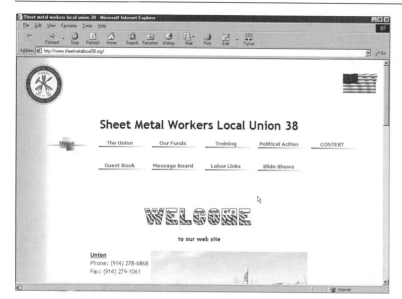

Figure 6.4
http://www.
sheetmetallocal38.org/.

AAAAAAAAUUUUUGH! He Used Text Links

Can someone explain to me why using simple text links has almost become taboo? Almost every page I've been into lately (I wrote this in 1999) has done their best to stop text links from looking like text links. Figure 6.5 is an example.

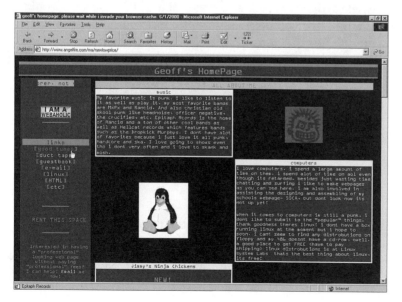

Figure 6.5
Links on the left.

This screen capture is Geoff's Homepage at `http://www.angelfire.com/ma/newlowprice/`. I'm sure Geoff is a nice guy and he did a nice little bit of coding here, but why did Geoff try to stop his links from looking like links?

First off, I applaud Geoff for even going with text-based links. The vast majority of pages these days seem to only use images as links.

Now, Geoff has links but has done two things to try and smooth them out, I guess. First, he has changed the color of the links away from the traditional blue. That's not a bad thing. Seventy-eight percent of those polled reported links could be any color as long as that color is blatantly different from the other text on the page.

Geoff also rid the links of their underline. This is a new trend in Web page design, to lose underlines on the links. I don't know that I like the effect all that much. The HTML Goodies readers polled suggested over half of them wanted to see links underlined. The underline denotes to the user that this specific text is a link. Obviously, it works in tandem with the placement of the text.

There are two times I really like links that are not underlined. The first is when a word within a paragraph is made into a hypertext link. The underline harms the block nature of the paragraph by moving lines of text farther apart from one another. In that case, a blatant color differing from the remainder of the text does enough of a trick to denote a link. The second is when the link receives an underline as part of a rollover effect.

I had a student hand in a page one time that went so far to hide that text represented links that she lost the underline and set the link to black, the same color as the text. You would have never known the text was a link had you not inadvertently run your pointer over it. Her thinking was that she just didn't like the look of blue-underlined links. It was a poor design decision.

Remember, your links do not have to be blue, just a blatantly different color from the rest of the text.

Links also do not have to have underlines. I've already discussed how placement alone denotes that links are links. However, think about an underline at some point, as when a rollover occurs.

Rollovers

You may have noticed in Figure 6.5 of Geoff's homepage that the text had highlighted when my cursor passed over top.

This is a great effect, it's easy to get, and you should think about using it if you intend to use text links on your page.

Figure 6.6 is another example of using the text rollovers on a page by Simon Husbands, "The Johnson Husbands" `http://www.isd.net/husbands/`.

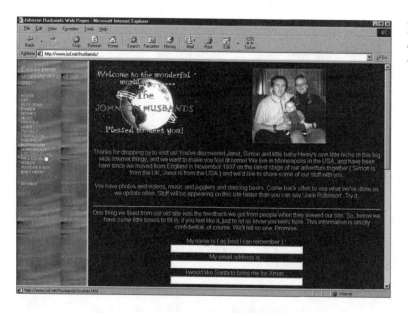

Figure 6.6
Look at the pointer on the left.

The highlight rollover effect is created through the use of Cascading Style Sheets (CSS). Here, copy this code from this page between the <HEAD> tags in your HTML document:

```
<STYLE TYPE="text/css">


A:link {color:black; text-decoration:none}
A:alink {color:red; text-decoration:none}
```

```
A:hover {color:blue; text-decoration:underline}
A:vlink {color:blue; text-decoration:none}

</STYLE>
```

The three lines of text deal with the page's link colors and if there is an underline, the color and underline when the mouse passes over the link, and finally the color and underline of links already visited. You can play with the colors and the use of an underline, or not, until the color scheme of your links fits into the look of your page.

Here's the basic concept:

- `a:link` affects all unvisited anchor flags.
- `a:active` affects anchor flags when being clicked.
- `a:visited` affect anchor flags representing visited links.
- `a:hover` affects anchor flags when the mouse is resting on them.
- `color:` sets the color.
- `text-decoration:` sets the underline.
- `underline` if you want one.
- `none` if you don't.

The effect is easy, offers assistance to the user during navigation and since the effect is produced through commands in the HTML document, it does not slow the completion of the page. What a deal! But, just like any other element on the Web page, if you decide to use rollovers, there are some items to concern yourself with. I have compiled some of my own opinions on using rollovers on your pages.

Joe's Rollover Opinion #1:

I feel that the link and vlink colors should always be set to the same color so that there is not a color difference between a visited and unvisited link.

Now, many people disagree with me because the way of the Web from the start was to offer a different link color for both. If that's the only reason for following the two-color pattern, I don't think it's a good enough reason.

In fact, I feel that the visited and unvisited colors should be the same even if you do not use rollovers.

I say that because when you set up a site, you decide on a color scheme and by allowing multiple colors to pop up in there, you break that scheme. If the visited and unvisited colors are all the same then the page always look as you want it to each time a user arrives, no matter what page he or she has visited in the past.

Furthermore, when you set two color schemes, even if both colors are complementary, your page often starts to look haphazard with just pockets of a new color here and there.

I just don't think that there is enough of a reason to let a user know they have already visited a page to set to different colors.

Highlighting Rollovers

It is possible to set the rollover so that the background is highlighted. You can get the effect by adding one more simple CSS command into the hover section of the previous code. That line then looks like this:

```
A:hover {color:blue; text-decoration:underline; background: #FFCC33}
```

Using that extra command adds a block highlight around the text. I think it is a wonderful effect, but if you use it, use it correctly.

Joe's Rollover Opinion #2

When using the highlight method, the highlight color should not be at all shocking. It should be quite pale offering just a highlight.

Joe's Rollover Opinion #3

When using a highlight, the text hover color should not change. The highlight is the winner here. Only one color change is enough.

Joe's Rollover Opinion #4

Don't have your rollovers change font, size, bold, or italic.

Changing the font, the size of the font, or the text to bold or italic can be done easily. No, I'm not going to show you the code because you shouldn't do it. It is disruptive and, just like the use of an underline, can alter the elements around the text.

When you use a rollover, you are attempting to create navigation assistance, not put on a show.

The basic rule of thumb should be, if anything around your links moves when the rollover occurs, don't use the effect. It is too disruptive.

That said, I like rollover links. It's a good effect to use. I suggest you make a point of it.

No Text! Images!

People love to use images as hypertext links. I actually had to search a bit to find the previous examples using text links. Finding pages using images as hypertext links was a whole lot easier.

If you intend to use images for your links, there are a few things to keep in mind. Here is a page I think has used image links pretty well. I'm not saying this is the only way to use images as links; I just think the author thought out his use of links. Figure 6.7 is Gil's Pittsburgh Steelers page at `http://www.geocities.com/steelergil/`.

Figure 6.7
The team of the '70s.

The page Gil put together impressed me for a couple of reasons. First off, it loaded very quickly. The reason is because Gil used the same image again and again. See the Steeler helmet and Steeler logo being used multiple times?

By using the same image multiple times and then allowing the text underneath the images to act as the label, Gil kept the speed of his page load fast and didn't tax the server too much. Furthermore, by using the same image, he schooled the user that that specific image means a link. In all subpages, when the user sees that image, he knows it's a link.

It's the same idea as running a series of long, thin rectangles down the left side of a page. That long rectangle is seen and accepted by the user as representing a link. No matter what page the user is on, that image format means link.

Design Goodies Survey

HTML Goodies Survey Question: Should a hypertext link produce text in the status bar when the mouse passes over?

Yes	67%
No	5%
Doesn't matter	28%

N=486

It appears that respondents would like text to appear. The only problem is that when questioned further, the majority of those polled said they wanted the link URL to be the text. That's what you get by default without any extra programming. The second answer given was a description of the page. Don't be so quick to use JavaScript to get text down into the status bar, but if you do, don't be cute with the text. Use the text to help with navigation rather than to try to produce a smile.

Often, I see pages that use images as links that use a different image for every link. That makes for a very slow download time. Gil's page is quick, stays loyal to his killer app, and looks pretty good.

Gil, I would, however, make a point of putting in text links as well as image links in case someone who doesn't use images strolls in.

But what of using multiple images?

It can be a concern, but if you want to use multiple images to represent specific links, just make a point of keeping the images small enough that they load quickly. Also, make a point of having the image represent the page it is linking to. Figure 6.8 is an example I really like.

This page, built for the Good Shepherd Lutheran Church, uses images as links. Each image is quite small but carries a good deal of detail. Each represents the page it is linking to. Each is set into a stained-glass motif so it goes to the site's killer app, but then look underneath. There you find text equals to the previous image links. It's a good use of multiple images acting as multiple links.

Only one concern...get the links up higher. They are in the wrong place on the page. Smaller screen settings chop them off leaving the links below the gatefold.

Figure 6.8
The Good Shepherd Lutheran Church by Don Titus.

Rollovers (Again)

This is why image links have become so popular. I guarantee it. The image rollovers are so much cooler than the text rollovers that people want them. If that's you, think back to the discussion regarding whom the Web site is for. You may think the rollovers are cool and from your hard drive they may load up lightning fast, but how does the page work on the Web? Do the images come in quickly? Does the rollover start right away or does the user have to leave his pointer on the image for a short time so that the rollover image loads?

Oh, these image flip rollovers are popular, but again, just as everything previously mentioned, there's a correct and an incorrect method of using the rollovers. There are elements you need to be concerned about.

By the way...I have a full tutorial on image flip rollovers at `http://www.htmlgoodies.com/tutors/imageflip.html`. Stop by and grab the code to get the effect.

Be concerned about this: To begin with, keep in mind the size of the images. If you produce a rollover on each hypertext link, you're asking for two images every time you create a link. That doubles the number of times your server is being asked to deliver a file. Go with images that are made up of the least amount of bytes yet still look good.

Be concerned about this: Now, let's talk about those rollovers. Stop and think. What is the purpose of the rollover? It's to highlight the link the user's pointer happens to be resting upon, yes? Yes. Then why would you create a rollover that changes the image completely? I've seen pages where the image link has a small button that read Links. Then, when I put my mouse over top, the image changed to Bill the Cat from the Bloom County cartoon.

What did that have to do with anything?

That link-to-cat flip was image flip for the sake of image flip. It wasn't meant to help the page or the user. It only showed the author could make an image flip. My bet is that if I had asked the author why he made such an odd flip, the answer would have been something like, "I thought it looked cool."

You may not have noticed it but the screen capture of the Good Shepherd Lutheran Church has a rollover set on their images. If you look at the image the pointer is on, you see a little shading appearing on the right and bottom sides of the image. It's subtle, but effective. It works a great deal like the highlighting behind the link in the previous text rollover. I knew I was on the image, but the flip wasn't so prevalent that it took my mind off what I was doing.

That's the concept. The fact that the image flipped is not the big deal. The flip should act as support for the links because it's the link that really matters. Don't go for a huge change in your image flips. A slight change is enough.

Figure 6.9 is my personal university homepage at `http://www.selu.edu/Academics/Faculty/jeburns/`.

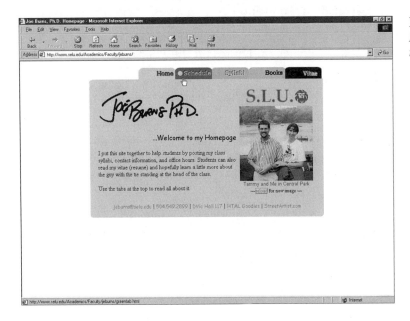

Figure 6.9
Dig that beautiful wife of mine...

The tabs along the top are image rollovers. Notice my cursor is on the second tab marked Schedule. Do you see the rollover effect? A dot has popped up. That's it. Nothing more was needed. The image did not need to be changed dramatically. That little bit was enough.

Be concerned about this! I just want to drive this point home. When you create an image flip rollover, you are interested in assisting the user through his navigation. There is no need to have fireworks every time the mouse pointer rolls over the link. A subtle change helps greatly.

Alter the Link Representing the Current Page

Let's say you have a list of links down the left side or across the top. It really doesn't matter which as long as the links are up high; go to the page's killer app and help the user to navigate.

The user clicks on the link marked Photos. That user is then transported to the photos page. Now. Think about your navigation. Is the link that leads to Photos still visible? It should be. If it is, is it still a hypertext link?

That's a very common mistake new Web designers make. Once the new designer has a navigation bar or system he likes, he copies and pastes that system into every page. That's smart. Every page should carry consistency and a similar navigation bar is a good method of keeping that consistency. The problem is that every link is still active with a simple copy and paste of the navigation bar. This happens a great deal when a designer uses a frames format whereas the navigation bar sits in a frame and never changes. Every link is always active.

Thus, a person who clicked on Photos can click on Photos on the Photos page. It just reloads the page.

"So what?" you may ask. "Why would users click on the same page they are already on?"

They may not, but then again they may. Why not use that bit of information to your advantage? Set up your list of text links or image links so that the link representing the page the user is viewing is somehow changed. Make the image darker or lighter. Make the text bold or maybe put a little arrow image next to it. I've even seen pages where the link had "You are here" written on top.

If nothing else, when the user is on the Photos page, don't allow the link to the Photos page to be active. On the contrary, alter it so that it aids the user in his navigation. Use the navigation bar or system you set up to prominently proclaim that the user is, in fact, viewing the Photos page.

It's a little thing, but a nice touch to your assisting the user by "providing clear navigation mechanisms."

Never More Than Three Clicks Away

Someone is going to read this section and write to me and ask why this portion wasn't the first topic in the chapter. The reason I didn't place this first is because I am putting this book, and thus, this chapter, in an order of importance. It is more important to first discuss when links should be placed on the page, and then to discuss how those links would look or appear to the user.

Now I begin to cover the concept of how many links and how often to offer them.

A well-designed Web site has a well-thought-out navigation system. If the author has taken the time to think out how his users move through the site then the navigation should be immediately recognizable and easy to follow. The navigation system should also allow that a user should be able to get from any page on the site to any page on the site in three, or fewer, clicks.

When designing a roadmap for a site's navigation, there are three basic formats, The Spider, The Hierarchy, and From All-to-All. Each has its own pros and cons. Let's look at each.

The Spider

The Spider is a navigation system whereby all roads lead to and from the homepage. HTML Goodies ran like this until it became a bit of a monolith. The concept is that the homepage acts as the main dissemination point. There is a link to all pages from the homepage and all subpages link back to the homepage.

No matter what page the user is viewing, he can get to any other page in two clicks. The first is back to the homepage, and the second is then to the desired page.

Pro: It's extremely easy to understand and navigation can be done in just a couple of clicks.

Con: There always seems to be an intermediate step. You must go back to the homepage each time. That can get dull after a while.

A site containing a small number of pages can get away with this pretty easily. The big concern is to remember that each page must have some form of back navigation.

A site containing a small number of pages might also be able to get away with putting links to all the other pages on each of the subpages. This is the all-to-all I talk about in a moment. That way each page can link straight to the next page. However, this doesn't work very well when the number of pages starts to get up around ten or more. If you are going to follow this format, make sure your site stays small in terms of pages.

Remember that not only do your users move forward through your site, but they also want to move backward. Give them the ability to do that. I have back navigation on the HTML

Goodies site that always goes back to the homepage. I want to always take them back to square one. I am offering a quick way to get back to Go, collect that $200, and start anew.

When you create your back navigation, make sure it sits at the bottom of the page and make sure it's consistent. If on one page you use an image that reads Back then use that every time. If you go with text links then use the same text every time you create your links.

In short, you got me here...now give me a way to get back.

The Hierarchy

The Hierarchy is best described as looking like a flow chart. The HTML Goodies site was set up in a hierarchical format when it became too large to act as a spider, too many links on the homepage.

The Hierarchy format sets pages into groups. Yahoo! is in a hierarchical format. On HTML Goodies, I broke my pages into three groupings. One was called tutors. Those tutorials deal specifically with HTML. The second was called beyond. Those tutorials dealt with elements not specifically HTML such as CSS and JavaScript. The third grouping was named primers and it included only primer tutorials.

Under each of the groupings were further groupings. For instance, under the primers group were the three groupings: HTML Primers, Banner Creation Primers, and JavaScript Primers.

To represent the hierarchy, I broke out the first two levels on the homepage. I had the first grouping, Primers, and then underneath, the three smaller groupings, HTML, Banner Creation, and JavaScript (see Figure 6.10).

The concept of the Hierarchy format was to create a logical flow into the site. The user would arrive at the homepage, click to go to the first grouping, choose a smaller grouping, and finally to the tutorial he desired.

All back navigation returned to the homepage to start the flow over again.

Pro: The format is logical and guides the viewer. It also helps the design to keep elements straight in the site itself.

Con: The format creates a great many clicks often breaking the three-click rule of thumb. You must be aware not to make too many levels of hierarchy. Also, as was the previous case, the user cannot quickly jump to a specific element from each page.

The hierarchy format is best when a site contains a great many pages that fall into specific groupings all by themselves. You cannot force these groupings. The grouping must be blatant and obvious to the user.

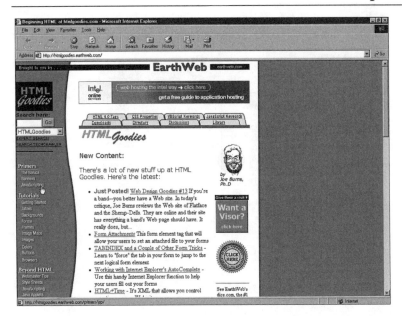

Figure 6.10
See the hierarchy down the left side?

Sites that contain a great number of pages may want to also have what I term a master page. This is a page that simply lists every page on the site. The HTML Goodies Master List is huge yet many people report they use it a great deal after they know the site from following the hierarchical format.

My Master List page can be found at `http://www.htmlgoodies.com/tutors/master.html`.

From All-to-All

The From All-to-All format is just what it says. There is a link from all pages to all pages. I don't know that it requires any further explanation than that. Every page carries a navigation bar or system that links to every other page (see Figure 6.11).

Pro: You are one click away from any page on the site. Having a great many links on each page helps when your page is catalogued with search engines. Not only is the page catalogued, but every page that is linked from it is taken as well.

Con: If the site contains a small number of pages then this might be the way to go, but sites that offer great numbers of pages easily get bogged down in link after link after link.

The all-to-all format works best with sites that contain pages that constantly change and die away. News sites often use this format. Surf CNN and note the number of links on each page. No matter what page you're on, there are links all over it. The top headlines in numerous categories fill the page. That's the best time to use this format. The reason is that the links aren't around for long and act like newspaper headlines.

Figure 6.11
The CNNSI.com is a pretty good example of linking all to all. The navigation bar and all the links follow from page to page.

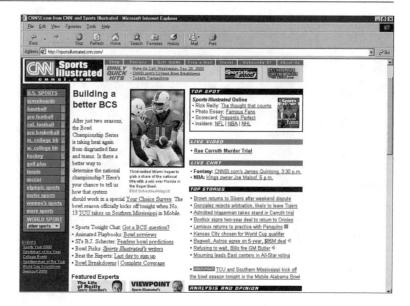

Go for a surf around some of your favorite news and sports sites. I bet you see the all-to-all format used a great deal.

Most personal and corporate pages do not update fast enough to go to an all-to-all format. HTML Goodies updates weekly and I don't feel it's a fast enough turnover to warrant leaving my hierarchical navigation system.

I also believe that the turnover in a site using an all-to-all format would not suggest a Master List page as the links would come and go way too quickly.

Site Maps, Master Lists, and Search Functions

I mentioned the concept of a master list earlier when using a hierarchical or all-to-all format. Do you need one of these elements on your site? I didn't ask if you wanted one of these elements—I asked if you need one of these elements.

Smaller sites that use a spider format don't really need any of the elements because the format itself is acting as a site map. All that can be seen is right there on the homepage. You might argue that a search function is required, and maybe it is. The choice is up to you. Do you really offer the format of information that people would want to search for? If so, then a search engine might be for you.

I am really speaking to sites that offer a great number of pages or information that is fact-based.

I believe that a large site should contain either a site map or a Master List. What's the difference?

A site map is just that. It is a visual map (see Figure 6.12). It shows the site as if it were a road map. Links from page to page are displayed and the user can see how the site flows. It is visual.

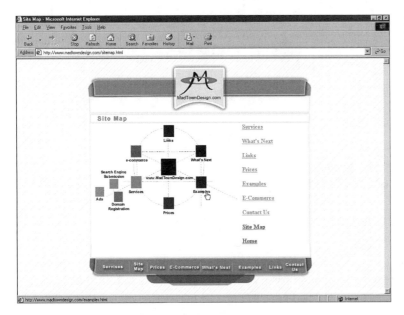

Figure 6.12
The site map at
`MadTownDesign.com.`

On the other hand, a Master List is just that. A list. It is a simple series of links that show all of the pages and allows you to jump to those pages in one fell swoop. Usually the links are grouped together to allow ease of use, but it's usually not much more than that. A Master List is a list. That's all.

You should use a Master List when the number of pages becomes far too large to show in a visual. Often sites have a Master List but refer to it as a site map.

That's fine as long as the functionality is there. Figure 6.13 is an example.

A search function seems to be the king daddy of the three. I have a search function on HTML Goodies and it is used by almost two of every three visitors. A full 64% of those polled by HTML Goodies said they would rather use a series of link menus to find information than to use a search engine. I set up this beautiful hierarchy format and most people use the search. Oh well. That doesn't make the navigation format any less important. One out of every three people still use it.

Figure 6.13
The site map (Master List, actually) at `Apple.com`.

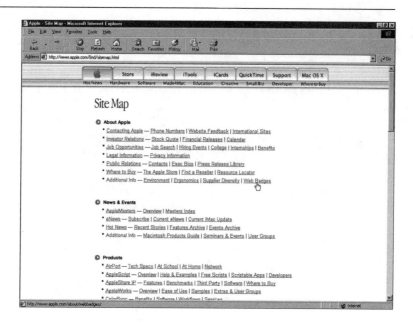

If you choose the search function, here are a couple hints before you find out on your own:

- **Hint 1:** Searches use CPU power by the bucket load. Make sure you are on a powerful server. You may want to see if the server you have chosen even allows you to set up a search function.

- **Hint 2:** Set up your search function so it searches the pages that are on the site at the time of the search. That pretty much leaves out JavaScript-based searches where you need to update the database yourself every time you change or add a page.

If you feel you're going to use a search, I would seek out an ISP that offers such a function before you get underway. Searches are difficult to set up, especially if you intend to use a CGI-based search. If the ISP already has a search function in place, you're way ahead of the game.

Ad Banners, Ad, Banners, Friendly Neighborhood Ad Banners

Ad banners? Huh?

Wait. I thought this was the chapter on links. Ad banners aren't links. They're images. Obviously, someone has made a true copyediting mistake.

My answer to that is yep and nope. (My parents were raised on a cowboy ranch.)

Yep, ad banners are images. However, nope, there has been no mistake. Any discussion of ad banners belongs here in the links sections.

I asked you to take the time to think about every element that you put on your page. Stop and think why someone might put an ad banner on one or more pages.

It might be placed to gain some money or to hopefully increase traffic to the site, but the designer, banner trade site, advertiser, or whoever placed the ad wants someone to click on it. That's a link. The discussion of ad banners belongs right here.

Design Goodies Survey

HTML Goodies Survey Question: Have you ever put an ad banner from a "banner-trade" site on your page?

Yes   74%

No   36%

N=483

Follow-up question: If yes, what was your reason for doing so?

Increase Traffic   54%

Make Money   15%

Improve the Look of the Site   4%

Other   26%

N=344 (99% total because of rounding)

The ads are out there. People seem to like them and have many reasons for putting them on their sites.

An ad banner is a link. An ad banner is bright, and happy, and colorful, and animated so that it draws attention.

The person who has the ad banner on his site wants a user to click on it. People can argue semantics with me all day on this, but keep in mind that an ad banner is a link and it should be treated that way.

If you place an ad banner using one of those banner trade sites, don't you want someone to click on your banner? You want someone to click to come to your site. That gains you more traffic. The problem is that far more people post ad banners than click on them. Over 70% of those polled said they click ad banners rarely or never.

Right from the start, allow me to say that I am in no way against using an ad banner. There are people out there that believe that putting ad banners on a Web site is akin to selling your soul. Not me. I like ad banners, I think they can be helpful and they are what keeps HTML Goodies free to the public. I just think designers need to learn to use ad banners correctly.

Take a look at Figure 6.14.

Figure 6.14
What is most important on this page?

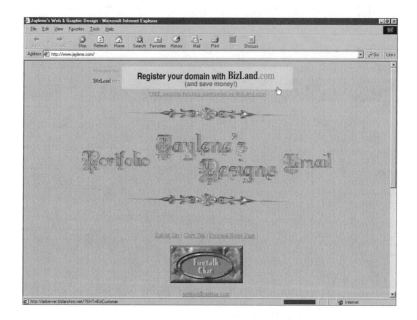

This is Jaylene's Web and Graphic Design at `http://www.jaylene.com/`. I really liked the look of the site. Jaylene obviously knows what she's doing. The text is readable—it melds nicely with the background which is a nice color. The entire look and feel of the site suggest an older American feel. I like it. The purpose of the site is to show her work as a designer. It does that pretty well.

Now, what's the most important thing on the page shown in Figure 6.14? The answer is...the ad banner for BizLand.com.

It has to be the most important thing. It is located at the highest point on the page. Not only that but it is set aside from the rest of the page almost as if it were the banner header for the page. It's a different color from anything else on the page and it's the only animated thing on the page.

It has to be the most important thing. I can't help looking at it.

My guess is that Jaylene does not want that ad banner to be the most important thing on the page. Going through the site, I see that that's the only ad banner. My guess is that her site is housed on the BizLand server and she has to have the banner up. But why would BizLand put the banner there? It takes away from the rest of the site.

Isn't that the point? What does BizLand want? They want someone to click on the banner so that user goes to BizLand and hopefully signs up for housing so more banners can be put up and more people will click and come to get more housing.

Links, links, links...

So, what could Jaylene do to minimize the effect of the ad banner and set her site as the most important thing?

I would suggest she move the banner if she can. There's a lovely open space just below her second page separator image. Put it there.

Ad banners are a part of the Web and they do good things for a lot of people, but that doesn't mean you have to give every ad top billing. I've always wondered why people who don't need ad banners often get them and place them right up top for all the world to see. The ad banner is begging to be clicked. Someone who puts the ad first is saying, "Thanks for coming to my page, now click to leave before you read anything."

Nestle, Nestle, Nestle

Ad banners are not the most important thing. Your page is the most important thing. That ad banner is a helper. It is not the end all.

Your site, your identifier, should occupy that coveted top-left position. If you include an ad banner, it should nestle into the page, not push it down a couple of inches. (Take a look at Figure 6.15.)

Take notice of where the top ad banner is sitting. Yes, it's up top but what is the most important thing on the site? Well, the HTML Goodies logo is occupying the upper-left corner. The parent name of HTML Goodies, EarthWeb, is taking the banner across the top. After the page denotes what's really important then the ad banner shows up.

Take notice also that the ad banner is not set aside or trumpeted in any way differently from any other element on the page. In fact it looks much more a part of the page than does the ad banner on Jaylene's page because the ad is nestled inside the page rather than being plopped up top before the page gets started.

Now let's go to the other side of the extreme and check out Figure 6.16.

Figure 6.15
This site looks familiar.

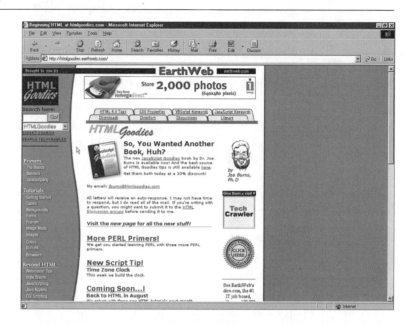

Figure 6.16
Here, ad banner; here, ad banner...

This is a nice site, Britt Technologies at `www.britttechnologies.com`. There's an ad banner on this site. You don't see it? Okay, then, let's scroll down a good bit of the page (see Figure 6.17).

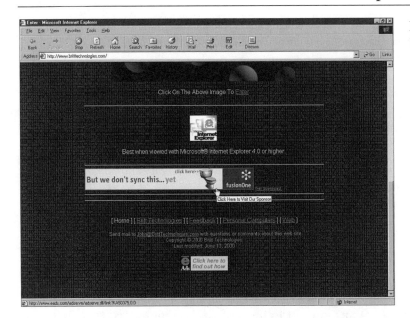

Figure 6.17
There it is.

Not knowing the author of the page, I'd guess this ad banner was placed specifically to draw new people to the site. I bet there are Britt Technologies ad banners floating around out there as part of the banner trade program.

The problem is that those trade programs work by the number of impressions or clicks the ads get on your pages. The placement of this ad, while well out of the way, makes the use of the ad basically worthless. Look again at Figure 6.17. Why would I scroll down to the ad? The identifier and all the links are right there for me. I have no reason to scroll, therefore I never see the ad.

In this case, the author has gone to lengths to get that ad out of the way. In fact, he had moved it so far out of the way that it's not worth having on the page. I would lose the ad altogether. It's not helping and it's slowing the page's completion.

If You're Going to Play, Play!

I had a music teacher one time that used to say, "If you're going to play, play." He meant that if you're going to make the decision to do something, do it. Ad banners fall perfectly into that statement. If you're going to use them, use them. Place them so that your site is still the most important thing, but still place them so that the user can see them. To decide to use ad banners and then do your best to hide the ad doesn't make much sense.

If you're going to play, play.

Yeah, but how much do you play? How many ad banners on a site is too many? There's no good way to answer this question with a number. If I say three then three is the number you shoot for. No matter what the page looks like, three banners end up on the page.

The best way to answer that question is, how many do you need? Think about your purpose for having the ad. Do you want money? Do you want to increase traffic? Do you want your site to look more professional?

Remember that more banners do not necessarily mean more user activity. If a user does not click on one banner, giving him a choice of three won't work any better.

So, how many do you need? If money is the concern, how many ads cover your costs? You want the lowest number for the highest amount of money. Remember that it's your site that is important. The ad banners are there to pay the bills, not to be the end all.

The same goes for an ad banner that is meant to increase traffic. One works. Two does not work twice as much.

If you're putting up an ad banner to make your site look professional, one is enough.

Just about any page can get away with one ad banner. The ad, no matter its size, can be nestled into some area to allow the site to remain the focus. Once you have two ads, now you need to find two places to nest them. Three require three areas of nesting. At some point, the ad banners win out simply because of space they cover. They become the focus of the page. You can't help it.

Before you undertake putting ad banners on your page, ask yourself if they are really and truly needed. Unless you're attempting to make a living through your site, the answer is probably no. There are other methods of increasing traffic.

How many ad banners do you need? You know...the number zero is a viable answer. You may not need any.

If you do decide to go with an ad banner, remember that your site is what is important, not the ad. Don't give away the most important part of your site to an ad if you don't have to.

Some Final Thoughts on Links

I want to wrap up this chapter by throwing out a couple of link concerns that didn't fit neatly into the previous discussions. Keep these in mind when choosing what kind of links to put on your pages.

If You Use Frames, Don't Be a Para-site

A para-site (parasite) is an author who uses frames to keep people from leaving his Web site. Usually the author sets up the traditional two-column format and offers links on the left to appear in the right. The link might take you to NBC.com, but the site opens up in the right side of this person's frame setup. Ugh.

If you offer frames, make a point of opening links that go off-site in the full browser window. Do not open off-site pages in the right frame. It usually messes up the look of the off-site page and makes the user feel trapped in your site.

Be nice. Don't para-site.

Make Sure Your Links Work

If you make a link, test it to make sure it works. Those polled reported that as one of the worst things that can happen when visiting a site. Many reported losing respect for the site and some said they would leave because of a Page-Not-Found error.

Links: Use Them

Finally, let me state what you might feel is a rather obvious statement. You have the ability to use hypertext links, so use them.

Ninety-two percent of those polled said they would rather click to go to a new page for more information than to scroll down a long page.

Users love to click. They're not thrilled about scrolling. Use that knowledge to your advantage. Break your content up into small bites that the user can quickly digest.

Don't try to get everything onto one page. Use multiple pages and let the users click. That clicking gives them a sense of forward momentum. It makes users feel like they're doing something, like they're making progress. Scrolling doesn't give the same feeling. In fact, it gives the opposite. It makes users feel they are stuck in the mud.

Links. Use them.

Site Critiques

1. Sand Seekers/Author: Anthony Dattoli

`http://www.sandseekers.net/`

Load Time: 18 Seconds (after-effect), 57kps modem, cleared cache, 7/11/00 1:31PM.

My Screen Size: 1,024×768

Browsers Used: Internet Explorer 5 and Netscape Navigator 4.5

Figure 6.18
Where the seekers roam.
(Color Plate C.16)

Concept: Welcome to the Delmarva Peninsula, at least on the Web. The page is intended to be a quick information spot for all that goes on in and around the Delmarva area.

Praise: After rolling through the site, I think the author meant this to be a site specifically for those from the Delmarva area. It doesn't look like a tourist site. I would have expected a great many more travel and direction links if that were the case. The site is well written and works quickly. I'm not from the area so I can't vouch for the information, but it seems as though there is enough sponsorship that the site is at least somewhat supported by the community. The link marked Classified has a good many listings from local people selling all sorts of items.

Concern: The first thing I noticed was that the site looks a great deal like Yahoo!. I compared the two pages and the Delmarva site has used the same text font, colors, and format. When you click on one of the links, the site resembles the Yahoo! results page perfectly down to the ad banner placement (see Figure 6.19).

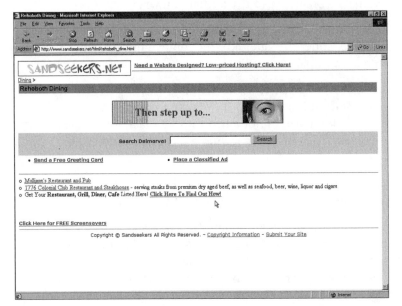

Figure 6.19
Does this look familiar?

Yahoo! is a very well-written site, but taking their two-column format and color scheme might be a little too close to copying.

Suggestion: I would look for a different look in the color scheme. I don't know that Yahoo! would ever make any comment, but it's better to be safe than sorry.

Concern: The site actually starts about halfway down the page. The four links offer screen savers and cards and the like. Each is part of the site but why they became the featured links I'm not quite sure. Then there are headlines, a fix for Melissa, the date and time, and then two buttons that don't work. Then the site gets started.

Suggestion: Think about why someone would come into a site like this. I don't believe it would be for a screen saver. The classified ads and possibly the postcards, but should they be featured? I don't think so. I would move all of that well down the page and get more of those links and small sponsor ads higher on the page.

Concern: Speaking of those ad banners, everything else on the page is geared to local. Those ad banners are pointed at the main sites for many of the companies. There's no redirect or CGI tracking involved. Are those ads being paid for? I ask because it's actually fairly common for people to put advertising banners on a site to give the site some credibility.

Suggestion: If the ad banners are paid for, keep them. If not, lose them. Use the space they free up to offer links and maybe break out of the format you've chosen.

Concern: I have the same question about many of the feeds you have linked on the page. I see two scrolling headlines (one is under the gatefold), the top five movies, stock tickers, and the results of a poll I can't seem to participate in.

Suggestion: Seriously consider if any of these feeds are helping the page. Would someone come to your page to get the latest headlines? Would they come to get the latest stock numbers? I would suggest they wouldn't. That's not a bad thing. In fact, losing the feeds helps the page load faster and, again, frees up space for more local news and events. I think people might come to your page for that.

Overall: I noticed that the Web design company that created the site keeps popping up on subpages. I'm also guessing that the author is actually that design company.

What you have here is a good page. The idea is sound and the coding is sound. What you need to do is break out of the Yahoo! format and look seriously at each element on the page and ask yourself if it is really something you need. The fact that you want the element on the page is not enough to keep it there. Be honest. If the element doesn't add to the page, it's harming the page. Lose it.

2. Otis Delivers/Author: Karen Samuelson

http://www.otisdelivers.com/index.html

Load Time: 14 Seconds (after-effect), 57kps modem, cleared cache, 7/11/00 1:59PM.

My Screen Size: 1,024×768

Browsers Used: Internet Explorer 5 and Netscape Navigator 4.5

Concept: Okay. There's this guy named Otis. He delivers things. Specifically, he delivers musical equipment. No gig too big. No haul too small.

Praise: I arrived at this page after looking through what seemed hundreds of other Web sites up for review. After a short while, Web sites all start to run together and all start to look the same. The reason I chose this site to review was because it jumped out at me. It set itself aside from the others, I think, through sheer simplicity.

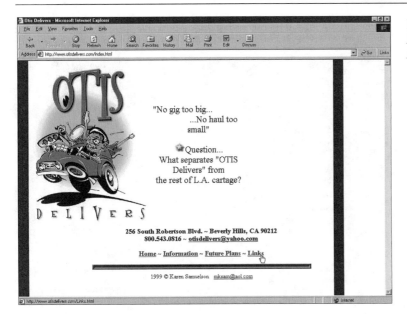

Figure 6.20
Here comes Otis! (Color Plate C.17)

The site is what it is, a business card for a guy who wants to deliver musical equipment around for bands. That's all, nothing more. There's no guestbook. There's no picture page. There's no chat room. There's none of the elements that have become so commonplace on people's Web sites.

My main purpose for showing this site, as part of the critiques, is to show that content is, and always will be, the most important thing on a page. I knew what this page was all about after looking at the homepage image. I didn't need to read the text. Read the text? There's hardly any there. I think the entire site has 200 words.

The most important page to the business even has few words. This would all fit nicely on a billboard (see Figure 6.21).

But...that's all that was needed. The price is the thing everyone wants to know. This trumpets the price instead of putting at the bottom of a long scrolling page filled with text. The page even carried the star with it to indicate that the price is the answer to the question with the star from the homepage. It told the story, it told it quickly, and the site finished its purpose. This is a killer app speaking for itself.

Concern: There is a link on the homepage in the form of a star just before Question.... I missed it. I think a lot of people might miss it.

Suggestion: Make the text a link. I would keep the black color, but still make the text a link. If you'd rather not do that then lose the star or add another image that reads something like, "Here's why...."

Figure 6.21
Hire Otis!

Concern: You have a links page. Why? I can see that the links really don't have anything to do with Otis, so why add the page? I see there is an image people can download to put on their site, but that's at the end of a lot of other links. My guess is those sites are also sites created by the author of the Otis site.

Suggestion: If that's the case, and that's the only reason for the page, lose it. I came to hire Otis.

Overall: I like this site. Writing a site like this took guts. Too often today people don't think Web sites are worth their salt unless they are jam packed with links and things for weary Web travelers to do. Take this site to heart. If the author, Karen, had filled this site with chat rooms, and images of Otis with his friends, a counter, four or five ad banners, and a guestbook, it would have harmed the site.

This is the value understatement at its best. When you think about what elements should be on your homepage, remember Otis. Use only what you need.

3. The Wilma Theater/Author: Anne Shuff

http://www.wilmatheater.org/home.html

Load Time: 25 Seconds, 57kps modem, (cleared cache, 7/12/00 9:10PM.

My Screen Size: 1,024×768

Browsers Used: Internet Explorer 5 and Netscape Navigator 4.5

194

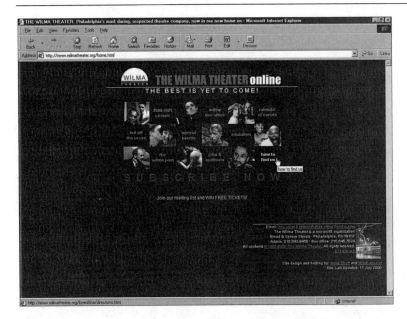

Figure 6.22
The Wilma Theater Online.
(Color Plate C.18)

Concept: This is basically an e-commerce site that promotes the Wilma Theater. Yes, there are a great number of pages that promote information, education, and other topics, but all that is geared to the selling of tickets for the information. I say that because I was on a committee that posted a page for a theater at one of my universities. We offered a lot of great information including cast photos and reviews, but we all agreed that when all was said and done, the main purpose of the site was to sell tickets, either online or by getting people to the theater. That's difficult because, at the same time, the site must be both a Public Relations and a business center. I think the Wilma Theater site has done it pretty well.

Praise: I remember one of the main concerns of the woman in charge of the theater I worked with. She said she wanted the site to look dramatic. She was never able to tell us exactly what that meant. I don't know that we did it, either. The Wilma Theater page understands it.

I'm not always a big fan of black backgrounds, but this one works. There are only three colors on the site: black, red, and white. Yes, there is some yellow text that pops up and the picture in the lower-left corner has some purple, but those colors are quite secondary to the main three.

To that end, the use of black-and-white photography looks like it represents a theater. The visual quite represents what the page represents.

In the last critique I discussed the value of understatement. The Wilma Theater homepage also understands that value. Notice the logo, the identifier, is not a huge banner. In fact, it's quite understated. It's smaller than the grouping of links and images below. It would have been easy to create a very large wide banner to span the page, but the author didn't do that. She kept the banner small and allowed its placement, top-center, to denote the importance. It is the first image you see when scanning the page, but it is not at all in-your-face.

The method used to display the links also impressed me. Often links are a straight line of text or images across the top of the page or down the left side. I'm not saying that's a bad look, not at all. It just that those methods have become so commonplace that when someone steps outside the traditional, the effect is so much greater. Here, the author has pretty much made the links the page. I have a large screen setting, so some of the effect is lost. Smaller screen settings would get a much greater effect. Figure 6.23 shows the same screen at 800×600.

Figure 6.23
The Wilma Theater Online.

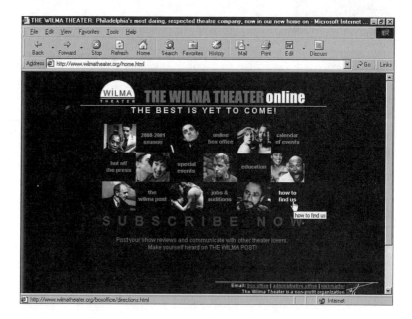

In addition to the design, a lot of textual information has been added into the page without it displaying right off. For example, the author has made a point of using a great deal of text in the ALT attributes of each small picture. When you pass over, you get the names of the actors, the play, and sometimes more (see Figure 6.24).

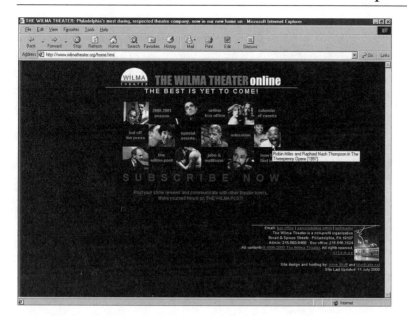

Figure 6.24
That's a good use of space that doesn't really exist.

I remember when I was first learning Web design. A professor told me that good Web design was useful, helpful, and contained a surprise. The surprise isn't always something great and wonderful, just something to make a person chuckle.

On the HTML Goodies page, if you roll over my picture, the Tooltip box reads "Handsome Guy, Huh?" I saw a page one time that had a lamp. When you passed over a specific link, the lamp turned on. Still another had a site map that was drawn out like a spider's web. Every fifth person was treated to an animated spider dropping from one of the arms of the web. Again, the surprise doesn't have to be much, just something that makes the user smile.

The Wilma Theater has such a surprise on each of its subpages, such as the one shown in Figure 6.25.

I attempted to catch the logo in the upper-left corner coming into place. When the page loads, the logo slowly rises up into place from the bar beneath. I liked it.

The subpages all follow the previous format. It was actually refreshing to get back to a white background. The author kept her color scheme, but on each subpage made the predominant color white instead of black. That's good not only for the eyes but also because a black background makes printing difficult. Each of these pages can be easily printed.

Figure 6.25
The logo on the left pops up.

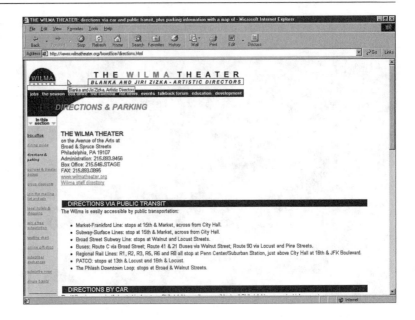

I captured the Directions and Parking subpage because it showed that the author thought outside of just the theater. Notice that not only can you book tickets and get to the theater, but there is also a dining guide, local hotels, and shops. From this one page you can plan out everything except what you're going to wear.

Notice also that on the subpage the author has made a point of softening the black bar across the top. When the bar gets to the left edge of the screen, it slopes downward rather than meeting at a right angle. That softening is becoming very popular on the Web. It does add another image to most pages, but I think the effect is well worth it.

Concern: I haven't too many. My main concern was the applet running on the homepage. To begin with, I thought it slowed the completion of the page by about five seconds. While it was downloading, everything seemed to stop. Once it had come in, then the page began to again pop to life.

Suggestion: Is it possible to add straight text links to the page that represents the pages the applet is running; a short line across the bottom, possibly? I'm not saying the applet is bad. In fact, it looks nice, but it does slow the page coming in.

Concern: Previously, I gave praise regarding the animated logo on each of the subpages. I do like it, but the animation is a loop. The logo appears, disappears, and reappears again and again. It gets a tad annoying.

Suggestion: Open the animation again and remove the loop command. Set to only animate once and stay once it's up there.

Overall: Gosh, this is a good page. I like it on so many levels because it doesn't follow the traditional page design formats and still performs its killer app well. The design is understated allowing the Wilma Theater to shine rather than the page. That's hard to get across to a lot of new designers. What you are designing the site for is paramount, not the site itself.

If I were to make a final nit-picky comment, I would ask if it were possible to change out the small black-and-white images on the homepage. Could a small JavaScript be attached to each so that one of, say three, different images came up? You would need to set three images for each section so that the same image wouldn't come up twice on the same page, of course. I don't know that it would be much of an improvement, but it's something to think about.

Chapter 7

Images and the Visual

Because this is the very beginning of the chapter, let me state this right up front: Your page does not require any images. That may send some of you reeling, but it's true. Your page does not require one image to be successful.

Think about it. How many times have you gone into a site simply because there were images there? I don't mean in order to download the images, I mean simply going into a site because the site has images. Maybe you've done this to see images of a sporting event or a friend, but for the most part, it's the content you're surfing for rather than the images, yes? Good. Now, use that information to your advantage.

Contrary to my rant at the beginning of the last chapter, images are what made the World Wide Web (WWW) the most popular portion of the Internet. Hypertext links may have made the Web nonlinear, but it was images that hit the homerun, down by three, bases loaded, two outs, two strikes, and the bottom of the ninth.

I still remember surfing the Web before it allowed images. I turned to the guy next to me and said, "You know this thing would really take off if I could just get some pictures on it."

I said that! I really did. Okay, you don't believe me, either, but I did. Once the browsers that supported images started coming out, the Web had no choice but to succeed. As soon as people knew they could put pictures of themselves and their cats on the Web, there was no stopping people from posting those images.

Design Goodies Survey

HTML Goodies Survey Question: Does a page have to display an image for you to consider it to be well done?

No   65%

Yes   35%

N=486

You don't always have to have an image. Make a point of using images when needed, not when you can.

And often they didn't stop. Pages began to get bogged down with image after image after images after image. Ugh, I would wait for what seemed like days for a page to come in.

There weren't as many pages on the Web back then as there are today so you actually did wait a little longer than people do today. Plus you thought a 28.8 modem was a speed demon. My first computer, a Tandy, has a 2,400bps modem. No kidding. Really.

When you hear people throwing around numbers such as 28.8 and 57K, do you know what they're talking about? They're talking about modems and how fast that modem translates analog information, from a telephone line, into digital information so that the computer can use it.

The size of a person's modem is stunningly important. For example, let's say you create an image that's 60,000 bytes. Most hip programmers say the image is 60K.

A 28.8 modem exchanges 28,800 bytes of information per second. That something is called a baud rate. It takes that 28.8 modem, under the very best of circumstances, 2.83 seconds to download that image providing that everything is working correctly. 60 divided by 28.8 is 2.83. Get it? That same image would be downloaded by a 57K modem in just over a second. See why the higher modems are faster?

Now let's say you have ten images, all 60K, on a page. That page would take almost 21 seconds to download through a 28.8 modem. It would take almost 12 seconds on a 57K modem. You may remember that the average time a person waits for a page to load is 15 seconds. Those ten images just put you out of the running with many viewers.

Now here's something you may dislike even more. Many surfers are still running 14.4K modems.

Did people need all those images? No, of course not. People put up a ton of images because they could. At that time designers weren't really concerned about copyright like they are today and images were thrown around the Web like crazy. Pages were chock-full of images. It just got silly.

Here's my point. Images are support. They are not the main push of your pages. You should use images on your site in order to spice up the content, to describe the killer app, to aid in description, and to help the user.

Yes, I know you can get three hundred different images of dinosaurs. That doesn't mean you should use them all. One probably gets the point across.

I'm not interested in telling you how to create your own images. There are other books that do a wonderful job of teaching that. To put that in this chapter would be to only skim the surface and that's not good. I am interested in your knowing how to use images correctly when designing your pages. In this chapter, I discuss when to use images, how to place them on the page, and where they fit into the overall scheme of your site's killer app.

The Golden Rules of Images

I'm not going to talk a great deal about images, but I think I would be remiss if I didn't hit the basics at least once. The following 10 statements are things you should already know and should already be doing, but just in case you might have forgotten, here they are again.

I call these "The Golden Rules of Images."

1. Big Images Are Not Better Than Small Images

I speak the truth here. If you need to make a choice, use images that are smaller first. Do your best to use an image that is small enough to still allow the user to see the detail, but not so small that it blurs the image.

I make that suggestion not only because it helps your page load faster but also because people simply won't sit through a large image downloading. Sixty percent of those polled in the HTML Goodies survey said they would stop a large image from downloading and go on rather than wait for it to come in.

Is bigger better? Nope.

2. If You Do Have Large Images, Let the User Choose to See Them

Sometimes you just have to have large images. A picture showing a lot of faces, a product, or a landscape might require a larger size in order to keep the detail. If that's the case then give the user the ability to choose to see the image if they want. Make links to larger images or make thumbnails of larger images so that the thumbnails load quickly yet the user can click to go and see the larger image. Don't force big pictures on anyone. Users simply won't stand, or sit, for it.

3. Denote Every Image's Height and Width in the Code

This helps the loading of the page because if you set a HEIGHT and a WIDTH inside of each image's flag, you allow the browser to load the page leaving holes where the image later loads. This allows the user to see the most important part of the page, the text. The images that support that text load later.

The code looks like this:

```
<IMG SRC="image.gif" HEIGHT="##" WIDTH="##">
```

Of course, the pound signs are replaced by the height and width of the image in pixels.

If you don't know the height and width of your images, try opening them in an image editor. The height and width should display. If you don't have an image editor, or better yet don't really know how it works, you can find the height and width using Internet Explorer. Open either the image itself or a page that displays the image in Internet Explorer. Once you see the image, fully loaded, put your pointer on it and right click. A box should pop up. In that box, choose the last line, properties. The height and width are displayed there.

You can also get the height and width of an image from Netscape Navigator. Once again, open a page in Navigator that contains the image. One it has loaded fully, right-click upon it. A box should pop up. When it does, choose View Image. The image then appears by itself and the height and width are in the title bar.

Figure 7.1 shows the HTML Goodies homepage with the inline images turned off so you can see the boxes created by the use of the HEIGHT and WIDTH attributes.

Here's another suggestion you might find useful. I set every image to its exact HEIGHT and WIDTH. However, a few designer friends of mine say the images look better if you set the HEIGHT and WIDTH two or three pixels short for each setting. They say it offers just a bit of extra compression. Give it a try. See if you like the effect.

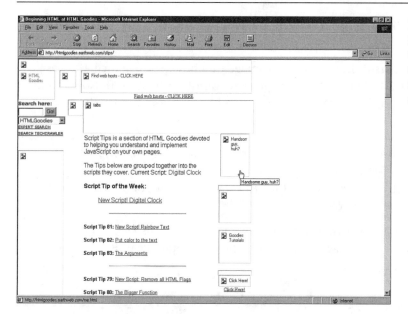

Figure 7.1
HTML Goodies comes in text first, leaving room for the images because of the use of HEIGHT and WIDTH attributes.

4. Always Use the ALT *Attribute in Your Image Flags*

That ALT attribute not only produces a yellow ToolTip box when the mouse passes over an image. It also produces the text found within the boxes shown in Figure 5.1. The ALT attribute also helps people who are surfing without their images turned on. Over 10% of those polled in the HTML Goodies survey said they surf without images most or all the time.

The ALT attribute also helps by attaching text to the image so that those who are surfing with disabled-assistant browsers can be helped. The browser reads the text associated with the image and tells the user what the image represents.

To that end, use text in your ToolTip that describes the image rather than something flippant.

The code looks like this:

```
<IMG SRC="image.gif" HEIGHT="##" WIDTH="##" ALT="ToolTip text goes here">
```

5. Never Resize an Image to the Point Where You Can See the Individual Pixels

I often see new Web designers trying to make an image fit a hole. For instance, the designer has to fill a space that's 200×200, but the image they want is only 50×120. No matter! Just resize it. Set the HEIGHT and WIDTH to whatever settings are required to fill the space.

Ugh!

The image gets blown way out of proportion and the lines that were nice and smooth become squared off and every pixel is visible. If you resize an image, go easy. You start to see pixels by just adding 20 to the height and width. After a certain point, you do more to harm the image than you do to help it.

What a lot of people don't know is that resizing goes the other way as well. You can make an image too small. Figure 7.2 is a page by Michelle Madonna titled Bean Bag Rags at http://www.beanbagrags.com/.

Figure 7.2
Too small and too pixelated.

Notice the bear image next to the pointer. It was resized to be exactly the same size as the others. The downsizing has made the image very grainy and hard to view.

Height and width helps with loading the page. If you want to seriously resize an image, use an image editor that can resize and keep the detail.

6. Odd-Shaped Images Should Have the Extra Portion Made Transparent or Set to the Same Color As the Background

Images are usually squared off. That's part of the nature of making an image. Yes, you can use a crop and shape an image, but that seldom happens. I sometimes see people create a logo that has an odd shape, yet leave the squared-off section of the image still visible.

If your image has round edges, but sits inside of a square, do your best to hide that square portion. Either make the background of the image transparent or set the background color of the page to the same color as the background of the image so the edges become hidden.

Figure 7.3 is a great example by designer Jonathan Kavalos on his Toonami Directory page at `http://members.aol.com/ahhgoaway/toonami.html`.

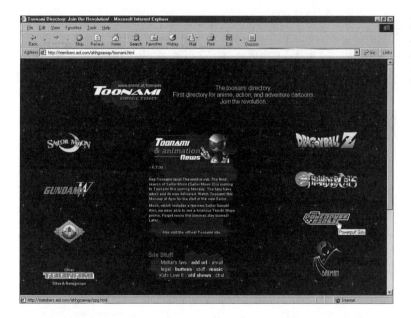

Figure 7.3
All the images are square, but the author made the square portions transparent to hide the square section.

Eighty-seven percent of those polled agree you should hide the edges.

7. Avoid Halos

This happens most often with animated images, or images that are sitting on a dark background. All the way around the image is a white "ring" of pixels. That's called a halo. Lose that at all costs. It just looks bad and reflects poorly upon your page. The HTML Goodies Survey had 43% of people reporting they thought less of the page if they saw halos around the images.

To rid the image of the halo you might want to re-create the animation setting the background to transparent or lighten the background of the page. Black backgrounds show off halos better than any other color.

8. Beveled Edges on an Image Mean It's a Link

Unless you intend to use an image as a hypertext link, don't make a point of beveling the edges to make it look like a button. It's confusing to the users.

9. Interlaced Images Are the User's Favorites

There are basically two methods of presenting an image to a user, interlaced (known as progressive in the JPEG format) and noninterlaced. Interlaced is when the image comes in blurry at first and become sharper with each pass. Noninterlaced is when the image comes in line by line from the top down.

According to my research, interlaced is the preferred method of presenting images. When you save an image in your graphics editor, you usually have the ability to set options. Choose to save as **Interlaced** if in GIF format, **Progressive** if in JPEG.

If it happens that you do not create or scan your own images and cannot assure that your images are interlaced, you're not committing any real sin. There is simply a preference toward the interlaced display.

10. Make Sure Your Images Work

The dreaded Internet Explorer Red X and the horrifying Netscape Navigator broken-image symbol are both death to a site. Users hate both with a passion. If you put an image on your page, make darn sure it works.

A full 92% of people polled felt a page that showed red Xs or broken images was poorly created and thought less of the site because of it.

This is an easy one to avoid. Make sure your images work. Check in both browsers just to make sure.

Support, Attention, or Just Plain Silly?

In Chapter 1, "Judge Not Lest Ye Be Judged," I talked about everything that you use on a page going to the page's killer app. In Chapter 3, "Begin the Design," I talked about so goes the homepage, so goes the rest of the site. The use of images is where both of those concepts truly come to life.

Let me state right up front, once again, that in terms of design, there are no hard tried-and-true image usage rules. Every Web site is different and every killer app needs to be addressed individually. What I am offering as follows are little more than strong suggestions. As you read, you may find statements you feel contradict each other. Just keep in mind that I am making those statements dealing with different Web sites. What works for one may not work for another. Something that would be death to one site may lift up another.

Each site is different, thus, each site's use of images is different. When you finish reading this next section, what you have is a series of examples and suggestions that you can use to draw out your own use of images.

Just remember, your images are not for you. They are for your users. Help them.

Support

I have gone on and on about how text (content) is the most important physical part of a Web page. That text delivers the message, the killer app, and whatever else the author wants the site to get across. Then come the images.

If you've written your pages correctly, using HEIGHT, WIDTH, and ALT attributes on all the image tags, the text comes in first and the images follow. Those images draw attention. They direct the eye and give the user information about your page. You have a killer app to think about. Choose and position images so they point to that killer app.

The images of a page describe the topic and mood far faster than any of the text or titles. That's a given. Here are a couple of examples to show what I mean. I know Figure 7.4 is hard to not look at, but if you can, just quickly glance at it and then jump down and start reading again. Ready? Go!

There are really only two important images on the page. One is in the upper-left corner. That's the one you probably looked at first. Then there's a fish image on the right side under the title. Yes, there are two other images, but they're pretty nondescript. You might not get anything off them.

Even if there were no text on the page, you probably would have figured out the site's basic concept. It has something to do with religion. Without the text you might not be able to pick out the faith or the topic, but you would know it has something to do with religion.

It's actually the homepage for the Montgomery Brethren In Christ Church in Mercersburg, PA fount at http://www.bic-church.org/allegheny/montgomery/index.htm.

I chose this page as my first example because I was proud of the author for not filling the page with images. There are a lot of free religious images on the Web and I have seen a lot of church pages simply filled with images.

Figure 7.4
Don't look too long.

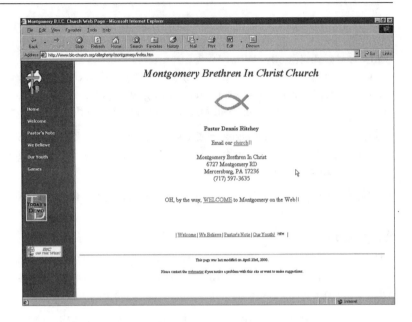

This page proves you do not need a ton of images to get a point across. Basically, two did it. The fish and the cross draped with cloth suggested religion. They pointed to the site's killer app and helped to describe it. You'd go to the text to find out more specifics. Okay, let's do another one. You can look at Figure 7.5 a little longer if you'd like. It's the genealogy page for James Stevens' family tree. The page has since been taken down.

Figure 7.5
What can you tell about James just from the images?

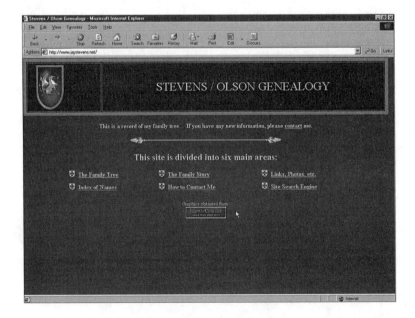

I liked the look of the page because of the use of older-style images. They look like shields and spears from days gone by. They really fit in with the motif of a page exploring the past.

Let's go a little bit further. What can you tell me about James Stevens' background? Where did his family come from? If the images are any indication, James' family is from Europe. The shield and the lion images look like something a king or a royal family would use. The squared cross on the shield looks like something from the Crusades. If the images were Asian in nature, I would suggest James came from the China or the Pacific Rim. If the images used Cyrillic letters, I would suggest James hailed from Russia.

According to the pages of the site, James came from a "farming community of Moorlynch, Somerset, England."

The images portrayed not only the fact that the page was devoted to genealogy, but more-over, that James was English. Why? Because James chose images that suggested his heritage.

It's a great use of images.

Okay, Figure 7.6 is another one. What does this page deal with?

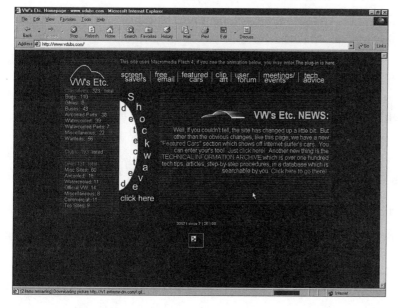

Figure 7.6
Is this a shockwave site?

This is Taylor Nolen's VW's etc. site at `http://www.vdubs.com/`. My wife would love this page. She has always wanted a vintage Volkswagen (VW). I wonder if she would have stayed in the site, though. I say that because the images don't really scream out VW. Yes, I see the VW logo and the one single line giving the outline of the car, but it's that shock-wave image that really takes precedence over the site. In this case, the image drew attention and harmed the page's perception.

Which leads me to my next area of image consideration.

Attention

The images on the VW page do support the killer app, but the author has made one big mistake, and I mean big. His images are sized so that the largest image draws the attention. That's the shockwave image. In addition, the shockwave image is animated. My eyes were drawn right to it.

The problem is...that image has nothing to do with the page's killer app.

When I first came in, I missed the topic of the site because the shockwave image did some razzle-dazzle and I missed the topic altogether.

I love the images the author has chosen for the site, but his image usage misleads me into thinking the site was something that it wasn't. The fix might simply be to make the shock image much smaller and make the VW images more prominent.

I have stated that images are used to define the site's killer apps. However, as the last example suggested, images are also used to draw the eye. I've talked about using too many text alterations to draw the eye being confusing. Here you've seen an example of using an incorrect image to draw the eye. It can be equally confusing.

When the VW page first opened, my eye went right to the largest image. It was located off to the left and high enough on the page that it took my attention right away. I missed the much smaller, and more important, VW image that was supposed to get my attention.

Yes, I know I said that the eye moves left to right and also down the page. I try, as you do, to do that every time I log into a page, but if the author has gone out of his way to draw my eye, the pattern can be broken and I can be pulled to a different portion of the page. Sometimes that's good and sometimes it's not. This time it wasn't.

When I discuss images drawing attention, I'm really concerned about three elements, placement, size, and movement.

Placement

Image placement is important and not overly difficult. Think about how a user's eyes roll across the page. Top to bottom mainly, and left to right. That means, in theory, the images you feel are most important, the images that identify and describe your site, should be placed in a sort of hierarchy. Those you feel are most descriptive should be higher than those that are not, more to the left than those that are not.

Obviously you cannot always keep a perfect hierarchy, but at least keep in mind that user perception is user reality. By placement, you suggest prominence.

Dig Figure 7.7.

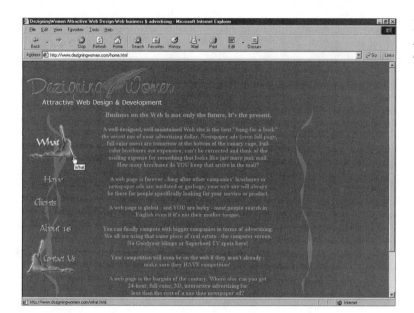

Figure 7.7
I waited for that image to come in.

This the homepage of Dezigning Women Attractive Web Design built by Yael Gilmor at `http://www.dezigningwomen.com/home.html`. Yael informed me she learned everything at HTML Goodies and parlayed that knowledge into this design company. Cool.

The page didn't load in order, top to bottom, the first time I went in. In fact the logo in the upper-left space loaded last even though it was first in the code. The reason for the last load might be that it was the largest image of the bunch in terms of bytes or it may be that Web congestion simply disallowed the server to deliver the image until last.

Either way—I waited. Have you ever done that? The rest of the page loads up and you can go on, but you wait for the top image to load. I find myself doing that a lot, because that image has to be important. It's in the upper-left corner. I had to mean something. So I wait. It finally popped in, I was at ease and I could go on.

That's placement for ya! I sat and waited because I knew the image was important. Its placement suggested it. Figure 7.8 is another example of image placement.

Figure 7.8
I was sent to the logo.

Here's a typical business page. Businesses like their pages to be a little low key, yet still look useful. I chose this page because, even though the logo is on the right, it still works well. I think the fact that it is up high has a lot to do with that.

This is the IRC Global page at `http://www.ircglobal.com/` written by Arnold van Klinken. Arnold broke the mold of putting the logo in the upper-left corner, but look what else he did.

The logo sits in the right, but through the use of a wide image with horizontal lines, he directs your eye right to the logo. Had the lines in the blue bar been vertical, you would not have followed it along quite as easily. By understanding the eye moves top to bottom, left to right, Arnold drew your eye to a blue bar first and then used that bar to pull your eye straight to the logo. It's a great effect.

I do have some trouble with that ad banner placement but I get into that in a moment.

One More Note About Placement

I've mentioned this before so I won't harp on it again, but the placement of your links is just as important as the placement of your images. If you keep in mind how the eye moves across the page, you know that links should be up high. There's a reason why the traditional place for links is sitting on the left side of the page in a vertical row. That placement is most comforting to the eye and it suggests prominence. It even matters what link is sitting highest in the list of links. The highest, usually the homepage, is perceived as the most important. Importance diminishes as the list goes on.

It's the same with images. Importance diminishes as the page rolls on.

Size

This one is pretty easy to explain. Look at Figure 7.9 and tell me where your eyes went right off.

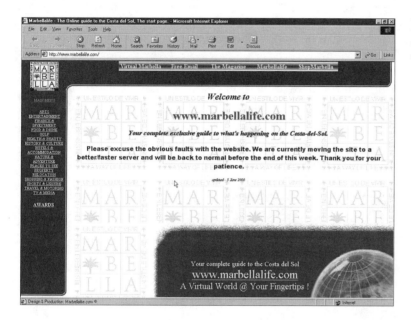

Figure 7.9
Zip! Where did your eyes go?

I bet they went right down to the lower-right corner, right? The author is Paul Denham. This is his page Marbellalife, a guide to Costa Del Sol at `http://www.marbellalife.com/`.

The page is constructed very well so that it resizes itself to almost all screen settings. I tried to make it mess up, but it didn't. I bet your eyes went right to the large globe image. They traveled across the entire page to get there, too. That big, colorful image grabbed your attention right off.

It's the biggest thing on the page. It won.

Please understand I am not saying this is bad. In fact, this is pretty darn good. The author broke with tradition but did it correctly. Notice he even has his titles down there with the globe because he knew the globe would grab the attention. It's a very clever idea.

Now, use this information to help you construct your own page. Know that large images often grab the attention first, even if the eye has to pass across a larger portion of the page to get to the larger image. That means when you are choosing images, using an image that is larger than your identifier might cause people's eyes to draw to that larger image missing your logo. Remember? That's what happened with the VW bug page.

Big images often win. Use that knowledge to your advantage.

Just keep in mind my #1 Golden Rule: Big images are not better than small images. Here's an amendment: They just tend to draw the eye.

See? I told you I would contradict myself depending on the site.

Movement

Some might call this animation, but the term animation doesn't fit anymore. These days, people can create fantastic movement across and through their pages rather than just a single image dancing around in a confined area. The use of Flash, applets, and DHTML go way beyond the simple, confined movement created by animation.

That movement grabs the eye. Figure 7.10 is a well-done example.

Figure 7.10
Even though the image is static, where do your eyes go?

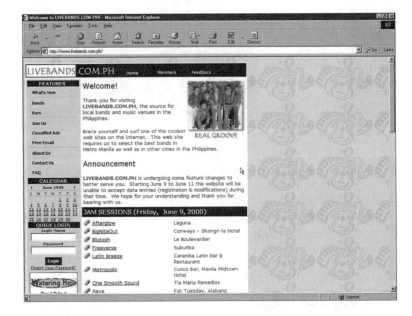

Did you by any chance look at the image over on the right? This is a page by Antonio A. Carganilla titled Live Bands at http://www.livebands.com.ph/. The image on the right looks a little fuzzy because I caught it dissolving between images. This is a page that promotes live bands in the Philippines. Antonio is an agent and created this Web page to help him drum up business.

So, ask yourself, what is most important when someone stops into this page? The bands! I have a club and I need someone to play that night. What Antonio did was use an applet to have a series of his band's publicity photos dissolve into one another. That way, a visitor to the site can quickly see the bands and what they look like.

Granted, Antonio has his logo in the upper-left corner. That's good. I have no doubt that when users stop into the page, they see that logo and the title of the band is reinforced, but past that, what is important? What should gather attention? The bands!

That animation drew attention and helped the site's killer app. It's a great use of design and movement to draw attention.

In addition, Antonio was smart to keep the images small. I'm sure he could have made the animation three times as large, but didn't. Had he done that, it would have done more than just draw attention; it may have overtaken the page.

And it may have taken a long time to load.

Movement draws the eye. It brings attention. That's why movement for the sake of movement is not a good thing to have on a Web page. Take a look at Figure 7.11.

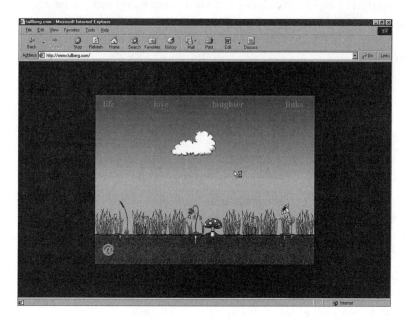

Figure 7.11
I've clicked on clouds from both sides now...

See that cloud? You won't notice it here, but the cloud is slowly making its way across the page, left to right.

I clicked on it. I right-clicked on it. I clicked to grab and move it. I called it a dirty name. It didn't do anything.

This is the Personal homepage of Erik Tullberg at Tullberg.com. It's a neat design, granted. I would liked to have seen some more identifiers so I knew where I was, but the page is still pretty nice.

But that cloud, that cloud. It rolled across the page, slowly and methodically. Of course, it drew my attention. I tried to make it do something, anything. I kept waiting for something to happen, something to blink, make a noise, or blow up.

Nothing.

Does the cloud go to the killer app? Well, yes. It fits the motif. Does it add to the page? Yes. Does it add some support? Visually, yes.

Does it harm the page? Yes.

If other surfers are anything like me, they are going to be drawn to the cloud and want to do something with it. When they find out it does nothing, ugh! It's upsetting and they think less of the page.

This could very well be the highlight of the site. Make the cloud active and have it be a link to get deeper into the site. I would have loved that. It would have tied the entire page together perfectly. Now, as it stands, it's just motion for the sake of motion and that's not overly good on this page.

Placement, Size, and Movement

Images are support for the page's killer app, but as I've just talked about, they can also do wonders by drawing the eye and making the user see or do something.

When choosing to put an image on your Web page, make sure it has a purpose. Make sure it does something to help the page, to aid the user in understanding the site's killer app.

The hardest thing about teaching how to use images is that there are no hard or fast rules. Some of the previous sites seemed to break the rules, but the effect worked. Remember that your site is different from any other site on the Web. Your use of images may differ from the page your friend is putting together.

Just make sure that all your images are adding something to the page. Make sure they have a purpose for being on the page. Without the image having some sort of purpose, either to add support, gain interest, or draw the eye, using the image is, well...silly.

Just Plain Silly

Let me ask you to remember back to some of your past surfing experiences. Have you ever gone into a page, usually a personal page that looked pretty good but had this one image that just didn't fit? Let's say the page was dedicated to a rock group, yet over on the right side was an animation of a kitty, or a spinning globe, or something else that just didn't look right.

I see these wayward images a lot when students put together their first pages. One example I remember distinctly was a page created for the career development center of one of my schools. There, on the bottom-right side of the page was an animation of a girl in a bikini diving into a pool. The animation was looped and she dove and dove and dove and dove.

When I found the author and asked why he would put that on the page, I received the same answer I always get.

"I liked the image."

I went on to ask what a bikini-clad girl diving into a pool had to do with careers.

"Nothing. I just thought the image was cool."

Remember this. If the only reason you're putting an image on a page is because you like it, you think it's cool, or it simply makes you happy, don't use it. Images are support. They are to help your site's killer app by describing mood and topic.

Now, let's get into what's behind it all. Backgrounds.

Nice Background. I Wish I Could Read the Page

When you decide to use a background, ask yourself this one question:

> Does it add anything to the page?

If the answer is something other than a resounding yes, then lose it.

Backgrounds are so popular, and so easy to deal with, I wonder why people ever have problems. Actually, I don't wonder. I know. The previous text explains it all.

You've all done this. You enter a page that uses this wild, freaky, swirling, green background. It's filled with detail and colors and other junk. You can't read the text to save your life even though the author has done his best to set the letters to a bright yellow just to attempt to overpower the background.

Design Goodies Survey

HTML Goodies Survey Question: Do you find background images:

Obtrusive: 32%

Unobtrusive   31%

Doesn't matter: 37%

N=494

Backgrounds don't really register a great hurrah or jeer by users. If you decide to use one, just be sure to use it correctly.

Why, oh, why would the author use such a background? You know the answer.

"Because I thought it was cool."

Cool backgrounds are not enough to keep someone in your site. When have you ever said, "I can't read a darn thing, but wow! What a great background."

Have you ever been in a casino? Did you notice the carpet on the floors? Often the carpet is a horrid, very detailed pattern that repeats again and again. The purpose is to get your eyes up off of the floor. That terrible involved pattern is meant to stop you from looking. Why would you put a pattern like that as your Web page background? I said it before and I'll say it again, images are support. If they harm your site in any way, don't use them.

Backgrounds, both color and images, are actually pretty easy to deal with. Backgrounds can be split into three general categories.

- **Color backgrounds**: Those using just color
- **Image backgrounds**: Those that use an image either tiled or not
- **Split backgrounds**: Those that have a stripe of color or images down the left, and sometimes right side leaving space for the text

Color Background: A Quick Refresher

Color backgrounds are the easiest to deal with. They offer a nice flat palette to lay your pages across. Color backgrounds are easy to deal with in that they are unobtrusive in many ways. I would just suggest that you stay away from bright or primary colors. Bright or primary colors tend to dull the eyes. I know a lot of you hate the word but pastel colors really are the best colors to use for a background. As always, use a nondithering color, described in Chapter 5, "Text and Color," for your background.

Lately, the hip color for backgrounds is black. It used to be just plain white, but apparently things have changed 180 degrees. Black backgrounds do look cool and they allow for easily readable text unless you choose yellow or dark blue for the text. Those colors don't seem to go well. I have found white text on the black background shows up best.

The only problem with using a black background is printing. They don't print very well. If your pages are being created specifically so they can be printed, you should avoid using a black background.

Image Backgrounds

If you decide to use an image background, tiled or split, you then have one more area to be concerned about. Image backgrounds can be split further into how the backgrounds flow:

- **Vertically**: Image backgrounds that have mainly vertical lines
- **Horizontally**: Image backgrounds that have mainly horizontal lines
- **No movement**: Image or color backgrounds that do not suggest up or across movement

There are times when a background has a specific vertical or horizontal flow to it. Often, when a background image tiles, both a horizontal and a vertical can be seen. What you intend to put on top your background helps you decide what kind of background you want.

Almost all backgrounds are useful; all are good as long as you use the background correctly. I say almost all backgrounds because I do believe there are two background images you should avoid like the plague:

- Photo images
- Images that contain text

Using a scan of a photograph as a background is simply too busy. It gets worse when the author attempts to have a single image cover the entire background. It may look great on a smaller screen setting, but as soon as a user running a bigger screen setting shows up, the effect is lost and that beautiful sunset, or rainbow, or what have you begins to tile and the effect is blown. Furthermore, if you do use one large image for the background, you get just what I wrote, one large image. It takes forever to download. People just won't wait.

Some disagree with my suggestion that your background should not contain text. My thinking is that the users should be reading your page, not your backgrounds. Now let's look at a few backgrounds.

Figure 7.12 is the homepage of Lars Arnesen at `http://free.prohosting.com/~laka/index1.shtml`. I liked the page because of the image of Lars over in the left stripe. Anyone who would wear a wig like that has got my friendship. I don't know him, but I like him. Lars has chosen a background that fits the page, but he hasn't used it quite correctly.

Figure 7.12
I love the wig!

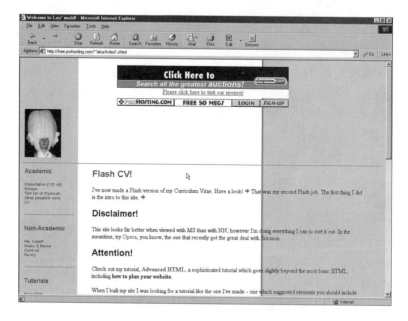

First off, what do you notice about the background? It fits into the split category. It's got that stripe down the left side and then another down the right. The background moves vertically. All split backgrounds do. The concept is usually to get the links onto the stripe and the main content onto the white section.

Design Goodies Survey

HTML Goodies Survey Question: Should backgrounds stay stationary or scroll along with the text?

Scroll along	27%
Remain stationary	41%
Doesn't matter	32%
N=492	

The use of the `BGPROPERTIES="fixed"` attribute in a page's body tag is very popular, but as you can see, doesn't add a great deal to a page. People seem to believe that if the text scrolls, so should the background image.

Often split pages do not have that secondary strip down the right side. The reason is to avoid the problem Lars just ran into.

Without even looking, I bet the distance from the left side of the page to the beginning of the right stripe is about 800px, give or take a few pixels. That leads me to believe that if I were looking at this page in 800×600, the background would render and the text would sit in the white column perfectly. Look at Figure 7.13.

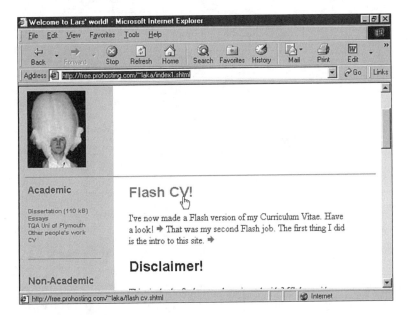

Figure 7.13
Ah! Perfect.

I like split backgrounds, I use one on the HTML Goodies site myself. My guess is that the split background came as a result of people wanting a frames look without the problems frames put upon a page. I also like split backgrounds because they offer a solid color for the text to sit upon yet add some secondary color to the page. One thing you have to be careful of is what happened to Lars. You need to contain the text inside of a table cell so that it remains inside the white section no matter what screen size the user has.

I also like split backgrounds because they move vertically. They create a gutter to guide the user's eyes down the page. It creates a focus on the text and helps things to keep moving along.

Just make a point of keeping the text on the correct part of the split.

Now let's answer the question. Does this background add anything to the page? I say, yes. Lars should keep it.

Figure 7.14 shows Allen Brooks' Beaufort Realty page at http://www.beaufortrlty.com/. This is a great example of a background moving horizontally. Yes, it has a tiled background, but notice the line underneath the logo that makes horizontal lines that keep the eye moving across the page.

Figure 7.14
How does this background move?

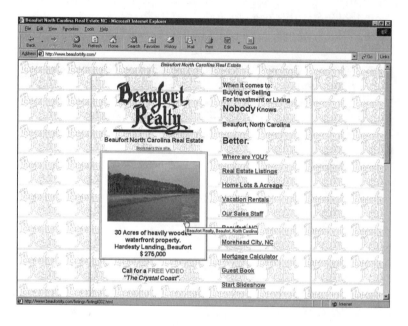

This is a very common background. An identifier image is made lighter, or embossed and is then tiled as a background. The thinking is that the logo tiled again and again reinforces the identifier. Well, maybe yes and maybe no.

I don't think the background on this page is obtrusive. I do, however, think it's poorly done. The identifier was put into a graphics editor, stripped of its color, and set to a semi-emboss using, I think, the contrast and brightness part of the image editor. The result is a grainy image that looks less than professional.

The background moves horizontally. That helps to move the user left to right, but the user would do that anyway with or without the background.

Finally, ask the question. Does this background add anything to the page? Maybe it would help to reinforce the identifier if the image were embossed in a more professional manner, but as it stands now, no. I would lose the background altogether. This is a nice page. I think the background takes away from it.

Figure 7.15 is a page by Sean S. Nordquist for Frank Emerson at http://www.frankemerson.com/.

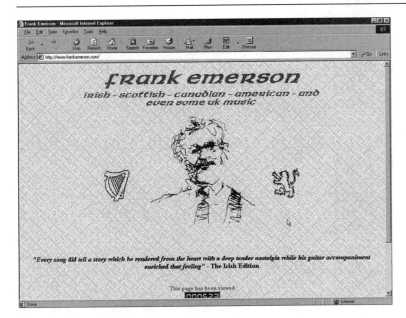

Figure 7.15
The background image helps to describe the killer app.

Right off the bat, I would suggest getting the links up higher on the page, but it's the background I'm worried about here.

I like this background for two reasons. First, it's not intrusive. There is a pattern, but that pattern is set on 45-degree angles so it does not interrupt the eye as it flows across and down the page. The color is pale and allows the elements on the page to stand out. The background is there but it's not at all overpowering.

Second, the background image acts to further identify the killer app of the page. The background appears Celtic. That, sitting behind someone who identified himself as an Irish-Scottish American, acts to reinforce the killer app to the user.

Does this background add to the page? Yes. Keep it.

Notice the background images in the largest section of this Web site by Shannon Watts for Management Consultants at `http://www.manageconsult.com` (see Figure 7.16).

This is an example of a vertical background. Yes, it is tiling, but the background images are all pointing up. The effect is that the user's eyes move across the page until they catch the background, and then their eyes are directed upward. It can be disruptive to the reader.

This Web page doesn't have a big problem because the background is very light and because of the type of business they're in, the background pointing up reinforces upward movement and that might be helpful.

I would test the page with a few people and if they didn't see a problem, I'd keep it.

Figure 7.16
Up, up, and away...

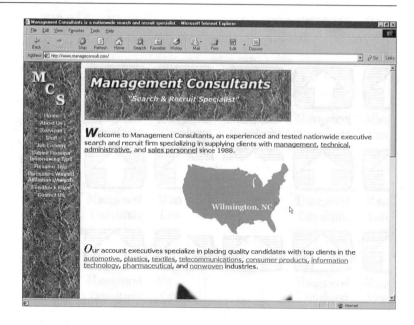

The Camp Herrlich Homepage by John Belansky at `http://www.campherrlich.org/` is a different story (see Figure 7.17).

Figure 7.17
Read up.

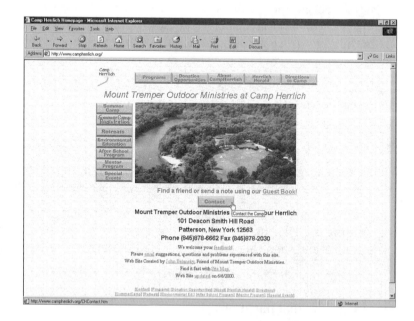

This is a well-built page that has a bad background. I can see the author is attempting to keep a green feel to the page since it deals with a camp. The problem is that once the user gets past the images and image links, the text becomes very hard to read. As the eye moves right, the lines on the page move up. It's a little difficult to keep focused on what you are reading.

Does this background help this page? No. A new background would do wonders for it.

So, to recap. If you choose to place a background, color or image on your pages, be very honest with yourself about the background. Forget if you think it looks cool, does it help the page? Also, as you learned from Lars previously, does the background look good in all screen sizes or does it tile poorly?

I often see pages that have used one large image as a background. In 800×600, the pages look great. In larger screen setting, the picture tiles and it just looks terrible. The sunset, or rainbow, or what have you stops and starts right up again.

So, try a few backgrounds. Look at each with a very critical eye. Try to read the text. Afterward, ask a simple question. Does the background add to the page? Unless the answer is anything but a resounding yes then lose it.

Site Critiques

1. The Eddie Fox Show on 103.3/Author: Leslea Burleson a.k.a. "Daisey Doodle Productions"

http://www.eddiefoxx.com/

Load Time: 23 Seconds (after effect), 57kps modem, cleared cache, 5/24/00 10:54AM.

My Screen Size: 1,024×768

Browsers Used: Internet Explorer 5 and Netscape Navigator 4.5

I know it looks like late-night TV, on channel 99, with bad reception, on a rainy night, but if you just hang on five seconds, it comes in. Really. Look at Figure 7.19.

Concept: Eddie Fox is a radio disc jockey and, like all jocks these days, needs a Web page. I was a jock for eleven years so I have a soft spot in my heart for those who take to the air-waves for a living, and it's a hard living, let me tell you.

Figure 7.18
Eddies Page! Wait! It's coming in...

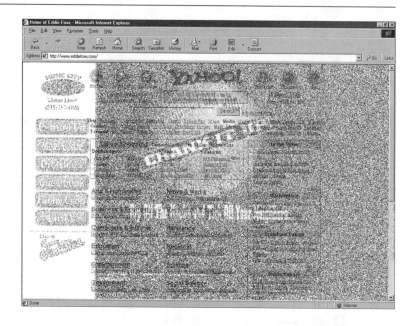

Figure 7.19
Here's Eddie... (Color Plate C.19)

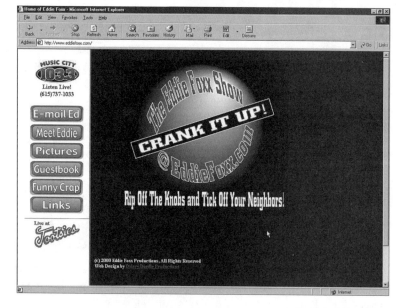

This is a traditional Jock-on-the-Web site. It has the basic elements that any fan would want to see, especially pictures. I can't tell you how many times I was told that I didn't sound like I look. I think that's good.

I like Eddie's site. Let's take a look at some of the good and the not-so-good elements of it.

Praise: First off, the site gives the impression that it is a frames site. It is not. It's a big table and I like that. The author, Leslea gave the impression of frames allowing the links to sit on the left side on top of a white stripe. What's more, she allowed the border to run down the between the two sections, but hid the top borders. That's a good look and some clever programming.

I like the links along the left side. I know nothing about the radio station where Eddie works, but I took it from the buttons that this was a country music station. I don't really know why, either. The buttons just looked like they would be associated with a country station even though Eddie had the rock format slogan "Rip off the knobs and tick off your neighbors."

The text on the buttons is large and a little blue. The one button reads "Funny Crap." That's not exactly family oriented, but I bet Eddie's listeners know the phrase well.

In addition, the "Funny Crap" page is not just Eddie spouting off. It's actually a message board where listeners can post and reply. I think I recognized the programming. It looks like the message board CGI offered on the HTML Goodies site. Cool.

Speaking of the buttons, look at Figure 7.20.

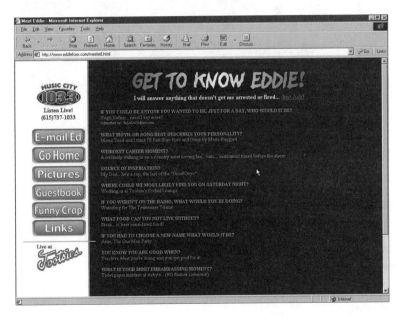

Figure 7.20
Notice the Button that reads, "Go Home."

I clicked on the button that reads, "Meet Eddie." Once the page came in, I noticed that the second button, the one I clicked, now reads "Go Home." It's a little touch, but it helps the user to know what page they're on and offers some easy back navigation.

Concern: To begin with, what is up with that snow effect when I first log into the page? Luckily, it only happens on the homepage. I've been to sites where the author put one of those Meta commands on every page. That meant every page went through a new and exciting effect to display. It became annoying very quickly.

Suggestion: This wasn't overly annoying, but I would suggest losing the effect. It's only cool once until the user has to see it every time he does "Go Home."

Concern: Take a look at the pictures page (see Figure 7.21).

Figure 7.21
No image settings to speak of...

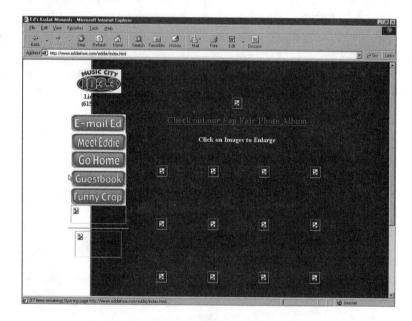

See how each of the images has a little broken image box that fills in? You need to program to avoid that, especially if you want to keep that frames look.

Make a point of setting each image's height and width within the IMG flag. In addition, I noticed there are no rollovers on the images. You need to also do that so that each image has a text equal.

Overall: This is a well-designed site that would run a lot smoother and faster with just a few minor changes. Leslea can be very happy with what she's put up here. The site contains good navigation, user interaction, and if you click on the station logo, a real audio feed.

Here is a piece of advice: Radio audiences are very fickle. The moment they get bored, they go somewhere else. You have put up a nice site here, but in the world of radio, fresh is only fresh for about three days. You need to make a point of updating this site often.

Hopefully, Eddie is promoting the site on the air. That's free advertising. I wish I could get that.

2. Pululahua: Rock from the Volcano/Author: Riccardo Perotti

http://www.pululahua.com/

Load Time: 18 Seconds, 57kps modem, cleared cache, 7/12/00 11:42AM.

My Screen Size: 1,024×768

Browsers Used: Internet Explorer 5 and Netscape Navigator 4.5

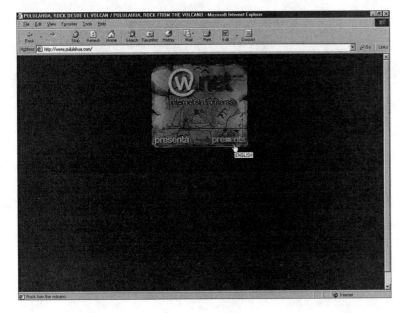

Figure 7.22
Not quite the homepage.
(Color Plate C.20)

I don't usually like pages that stop you before entering into the site, but I've said before, used correctly, there are not wrong design decisions. Notice that the page is not asking the user for a choice regarding Flash or frames, but rather for what language you'd like.

Furthermore, the choices are image links with rollovers. The Spanish link, "presenta," produces an Ecuadorian flag. The English link, "presents," produces a British flag. That's very clever.

Because my Spanish is rusty since being in high school, I chose to go into the English site (see Figure 7.23).

Figure 7.23
Very clean-looking pages.

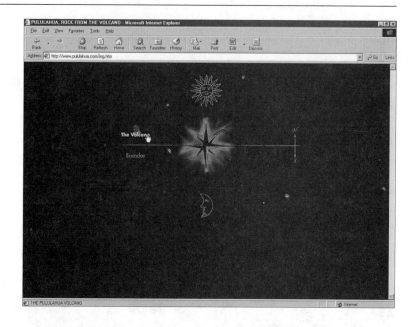

Concept: This site is dedicated to Pululahua, a volcano in Ecuador. Past that, there are links to information about Ecuador itself. I spent a little too much time reading through the site once I got into it. I should have been writing, but a good read takes you away from it all.

Praise: Forget HTML and site design for a moment. This is a well-written site. The text just sang. Points were made with few words and I enjoyed it.

The text itself is in a pretty gold color that cascades down through images that came in very quickly. Links were blue against a black background. Again, that's not always good, but the artist made a point of setting the text to a large Arial font that was easy to read. It looked like Figure 7.24.

The colors the author chose were gold against a black background. They seemed to fit the site perfectly. In addition, the navigation images were drawn in such a way that they appeared to have been lifted from an old sea map.

The author put some real time and thought into this site.

Concern: The author has some text in gray. I think the concept is to highlight the name of the volcano. The problem was that every time the color came up I thought it was a link. I tried to click on it. Yes, I know it wasn't blue like the other links, but setting text to a different color means a link. I just assumed it was a visited link.

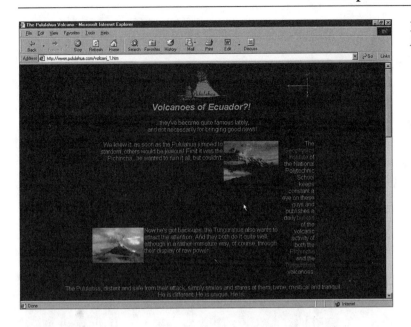

Figure 7.24
Easy to read.

Suggestion: I don't know that text color change is needed. Try changing that text back to the color of the surrounding text. It makes reading easier. If you simply must draw attention, try setting the text to bold.

Concern: The author is probably upset at this point because I haven't mentioned that the site also contains information about two rock concerts that occurred near the volcano. The concerts were titled Pululahua 1999 and Pululahua 2000. In fact, there are more pages dedicated to these rock concerts than there are dedicated to the volcano.

The problem is...I missed them. I bet most people miss them. If I weren't coming in specifically for information regarding those concerts, I might never get to them.

The reason is your link placement. The homepage actually does have two links to the concert pages. It's the sun and moon in Figure 7.22. I never knew they were links because my mouse never passed over them. I went right to the text seeing that as the page's navigation.

I finally found the concert pages from a link on the volcano page seen in Figure 7.23. The problem there was the links were way at the bottom, even under a link that took me to the top of the page again.

Suggestion: What is the purpose of the page, the concerts, or the volcano and Ecuador? If the concerts are what you want to push, and I believe they are, then you need to make their links much more noticeable. Follow the same patterns you currently have, but make the sun and the moon image scream that they are links.

Overall: This is a site the author can really be proud of. It's a very sleek, professional-looking site that is full of surprises and kept me very entertained and I didn't even know there was a volcano in Ecuador.

Shows how much I know.

3. BV Gallery/Author: Unknown

`http://bvgallery.com/index.html/`

Load Time: 20 Seconds, 57kps modem, cleared cache, 7/25/00 9:37AM.

My Screen Size: 1,024×768

Browsers Used: Internet Explorer 5 and Netscape Navigator 4.5

Figure 7.25
The BVGallery homepage.
(Color Plate C.21)

Concept: I spent a good deal of time in this site trying to make the concept of it more than it actually was. Since the word gallery was used in the title, I assumed there would be a sales pitch or at least a download pitch.

Nope.

This site is just what it states. It is a gallery. The author doesn't care to sell you anything nor does he appear to even want a great deal of recognition (he never asks for it). The site

234

is purely and simply a gallery of photographs and drawings. It is meant to be something to be viewed and enjoyed. That's all, and there's something very refreshing and comforting about that.

Praise: I was drawn first to the site's overall design because it was bold, clean, and simple. There's very little clutter and that makes for an enjoyable visit. I was pleased to see that the author was confident enough in the site to not add elements that weren't needed simply to fill that space. Too often I see sites that have these elements slapped on the page for no other reason, that I could see, other than to fill space.

The author of BVGallery kept it clean and kept the site's killer app in mind from start to finish.

The site gives the appearance of frames but in reality is just a large table. That's good because it only takes one page loading rather than the three a frames format would use. In addition, the text and links that cross over the color boundary never lap across the line. The table sees to that no matter what the screen size. Frames might have trouble adjusting to smaller screen sizes if the author isn't careful to take those screen settings into account.

Here, let me click on New York for you (see Figure 7.26).

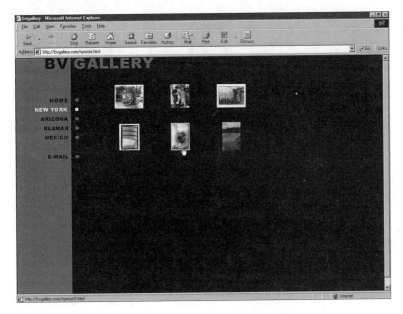

Figure 7.26
Color changes, format remains.

You might not be able to notice it on these pages, but the color changed from a deep burgundy to a richer blue when the page loaded. In fact, this happens on all the links. The design remains and the color changes. It's a clever method of carrying design across pages yet alerting the user that he is inside a new page. Notice also that now that you are inside the New York page, the link for that page remains on the left, but is now inactive and a different color further confirming that you are in a specific page.

I like the use of thumbnails rather than posting the big pictures first. Allow me to choose which one I want to see. That puts me in charge and keeps me happy.

Now, allow me to click on one of the images for you (see Figure 7.27).

Figure 7.27
The thumbnails remain.

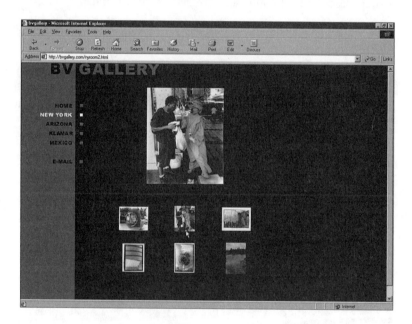

The author has carried the thought process used with the link on the left to the page and the image thumbnail. Notice that when I clicked on the thumbnail, the image came up, but the other thumbnails remained. That way, the user does not need to go back and back and back every time he wants to see another thumbnail full size.

Furthermore, the thumbnail of the image I am viewing still remains, yet it is not an active link. That's very clever and very helpful. It means creating an entirely new page for every image, but the effect seems well worth it.

Concern: I hit upon my biggest concern right off. What is this page for? Better yet, who are you? Can I take the images if I want? What am I supposed to do here?

The site is beautiful, but very confusing right up front. I know that sounds strange, but it's true. People like to be given instruction. They like to be told what's going on. This site seems a little too good to be true. You mean you're going to just show me pictures? That's all?

Uhhhh...why?

Suggestion: Put up another link. Make the link give a history and some instruction for the site. Also—explain who is Klamar. I liked his work, but I couldn't read anything about him. Offer me some textual support for what I am looking at. Again, I would make it a separate page. The image pages are fine as they stand.

Except...

Concern: None of your images have HEIGHT, WIDTH, or ALT attributes attached.

Suggestion: You really need to do that, without a doubt. That's a simple requirement for any image on any site.

Overall: You have a very nice site here, but it requires a little more support than what you've given it although the design is just great. I would keep that at all costs. It's so simple that it looks elegant and thought out. I saw in your letter to submit the site that you had the design suggested to you by a print designer. That makes sense. The site looks like it was created to be a handout at the first gallery showing.

Chapter 8

Hello? Anybody Here? How Many?

"I have a Web site," says one person.

"Oh? How many hits do you get?" says another.

Have you been in this conversation? I have. I find it funny that once a person gets a site up and running, the content often becomes a secondary concern. The big question people want to know is "How many people are coming to see the site?"

Why is that a concern? What does it matter if you get one a day or a million a day? Is the site any better or worse because only a few people come in? Let's say I had a site that pulls in millions of people a day. You specifically arrive and don't care for the content. It isn't what you're looking for. Would you stop, look at the counter that reads "eleven jillion people have visited this site since noon today," and rethink leaving? Maybe you would stop and ponder aloud, "Gosh, eleven jillion, that's a jillion more than the last site. There's nothing here I need, but I had better stick around. After all, eleven jillion people can't be wrong."

Please.

I find students, as well as designers, get overly wrapped up in the number of hits, clicks, page views, unique visitors, and so on, that they start to lose sight of what's really important, the content. Take my word for it. If you answer the five questions laid out in Chapter 2, "Before You Write a Word," outline the site and put forth an effort to offer solid content, the audience will come. It may take a little advertising on your part to get the name out, but once your site is discovered, the people will come.

But how many are coming? How will you know? What's a hit? What's a page view? Aren't they the same thing?

When the people come, will you make contact with them? Better yet...how will they make contact with you?

Should you have a chat room, ICQ, or just email, a bulletin board or a guestbook post? Italian or vinaigrette? Do you want fries with that?

This chapter discusses the concepts involved in tracking and making contact with the visitors that will come to your site.

Hits? Visitors? Impressions? Huh?

First things first, here are a few terms to learn before going on. I hear people talking about clicks and visitors and hits like they are interchangeable words. They are not. Each means a specific count and, if used correctly, can make a site seem a whole lot more important than it probably is.

Hit

A hit is a request of the server. That's it. That's all it means. Reporting the number of hits a Web site gets is actually a pretty lousy measure of site traffic.

Here's why—let's say I have a Web page. It's my homepage. That homepage has nine in-line graphics. That means, when someone allows the page to load fully, they see nine images on one page. It makes no matter how large the image is, just the fact that it's an image is enough.

That one page is equal to 10 hits. When a user logs in to the page and allows the page to fully load, a total of 10 requests are made of the server. One was for the page itself, and then nine for the nine images. That's 10.

Get it?

If the site has five pages, each with nine images and the user sees all five, that's 50 hits, right?

So! Now, the owner of the site gets into that "How many hits does your site get?" conversation. The owner reports 50. Technically, he's correct. There were 50 requests of the server to display five pages to one user.

One user. Fifty hits. If the owner added only one image to each page then he could report 55 hits.

Woohoo!

Do you see why hit is not a good measure of site traffic? If all I am looking for are big hit numbers, all I need is to create pages that are just filled with images and hope my user waits for them all to load. Ten viewers later, I could have hits out the wazoo.

The number would be impressive, but it wouldn't last long. I can't imagine graphics-filled pages that take forever to load will be a big draw for users to return.

Page Views

This is a better reading of site traffic. It is a tally of the number of pages the server offered up. It's basically still a reading of hits, but in this case we're only interested in the HTML page hits.

This eliminates the ability to cram 50 images onto one page and report large hit numbers. Page views at least allow you to see which pages are being viewed most often and better yet, allow you to track how many pages a user moved through while in your site. Thus, page views are often reported in two ways, total views and average number of views per person per visit.

When HTML Goodies first became a domain unto itself, my tracking numbers showed that I had an average of seven page views per person. That was great. The Internet average was around three. From that I could ascertain that I was not only offering something people wanted, but the site construction was inviting enough that people felt comfortable staying and moving deeper into the site.

Impressions

This is another word that is often misused. Some people might tell you that page views and impressions are the same thing—they are not. Page views count the number of pages a user views. Impressions count the number of times a user sees a specific element of the page. This is almost always a measure of ad banner effectiveness.

When HTML Goodies first began accepting ad banners, one of my first purchases was a server program that would place the banners, count how many times each was displayed, and count if the banner had been clicked or not.

We considered an impression when the ad server served up an ad. If a person stopped in, saw the page, but left before the ad banner popped up, then it was not an impression. The ad server must have served up the ad for it to be called an impression.

My ad server software wasn't overly expensive; thus, it wasn't overly sophisticated. Today it's possible to not only track total impressions, but also if the entire ad banner popped up or how many times a single unique visitor saw the same ad.

Unique visitor?

Unique Visitor

A unique visitor is just that, a visitor. I call them users. Your site may have served up 25 pages, but if one person looked at all 25 pages then you had only one unique visitor.

How you track return traffic depends on how sophisticated a system you want to set up. If you set cookies, it's possible to not only track a person arriving for the first time, but then also to track that person's returning.

In that case, unique visitors can be broken down even further into unique and return visitors. I've also heard them called comebacks.

So, what's the best method of reporting site traffic? Well, that depends on what you're trying to do with the report. If you're reporting traffic to advertisers, you probably want to let them know impressions or number of unique visitors. Each advertiser has a different plateau that your site must meet in order to begin seriously talking to you about placing ad banners. In case you're wondering, the general rule-of-thumb number is 10,000 unique visitors. Once your site reaches that level, you can consider yourself a serious contender to vie for that advertising dollar.

If you're simply trying to impress your friends or colleagues, then maybe you want to report hits. That is, unless they know what hits really are in which case they know you're simply inflating your numbers.

The problem now is that you can't report inflated numbers if you don't know what the numbers are. Yes, you could lie, but that's not nice. You need to somehow get a record of your numbers. Hmmmm. Let's see. You need a record. A count. That's it.

A counter!

Hit Counters

Now that you have a pretty good idea of what you are attempting to count, now you need to decide how to go about counting. The quick and easy answer is to use a hit counter (see Figures 8.1 and 8.2).

Figure 8.1
I am visitor 077365.

Figure 8.2
I am also visitor 077366.

Give me a moment. I want to be visitor 077777. That's my lucky number.

The page shown in Figure 8.1 and 8.2 is by Nancy O. Johnson who calls herself "The Mac lady." Stop by at `http://www.the-mac-lady.com/`.

Mac fans might really dig this site. Nancy used her counter in much the same manner as most designers. The counter is set high enough on the page so that it can be seen. She then added text to address the user in some way. Her text is a polite straight-to-the-point, "You are Visitor Number 0077366." She even went as far as setting the counter to fit in with the color scheme of the page. I just wonder if the counter is needed.

I ask that because I am not an overt fan of hit counters. In fact, if you remember back in Chapter 3, "Begin the Design," I listed counter as number two on my hit parade of things you probably want on a Web site but probably shouldn't have.

Please understand that just because I dislike counters it certainly doesn't mean that you shouldn't use them. If used properly, counters can be helpful to the author—I'm just not so sure about how useful they are to the users.

My concern over counter use comes from the years where I have seen counters used incorrectly, falsified, and displayed with any number of different images that simply slow the page. The basic concept of a counter is a good one—it's just that the problems I noted previously have given counters a bad name. In fact, as stated in Chapter 3, more than 50% of those polled said counters were not credible. Those who see the counter don't trust it nor do they put any stock in its reading.

If you do decide to use a counter, please be honest with me here. Whom is the counter for? It's for you, not your users. They may glance at the counter, but a big number is probably dismissed as false and a low number might be taken as a sign of a poor site. Those polled by HTML Goodies showed that 13% said a low counter number, below 1,000, made them lose respect for the site. In case you're wondering, over 80% reported that no matter what the counter reads, it doesn't matter to them. They don't believe the number anyway.

Can you tell me the good in using a counter?

"It tells me the number of people who came to the page."

It does? Really?

One of the first tutorials I ever posted on HTML Goodies was for the installation of a counter. Yep, I used to have one on every page on my site. (Hang head in shame here.) In fact, that counter tutorial was the first page to win an award. The problem was that no sooner than the page was up and running did people started asking how they could up the number themselves. You know, start at around 50,000 visitors just to give the site a little kick-start.

That's lying, isn't it? Plus if there are any actual visitors to the site, they might notice that the counter reads 50,004 one day and 50,009 the next. The inflated number actually won't fool anyone unless you go in every day and add a couple of thousand just to make it look real. Then what good is the counter? Unless you are a stunning record keeper, the counter has lost its purpose. It's no longer a counter but rather something you feel impresses people.

Sorry to say, it won't.

A student of mine placed a counter on her page. She spent so much time looking at that counter that it started to consume her. In fact, she went as far as to keep a record of her personal visits to the page so that she could subtract that number from the counter total to get a true reading. Each day, I would walk into class and there she would be with her note-book open adding another "That was me" hash mark to her personal visitor count. I wanted to suggest that she subtract that number from the counter at the end of each week, but that would mean the counter would start going backward. I can't imagine how that would have gone over. I kept the suggestion to myself.

So...What Do You Do?

To begin with, ask yourself if a counter is really necessary. Why do you want this count? There are certainly valid reasons. Maybe you do want to begin accepting advertising. Maybe you want to track visitors to find what sections of your site are the most popular. Maybe you just simply want to know how many people are showing up. These are all good reasons, but are they worth putting something on the page that most people feel is false?

If you want a count, my suggestion is to gather that count through what's known as your access log. Every site has one. This is a long list of every hit the server received. There's the word, hit. I guarantee your site has an access log. The question is whether you can get at it and if it's delineated for you.

Those of you on free servers are probably unable to get at your access log. Those of you on national ISPs such as AOL or CompuServe might run into the same problem. My sugges-tion is to get on a local ISP that allows you access to the log. It may take some looking but they're out there and they would love to have your business.

I know that seems like a bit of a pain. Just think about how important is the counter and how important is it that the count be correct? The access log is correct. It doesn't lie very well.

Once you find a site that offers you access, you then need a second program that delineates the log. The access log is little more than line after line of hit requests. Something must count through the log and make a statistical chart of visitors, impressions, and page views for you. A lot of ISPs already have such a program for you to use, but if not, ask them what program they suggest you use. Install it and you're good to go. If you have any intentions of setting up advertising on your site, you most certainly want to go this route. Most adver-tisers that I know simply do not accept a page counter as proof of traffic.

Aw, C'mon Joe! I Just Want a Lousy Counter

Here, here! You're right. This is your page and if all you want is a basic counter to keep a general eye on things then you should be able to have it. Again, I am not here to talk you out of anything, I just feel a little stronger about some elements than others.

All right, if you're going to use a counter, use it to your benefit. Using a counter is far more for the author than it is for the user even though a lot of people attempt to apply it to the user by writing text like, "You are Visitor something, something, something, something."

Once you agree that the counter is not really for the users then you can quickly agree that to make a point of displaying it as such makes no sense. So, rule of counter thumb number one:

1. Use the fastest-loading counter possible.

The fastest-loading counters are text-based rather than image-based. Figure 8.3 is a counter I found on Candy Torres's page "Virtual Candy" at `http://www.virtualcandy.com/`.

Figure 8.3
I am visitor 132113.

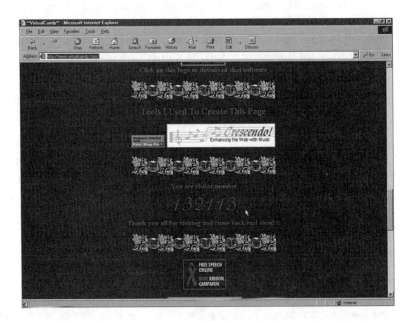

Each of the numbers is a single image. The counter is pretty and Candy has surrounded it with text, but the counter slowed the page. The server needs to service six hits before the counter comes in. I cleared cache twice, reloaded, and each time the counter images were the last to come in.

Candy should think about finding a counter that offers text that she can alter. Make the text numbers blue rather than slowing the page for six blue counter images.

2. Try not to use a counter that comes from a second source, or at least try to find the smallest, text-based counter out there.

There are a number of services out there that offer counters in return for posting some advertising on your site. Usually that advertising comes right along with the counter itself.

Marshall Rowe put together a pretty nice site with a free counter from FastCounter. It's down in the lower-left corner of Figure 8.4.

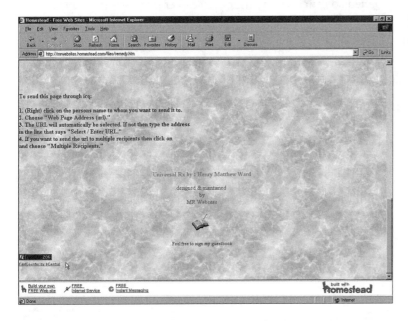

Figure 8.4
I am visitor 206.

The counter is text—that's good—but it also carries advertising and text in return for the free counter. This is actually a small amount of advertising in return for a counter. I've seen services that take up three times the space as the counter itself to tout the service.

Although it may seem this way, I'm not too concerned that someone gives up space to the advertising—what concerns me about using a free service is that the counter you use is located off site. You must attach to a second server to get your count returned. If there is net congestion or that second server is down, then your page stops. I don't mean it's slowed. It stops.

Find out if your server offers a public domain counter application that you can attach to. That way you can keep all your links on the same server and have less of a chance to stop your page from coming in. Plus, you only get the count. That's what you're interested in anyway, right?

If a counter isn't available to you, then make a point of looking at the counters offered by numerous companies. One might fit into your page better than another. They all count. You just need to make the most aesthetic choice.

3. Display the counter far down on the page.

Display it last if you can. Here's my thinking: If you place the counter last then it may very well be the last thing to come in; thus, the user can see the text and images above it first and be happy that the page loaded so quickly. The user may never even see the counter. That's fine. It's for you.

One downfall of placing it that low on the page is that people may leave the page before the counter has a chance to trigger and make the count. That's a problem, but remember that all counter readings should be taken with a grain of salt anyway.

Keeping those three objectives in mind, Figure 8.5 is a site by David Schneider he calls "Quiet Elegance Woodturning." Find it at

`http://hometown.aol.com/dschwdturn/qew/qewhome.html`.

Figure 8.5
Where's the counter?

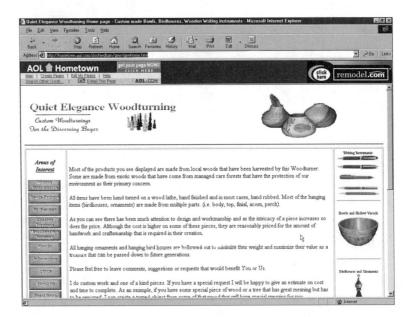

Oh, I'm sorry, the counter is a bit down the page. It's here (see Figure 8.6):

Figure 8.6
I am visitor 1591.

It's last on the page. It's straight text and the entire page came in before the counter got its count. David made a point of getting all of the important things up high. It would be quite possible that the next 10 people that roll through the site might never see the counter.

That's fine. It's for David anyway.

Thus ends my rants against and about counters. Again, this is your Web site. If you want a counter, you should have it. Just stop and think about what you want the counter for, to whom the count really matters, and where you should place it on the page.

Oh, one more thing, I have five figures of counters so far. You may have noticed that I listed the visitor number displayed on the counter for each one. Think back. Did the number mean anything to you? Did you care what number I was? When the number was high, did you think better of the site? When the number was low, did you think less of the site?

Remember that people who come to your Web site make those same distinctions regarding your count. Oh, sure, you could bulk up the number and have it start at say, 50 million. That might impress someone, but probably won't. You'd be lying anyway.

Since I keep giving tips I learned during my time in radio, let me give you another one.

"You can't get hurt by what you don't play."

If you put a counter on your page, you are inviting people to make judgments based on the count. However, if you do not put a counter on the page, no one will notice.

When's the last time you went into a page and asked, "Gee. I wonder what number visitor I am"?

Email Versus Guestbook Forms Format

Yes, it's email versus Guestbook—one night only. Get your tickets today!

As you continue this discussion of your relationship with your users, examine how your site offers users the ability to communicate with you.

During my time on the Web, I have noticed that the word Guestbook has started to become synonymous with email.

The link "Sign my Guestbook" has become quite commonplace. The problem is, a Guestbook really doesn't mean email, nor does email really mean Guestbook. I think the real problem is not the terms as much as it's the look of the page.

In fact, I have found out that often Web designers feel that a straight email link isn't professional enough for their site. They feel that a Guestbook format that allows someone to send email using form elements is a more corporate look. Of course, it takes longer to fill out a form, but the form does offer some really nice effects. I get into that in a moment.

Figure 8.7
A pretty nice Guestbook at the Centris Web Site
`http://www.centris.`
`freeuk.com/.`

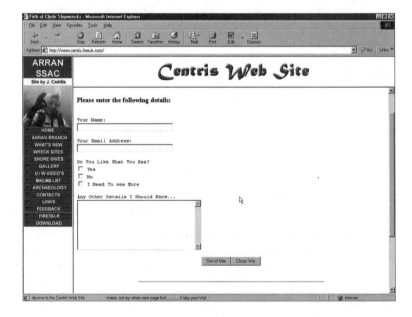

Furthermore, I think people have actually started to get the feeling that a Guestbook isn't as cool as it once was, so I am now starting to see the same Guestbook being renamed Feedback pages or Contact pages.

The problem is that that perception of Guestbooks being un-cool isn't actually true. Seventy-seven percent of those who answered the HTML Goodies survey noted they expect to see a Guestbook on a personal Web site. Only 31% reported they expected to see one on a business or corporate site. You may think a Guestbook looks corporate, but most viewers don't think it belongs there.

Why the difference? Why do people think a Guestbook should be on a personal Web site, but not on a corporate site? My guess is that the simple email link is quicker. It relies less on the server than a Guestbook page, especially if that Guestbook page has attached the output of the form to a PERL CGI that, in turn, posts a thank-you page. It's a great effect, really, but let's look at when that effect might be best used and when it might not.

Of course, in the world of the Web, perceptions change faster than you turn the pages of this book. So, which do you use, the Guestbook or the email link?

What Exactly Is a Guestbook?

Take a moment to remember back to the last time you actually signed a Guestbook. I don't mean a virtual Guestbook, I mean a real, honest-to-goodness Guestbook, with a pen.

My guess is that it was at a wedding, a birthday party, an anniversary party, or in a hotel or cultural place, right?

What do you believe was the purpose of the Guestbook? A Guestbook is there so that the people who put it there can go back and see who came to the party. It's there so that addresses are captured and correspondence can begin. If you sign a Guestbook at a museum, I guarantee you'll be on the next membership drive mailing list. If you sign the Guestbook at a wedding, my guess is that you'll soon get a thank-you card even if you're cheap and didn't bring a gift.

When you put an email link on a page, what are you looking for? You want email, period. You allow the user to decide what to write. The email link is there only to create a message to be sent back to the author. It's quick, it's useful, and it doesn't get in the way.

I am actually happier when I am granted a simple email link rather than a Guestbook link. The reason is that a Guestbook always asks questions I have no reason to answer.

Some of the most common are

- How did you find my site?
- What do you think of my site?
- How do you rate my site?
- How many times have you been to my site?
- Would you like more information about my site?

251

Notice a pattern? Often, those who set up Guestbooks also see their Guestbooks as a method to gather user information. In fact, some authors go as far as to attach JavaScript to their Guestbook so that the user cannot leave the page or submit the Guestbook without filling in every blank.

If you want to have the user take a poll then set up a Guestbook format page to act as a poll. Don't ask the user to sign a Guestbook and then hit them with extra questions. Be fair. If you want to offer a poll, offer a poll and hope people choose to take it.

Sticking poll questions in a Guestbook designed to communicate with the author is taking advantage of your users and it's not using a Guestbook correctly. Take my word for it, even the most loyal user gets a little miffed when you intentionally place a survey before him. I did five surveys for this book and many of the comments I received told me that they would fill out the survey this time, but in the future...knock it off!

Should You Use a Guestbook Format or Email Link?

Both, depending on the type of site you have created.

You should always have a simple email link on your pages, no matter if you have a Guestbook or not. There are numerous reasons such as

- I don't want to fill out a Guestbook form.
- I am using Internet Explorer Version 3 and your Guestbook form keeps messing up (it isn't until version four that IE starting playing nicely with basic HTML Guestbook forms).
- I am on AOL and your form isn't working (ditto previously).
- I don't want to answer these questions.
- I don't want my information posted.

That last one, I think, best promotes the argument. I talk about this in just a moment.

That Email Link

Email links should be simple and since it is a link, up high on the page. If I want to contact you, don't make me search around. I should be able to find that link pretty quickly.

The text you use for an email link is very important. The text must make it very clear that clicking fires up an email. Figure 8.8 is an example.

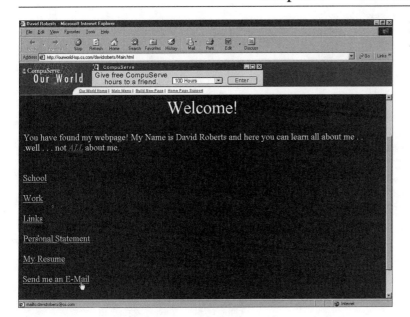

Figure 8.8
Mail me something, mister!

Dave Roberts has a personal page at `http://ourworld-top.cs.com/davidroberts/Main.html`. His email link is last in the long run of links. That's common. The reason I like Dave's link is that it's quick and it's hard to confuse this text with being just another link. The text "Send me an Email" pretty much spells it out.

I point out the use of the text because I have seen pages that use strange terms like "Make Communication" or "Click for me" or "mailman" to denote their email links. That may be being too clever for your own good. People may miss the pun, the joke, or the clever wording and not send you anything at all.

It is my opinion, and the majority opinion of those who answered the HTML Goodies survey, that the best text to use for an email link is the email address itself as in Figure 8.9.

Look under the book advertisement. There's my email. It's a text link and it's up high. By using the email address, you offer the user more than simply the ability to write—he can also copy the address to put into an address book. It is my opinion that using the email address as the link is the best method, but text such as "Click here to Email" is also very good.

Of course, it is also possible to use an active image as an email link (see Figure 8.10). Depending on the size of the image and how animated it is, I don't have a problem with it. However, over 30% of those polled said they didn't care for email image links.

Figure 8.9
Email address as link.

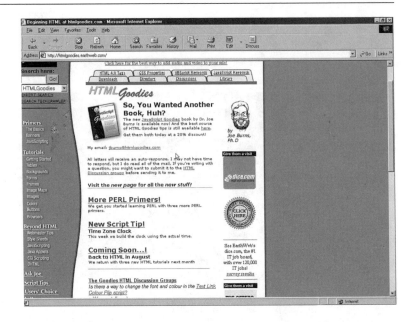

Figure 8.10
Active image email.

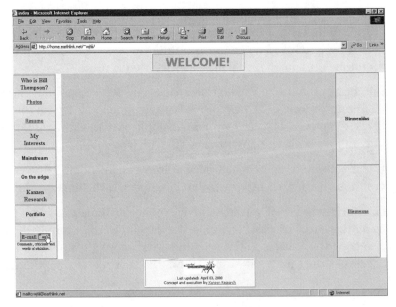

Figure 8.10 is a page by Bill Thompson at `http://home.earthlink.net/~wjtiii/`. Bill has gone with an image for his email link even though the other links on the page are text. That breaks the consistency a bit, but I have to hand it to Bill. He didn't go with one of the huge animated images.

Email image animation can be quick, a mailbox where the front opens and closes, or it can be huge, a letter being written, folded, placed in an envelope, sealed, stamped, and sent.

If you use an image for your email, take the same care with that image as you would for any other image and keep the purpose in mind.

The image must be representative of what the link does. The image must fit with the remainder of the page. If you have a classical feel to your page, it might not be good to have a little mail truck drive across the screen.

If the image fits and it tells what the link does, I don't have much problem with using it. I've used email image links in the past myself. Just know that about a third of those polled didn't find an image all that pleasing.

Email links are meant to be quick and easy. Text may be the best way to go, but this is your page.

That Guestbook

At this point, someone is probably angry because now they think they need to go in and drop the Guestbook from their page. Wait before you go in and starting erasing code. Let's talk first about how you're using it.

Rule number one: If you are using your Guestbook simply as your email link, then maybe you should lose it. The email link is quicker, upsets no one, and works on all browsers, all versions. The Guestbook might not.

So, when do you place a Guestbook on your site? You should place a Guestbook on your site when you intend to use the information as if it were written into a Guestbook.

The most common method of using a Guestbook is to set it up so that the responses people give are posted for everyone else to see (see Figure 8.11).

Here's Jerry David's site at `http://members.aol.com/Dedreo/index1.html`. Notice the two buttons there in the middle. One allows you to sign the Guestbook and one allows you to view what others have written. If you're going to use a Guestbook, this is one of the correct methods.

After enough people sign, you get a page that looks something like Figure 8.12.

This is the Guestbook response page from Amita Guha's Picture Of My Finger page at `http://picturesofmyfinger.com`. If you have a picture where your finger is part of the show, then send it in to her. I have sent one in already.

Figure 8.11
Sign it—view it.

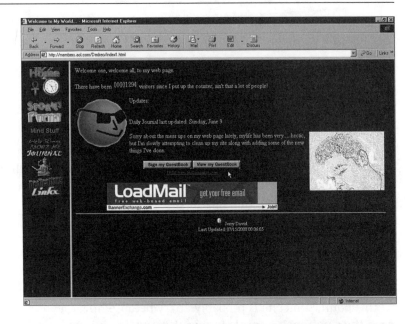

Figure 8.12
Love that site.

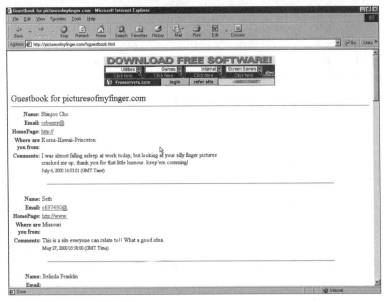

A Guestbook is something that should keep a record for everyone to see. The postings are the best part of posting a Guestbook. As long as everyone keeps the words clean, you should quickly produce a long page that fun to read. In addition, you receive a record of all the people that came and signed in. That's using a Guestbook correctly.

If you simply want a form element email system, then don't call it a Guestbook. Call it a feedback form or a contact form. Guestbook suggests you're going to post, or keep, the results. Or maybe you could just use an email link.

Or maybe I should talk about this a bit more.

Form Elements

There are other methods of using the Guestbook format. In each of the following cases, the forms aren't being specifically used as a Guestbook, but the format is similar. The user is being asked to put information into input elements such as text boxes and radio buttons rather than using a straight email.

In each case, the main difference between using form elements rather than email is that the information collected is kept and used for some reason other than simple communication.

The first is when you accept users for a mailing list.

Edward's developer site (see Figure 8.13) offers a newsletter correctly, using a forms format. Here the user can be very sure of what he is signing up for, can make some choices, and can submit the information himself.

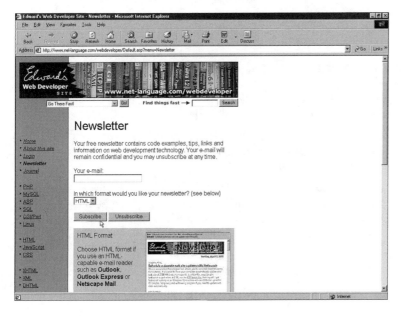

Figure 8.13

Edward Tanguay's Web Developer Site Newsletter Page at `http://www.webdevelopersjournal.com/`.

The second usage is when you set up a poll. As I stated previously, just make a point of informing your users that what they are about to enter is a poll. Often poll questions are hidden inside another Guestbook. I think the reason is that it's generally understood that online user dislike taking polls. If you offer a poll, be up front about it, understand that most people won't answer it, and be happy with the results you get. Don't attempt to force someone to answer the questions you ask. They might not care to give you the information you're requesting.

Finally, a form format is required when e-commerce is involved. I feel much more secure entering my information to form elements rather than one large text area box. When money is involve that information needs to be correct and entering it into form elements helps keep each piece of information separate from the other. Plus it makes it easier for the person doing e-business to break up the information using forms. He can separate the last name from the first name in order to more easily keep records.

Past those three uses, go with the email link. Your users will thank you for it.

To end this discussion of Guestbook or forms format versus email link, I want to suggest that if you post a Guestbook format you might want to skip all the extra JavaScript that forces someone to fill in a blank unless that blank is required for a very good reason. Please understand that a form used for e-busines—an order form, for example—is a different matter. There you may very well require specific elements to be filled in so the JavaScript prompts are useful. I am discussing an email contact form here.

It has happened to me that I have entered information into a form and skipped some of the text boxes only to be greeted by a JavaScript prompt suggesting I go back and fill in the blanks. I didn't want to so I put in false information. When the false information itself is tested and found not to be valid, another prompt came up telling me to try again.

I didn't. I left. The information the form was requesting was my phone number. No way. My phone number only goes out when I am making a purchase. A general Guestbook form does not need to have my phone number to work.

The moment you attempt to force an answer, you make users nervous and most likely scare many of them off. If the information you receive is incomplete, try contacting the user over email and requesting the data you need. Explain why you need the data and maybe you'll get it. If the explanation is short, maybe you should include the reason for gathering some data on the forms page itself.

Don't force anyone. That's setting up an ultimatum that you will most likely lose.

Chat Rooms

Chat rooms. The anti-newsgroup.

It used to be that only the largest of servers offered chat rooms. They were quite a premium element to have on one's site. Thus, everyone wanted one. There were often links on personal sites to larger sites that offered chat room capabilities just so that authors could proclaim they had a chat room.

I've been in a few chat rooms. I don't go often because I don't really enjoy that chat. If there are more than two or three people in the room then the questions and answers start to become to separated by other questions and answers that it gets hard to read. MTV once ran a show where they would play a video and scroll the posts to a chat room while the video played. The posts rarely made sense in relation to one another because people were answering other people while posts about the current video separated the answers while posts were still flying about the last video.

It became very confusing and the show was cancelled.

Today, numerous free sites offer chat rooms. You fill out a form, offer some information and in a short while, you've got your own chat room. Getting a chat room is so easy that Web sites offering links to a personal chat room are becoming commonplace.

Design Goodies Survey

HTML Goodies Survey Question: When visiting a site with chat features, how likely are you to go into the chat room?

Highly Unlikely	60%
Unlikely	20%
Neutral	14%
Likely	4%
Highly Likely	2%

Only 6% suggested they would go into a chat site. Now, that doesn't take topic into account, but this should make you think hard about putting a chat room on your site.

So, should you offer a chat room on your site? Well, that depends on what your site is all about and what you will use the chat room for. Above all else, when deciding whether to post a chat room or not, remember:

> People who use chat rooms are a very small portion of the Internet audience.
>
> Chat room users are very specific users.

To begin with, the percentage of people who regularly use chat rooms are a relatively small percentage of the Internet population. Offering a chat room would mean you would have to take a small portion of people away from their already established chat rooms or convert people who do not use chat rooms to people who do use chat rooms. That's a pretty tall order. Just about half of those polled reported they would never go into a chat room. Only 20% total reported they would go into a chat room monthly, weekly, or daily.

Where the decision to post a chat room might lean toward yes is the topic of your site. Successful chat rooms are very topic specific. If you have a personal page simply dedicated to your likes and dislikes, and you offer a chat room, I doubt many people show up. The topic is too broad. There's no real focus to the chat room. There's nothing to draw someone in.

Your site's topic, and thus the topic of the chat room, must be chat-able. I like to make up words like that. The topic has to be something specific that actually has the ability to be chatted about. You may say that any topic can be chatted about. That's true but broad topics are much more difficult to encompass within a chat than very specific topics.

Let's say you start a site that sings the praises of the Chevrolet Fleetside pickup trucks. This is the kind of page that might have a chat room. My bet is also that it would be successful, too.

Why? Well, because there's a specific topic. The topic of the page is the same topic as the chat room. People who go into the chat room would expect to find others who share the same interests, Fleetwood pickup trucks (see Figure 8.14). Seem silly? It shouldn't.

Figure 8.14
Chat about trucks.

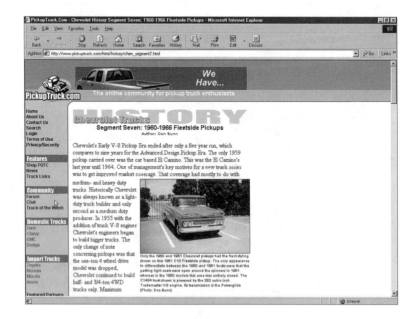

Notice the links on the left. There's your chat room.

One of the largest sites on the net offering chat rooms is WebMd.com. The site currently offers 45 different topics. You see a good many of them in Figure 8.15.

Figure 8.15
Good for what ails you.

The site has made a point of breaking down the topic of health into so many sections in order to keep the chat room focused. They could have just as easily offered only one chat room and called it health, but that would have had too many formats and too many different conversations all going on at the same time to be helpful. By keeping the topic small, they offer a better place to chat, and they have a great many chat users because of it. Plus you don't get some guy discussing allergies while another guy discusses that funny red thing on his forehead that won't go away.

So, there are your two concerns. Is the topic of your site specific enough that you feel it warrants the use of a chat room? If so, do you have enough traffic coming to your Web site to actually make the chat room viable?

If not, then maybe you shouldn't use it.

I gave this exact same speech to a class one time and a young man who wanted a chat room come heck or high water, said that he was putting one up anyway. I asked why and he said that he wanted to offer his users the opportunity to chat about what they wanted. Besides, it's only a link on the homepage. If no one ever clicks then the page wasn't slowed nor was anything misused, so there. He put a link on the page.

I really can't argue with the logic. He's right. It won't slow the pages nor does it interfere with anything on the page. It's just a link. It's just a link that probably is never used and if it is, only one person shows up. That's not much of a chat.

If your only reason for putting a chat room on your page is to have a link that reads, "chat room" then do it. You can always pull the link down later. I don't really understand how this shows that your site is better in some way, but it's your site and if you feel this makes your site appear more advanced then go for it. I'm just of the opinion that you don't put anything on your site that doesn't really belong or serve some purpose. Have you ever gone into a chat room where you were the only person writing lines like, "Is anyone here" and "Guess not"? I'm just wondering.

To that end, I know a lot of people that have chat rooms simply so one of their friends can pop in and the two people can chat. If someone else jumps in the mix, all the better, but the chat room is specifically for these two people. Some of them placed a link on their homepage, some didn't.

Remember Chapter 2—your site should have a single killer app. Does your chat room go to your killer app? Does the use of a chat room help what you're trying to do or are you simply placing a chat room because you feel it would be a neat thing to have?

Some might argue that the addition of a chat room wouldn't go against any killer app because the room would simply be a link on the homepage. If the user wanted to go, he could go. I guess there's some logic to that. It's not bothering anyone if they don't go.

But what if they do go and there's no one there?

Newsgroups

Newsgroups should be handled in exactly the same manner you handle chat rooms. If your site is specific enough and you draw enough audience to offer a place to post then pop up a newsgroup.

In reality, I like newsgroups a whole lot better than I like chat rooms. They are more organized, easier to navigate, and just make more sense to me. Then again, I was around when newsgroups were the chat rooms of the day.

I would put up a newsgroup long before I put up a chat room. In fact…I have. Check out Figure 8.16.

Post a question, answer a question and create interaction. A list of my five newsgroups can be found at `http://www.htmlgoodies.com/discussions/`. Stop in and get involved. You'll find a lot of interaction there.

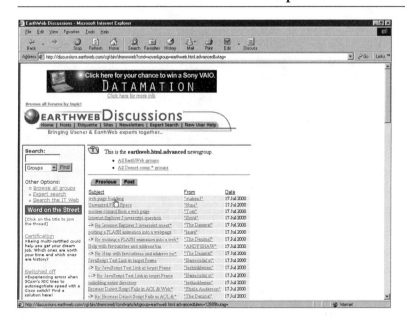

Figure 8.16
The Goodies HTML Newsgroups.

I post newsgroups for many of my online classes. I like them a lot. I think they go to my online class's killer app. They are helpful to my students, my users.

The problem is that today, newsgroups seem a bit antiquated to some people. Chat rooms are the way to go. They are immediate, real time. Newsgroups are slow and there's no personal interaction.

That may be so. All I ask is that you first decide if your site even requires a chat room or a newsgroup. If so, set it up and make a point of going in yourself a great deal. Users will be looking for the owner of the chat or newsgroup. You can always post a link to your newsgroup and if you receive little or no user involvement then pull down the link.

Here's to good interaction, and speaking of good interaction...

Instant Messaging

Instant messaging had a real heyday in about 1998 to 1999. That's when the software first came out and the entire world needed to get on ICQ, Pow-Wow, Hotline, Jabber, or any other platform that would alert you to the fact that a friend or colleague was online.

I was like everyone else. I jumped on the bandwagon and quickly signed up for a couple of the biggies. I enjoyed them for a short time, but then had to get off of them. I never had a moment's peace. Every time I came online, the people who had me listed got the word and the requests for chats came flooding in. I had to shut off the software for good. But that's me. I have a jillion people trying to ask me a question every day.

In terms of Web design, I like the Instant Messaging systems. I like that people have their ICQ number on the page. I think it looks professional and gives the impression the author wants interaction. I know a lot of programmers that keep in touch with each other specifically through ICQ. They use it before jumping their cellular phone. Believe me, that is saying something.

If you can keep up with the number of people contacting you or you only use the messaging systems within a small group of friends, then use it. Just understand that as your site grows, so does the number of people that want to talk. I would like to turn on the messaging system but it would never stop ringing. I do have some personal systems but goodness knows I won't be offering them here.

If you want your users to contact you, the messaging systems are a good, real-time method. Just keep your killer app in mind. Does the killer app collect people that would use the instant messaging? If so, then offer it.

Newsletters

I'm going to end this discussion of tracking and keeping contact with your users by talking about the latest and the greatest method of reaching out, the newsletter. It seems like everyone has a newsletter that you can get by simply leaving your email address behind.

Just like any other form of interaction these days, there are numerous sites out there that offer you what is known as a listserver. That server compiles a list of everyone who should get a copy of an email. There may be 500 names on the list. No problem, the listserver sends every person a copy of an email...er...newsletter.

If you decide to put out a newsletter, I suggest that you do go with a listserver instead of simply addressing one email to numerous people. The reason is just so that when the email arrives, the names of everyone who is receiving the email aren't listed at the top. The listserver hides the names and simply sends the email to a group rather than a person. It's safer for the people who receive the newsletter and doesn't create a huge chunk of names before readers can actually get to the good parts.

At the time of this writing, I have been putting out a newsletter for just over two years. I started a second newsletter just over four months ago. It is a weekly newsletter that carries sponsors. After having written a weekly for that long, I've pretty much seen everything that can go wrong with writing a newsletter. Allow me to share those concerns with you here and hopefully guide your decision to write, or to not write a newsletter.

First and foremost, remember that a newsletter is an intrusion. You are sending email to someone. You are intruding on their turf. Because of that, rule number one when deciding to put out a newsletter is this:

Newsletter Rule #1: Let Users Sign Up for Your Newsletter

Do not, do not, do not, simply send someone a copy of your newsletter without their first asking for it. I have gone into Web sites, purchased something or filled out a form to get some information and the next thing I know, I am receiving their lousy newsletter, and it is lousy.

I never asked for it. I just got slapped onto a list because I offered up my email address. Sometimes I get put onto newsletter lists simply because my email is prevalent.

People decide they want a newsletter and just add me to the list saying I should be giddy because I am receiving the first copy.

Pinch me. Am I dreaming?

I never wanted that newsletter. I never signed up for it. The newsletters I signed up for, I read. Them, I like. The ones that just showed up, I unsubscribe.

That is actually an excuse I have heard for putting people on a newsletter mailing list, "They can always unsubscribe if they don't want it." What? How silly is that? Do you actually believe you're building any kind of relationship with a user by starting with that kind of attitude?

Let your users sign up for your newsletters. If you only have two people signed up, then those two people get a newsletter. Don't try to build a following by tricking people into receiving mail. That is seen as an intrusion and people won't stand for it.

People sign up for my Goodies To Go! Newsletter; however, now and again someone gets on the list that shouldn't be on the list. A friend signed them up, I guess. The emails I get back from those people are awful. They call the newsletter spam and call me names. The emails are full of threats and nasty phrases.

Don't do that to a possible user. If they want the newsletter, they'll sign up for it. If they don't, do not force it on them. Sure, they can unsubscribe. They'll unsubscribe, write you a nasty letter, tell as many people as they can about your nasty practices and do much more harm than good.

Newsletter Rule #2: Send a Newsletter, Not Just Ads and Links

If you take on the responsibility of writing a newsletter, you have to actually write a newsletter. The first syllable in the word is news. I receive a newsletter that I never signed up for that I actually like to read because it never changes. It's the same information week after week. Come to my site. Here are my links. My site is cool. Another newsletter I receive comes from a music site. It's a giant advertisement. It's special after special. I don't consider that a newsletter. There's no news. It's a static format that never changes. I know what it reads before I open it. I won't unsubscribe because I just want to see how long these people can keep this up.

If you decide to undertake the writing of a newsletter, understand that you have taken on a task that takes a good deal of your time. I block out at least two hours every Saturday morning to write the Goodies To Go! newsletter. Usually, it takes me three hours to write.

A newsletter contains new information, new text, something that differs from last week.

Newsletter Rule #3: Weekly Means Weekly

If you offer a weekly newsletter, you need to write a weekly newsletter. The newsletter has to show up in mailboxes weekly. Newsletters aren't very good if they only show up when the author feels like it, or when the author has enough new information.

Some might say that when the newsletter comes doesn't matter because no one is going to miss it—so when it shows up, it's a welcome email. Actually, nothing could be farther from the truth. If you create a newsletter, with new content that someone signed up for, then consistency of delivery is crucial to building the audience trust.

The Goodies to Go! Newsletter goes out on Mondays. It happens like clockwork and the readers who've signed up look forward to the letter. If it is more than a day late, I get letters asking where it is. That's what you're shooting for. You want to provide a solid product, on time, to people that want it. That builds audience and that helps your site.

Newsletter Rule #4: Put It in the Newsletter—I Can Go to the Site Myself

Newsletters that offer nothing but teases and then links back to the site bother me greatly. First off, the newsletter arrives in my mailbox and it has advertisements. Then, I read a short paragraph teasing a topic. If I like the topic, I click on a link that takes me to the newsletter site where I am bombarded with more advertisements and get the rest of the story.

Don't do that.

If you're going to put out a newsletter, put out a complete newsletter. Give the user the whole story right then and there. They were nice enough to sign up and accept your information. Don't then put more upon them. Let them have a nice time reading your newsletter from beginning to end.

Newsletter Rule #5: If You Start a Newsletter, Keep a Newsletter

Too often people start a newsletter and don't really understand the time involved in writing or producing the piece. I have received a lot of newsletters that only showed up once or twice, and that was it. The author's desire to write a newsletter was quickly doused when the time frame began to come into play.

My suggestion would be to write four newsletters before you even get started offering them to your users. If you still have the drive after a month then maybe you should put out the newsletter. Plus, you have four ready to go out. If you can't stand the thought of writing another newsletter after those four then don't put it out.

Finally, you write the newsletter. I understand that other people want to contribute and when someone else writes something, that's all that much less than you have to write, but don't start relying on your audience to write for you. You should write your own newsletter. Guest columnists are fine now and again, but for the most part, people signed up to hear your words, not the words of someone else.

Think About It...

Putting out a newsletter is time consuming, but it is also a real joy when the audience begins sending in letters commenting on what you've written.

If you feel you have enough to say and you want to write then maybe a newsletter is for you. Just understand the time and effort that are involved before you get 100 subscribers and decide after four issues that you've had enough.

Back to the Top

Now that I've beaten through some of the most popular methods of tracking and making contact with your users, it's time to answer the question you're sure to get the next time you tell a fellow Web-head that you have a Web site.

He asks, "You have a Web site? How many hits you get?"

You answer, "Enough." Tell him that it's because you have great content. Then give him the address. Ask for a visit and feedback.

Don't worry. Your users will contact you, either through a Guestbook or an email link. If you offer the ability to contact, they will. The Web is a form of communication and people want to communicate. Give a user the ability to contact you and they most likely will.

Users are funny that way. They like to talk to the people they are visiting.

Site Critiques

1. Andrew J. Velkey, II, Professor—Mississippi College/Author: Andrew J. Velkey, II

`http://www.mc.edu/~velkey/`

Load Time: 9 Seconds 57kps modem, cleared cache, 7/17/00 1:40PM.

My Screen Size: 1,024×768

Browsers Used: Internet Explorer 5 and Netscape Navigator 4.5

Figure 8.17
*Good morning professor—
is this going to be on the
test? (Color Plate C.22)*

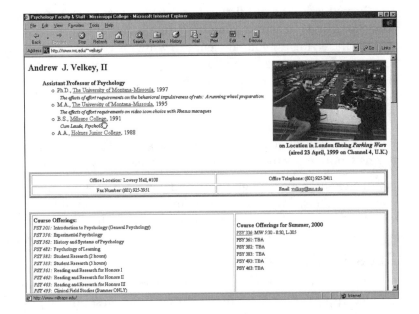

Concept: Every professor, teacher, or businessperson wants to have his own Web page. Why not? Web pages are becoming the business cards of 21st century, but they can be so much more than a simple card.

The last two universities I have worked for seemed heck bent on getting every professor up and online with their own page. I think it's a good idea—there's so much one can do with a personal homepage in an educational environment.

This is Professor Andrew J. Velkey's page. He's a professor of Psychology at Mississippi College. His page has the traditional pieces of information including his email, phone, office number, some Vitae information, some links, and to his credit, only one image.

Praise: I wasn't kidding about the "only one picture" comment. I am a professor and because of that, other professors often ask me to look at their pages. I guess there's something between higher education and use of graphics. Usually, a professor's page is either completely devoid of graphics or has so many it might peel off the screen through sheer weight. Professor Velkey only has the one image and it's enough. The site loaded quickly and it contains just about any piece of information one would want to know about Professor Velkey and/or his work.

Concern: When a professor, businessperson, manager, supervisor, or anyone, for that matter, posts a Web site, one of the first questions he must answer is, who will come to this page and why?

If you took the five questions in Chapter 2 to heart, you've already got answers to these questions. What about Professor Velkey's page? Who will come to this page and why? Well, if his page is anything like mine, students will be the majority visitor. Unless there's a good reason, colleagues usually don't trek to another professor's page very often. There really isn't anything there for them.

Students, on the other hand, need to see that page for various reasons, many of which Professor Velkey has touched on, but has not quite yet fulfilled.

I'm going to focus on just one aspect that students are forever harping on, syllabi. Professor Velkey has posted one syllabus, for PSY 336. I was impressed with the work. It's a nice thick syllabus that lays out a lot of the groundwork for the course. Students love that.

Suggestion: Post all of your syllabi. I know most of them will be out of date once they're up, but when a student is checking you out, he wants to see every syllabi from every class you offer. I don't know why—they just do. I guess it allows them to somehow gauge your level of difficulty. One student told me that there is a direct correlation between the length of the syllabus and the class difficulty. There's not a lick of logic in that, but seeing the syllabus was important to the student so I offer all of mine.

Concern: I am concerned about the flow of the content of your page. What is most important to the student, or prospective student that shows up, to read about that Professor Velkey he has to take next semester? He wants your location and wants to know what he is in for next semester.

Suggestion: Get your contact information first and your course offerings next. I have also found that providing a short narrative about your teaching philosophy helps a great deal.

On a businessperson's page, a business philosophy goes a long way. It gives future employees the ability to judge you and your ethics before taking the job.

Concern: After your second table, the page begins to stack. It starts to become a little long and a bit hard to read.

Suggestion: You have too much information on this one page. It needs to be broken down into the pages representing each of the headings that follow, Areas of Competency and Specialization, Research History: Species Investigated, Teaching & Research Activities.

In fact, I would suggest the homepage be your contact information, your current classes and then a teaching philosophy. Following the current classes, you could have a link to a page that lists all of your classes. Then there could be links to the elements listed earlier, your Vitae, and then your publications.

I don't know how you feel about posting your publications online. I have just about every paper I've presented or published on my school Web page and I have actually found success with it. People have contacted me to ask to use the text and/or cite the work. If you do not have strong copyright concerns, posting the entire paper, or at least the abstract, might be a smart move.

It is the same if you are a businessperson. Post your memos. Post your reports. I'm sure someone has used my work without citing me. However, I believe those cases are far outweighed by the cases where people did cite me and used my work properly.

Concern: Your syllabus and Vitae are easy to read online, but would be very difficult to print. The text breaks in strange places.

Suggestion: Rewrite your Vitae so that it can be printed and look professional. I make every one of my Web design students post their résumé so that possible employers can gain easy access to their work history. One of the concerns that came out of posting the pages was that online résumés were not laid out as nicely as those that were typeset. Yes, it's a little more coding, but it's worth it. Make your Vitae so that it prints as nicely as it displays.

Overall: You have all the information that someone would need. Well, maybe a few more syllabi and a teaching philosophy, but other than that it's all there. The page is just too long and too hard to navigate. Break it up. Put each section to its own page. Keep in mind your audience. Play to them. Give them what they want most, first, and don't make them scroll to find it.

Remember, people love to click. Scrolling is another matter.

2. Mrs. Burns' 1st Grade Class/Author: Ted Burns

`http://www.mrsburns.com/`

Load Time: 19 Seconds 57kps modem, cleared cache, 7/18/00 8:59AM.

My Screen Size: 1,024×768

Browsers Used: Internet Explorer 5 and Netscape Navigator 4.5

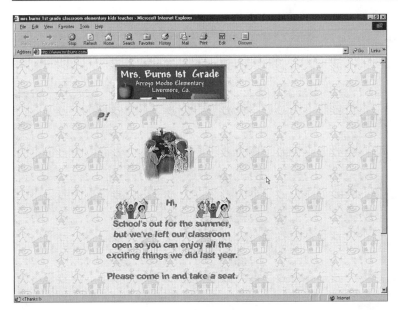

Figure 8.18
An apple for the teacher...
(Color Plate C.23)

Concept: From college professor, you go to the opposite end of the teaching time line to Mrs. Burns' 1st Grade (now 2nd grade since the blackboard keeps rewriting) Class Homepage. Ted, who I am assuming is Mrs. Burns' husband, wrote the site. This is a revolving topic site that changes every year Mrs. Burns gets a new class. There are pictures, awards (gold stars), and all the things that you remember from 1st grade.

Praise: Dig that background! I talked in Chapter 7, "Images and the Visual," about allowing the images to tell most of the story of the page for you. Without one piece of text you would know this page had something to do with kids and school. The main banner is a chalkboard with chalk text writing and rewriting itself. The image of Mrs. Burns is darkened. Just the apple is given a touch of red.

Without knowing anything about the page, you would have to assume this is a teacher's page. The apple, the blackboard, and the background are great. Furthermore, just off the page is the link that gets you into the main site. It asks that you "Please come in and take a seat."

How many times did you hear that growing up? When you click, you enter into room 17, which is, I'm sure, Mrs. Burns' room.

I'm not a fan of pages that stop you from entering the site, but this one is so well constructed that it's hard to dislike it. Ted had taken every single stereotypical grammar school idea, text, or image and put it all together to create a page that explains itself through image and text. Well done.

The main page carries the background across and continues the use of images to convey school (see Figure 8.19). The pencils as links are brilliant. Ted has even made them rollovers.

Figure 8.19
More images that convey school.

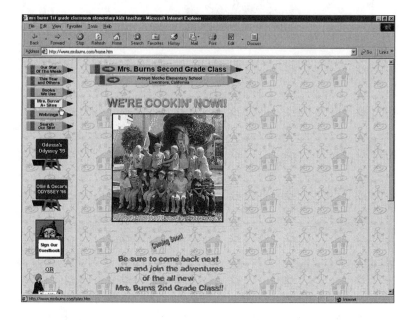

The text, again, works. Note the links text, "Mrs. Burns' A+ Sites." Get that school nomenclature in there.

When you delve deeper into the site, you get to Next and Back navigation represented by children looking in the direction you're supposed to go. Great.

I could go on and on about the use of correct images and text, but let me get back to the critique. What makes this site so good goes beyond the simple use of images and text—it's that Ted really understands whom this site is for, the parents. Yes, the kids may go in and others from the school district may go in, but this is built mainly for the parents.

In this site, there are images of the kids and the trips they took, like going to a Mexican Restaurant for Cinco de Mayo.

I think the biggest hit with parents would be when their son or daughter becomes the Star of the Week, as shown in Figure 8.20.

Hunter gets his own drawing, a list of the things he likes and gets to be the online star for a week. This is a winner. Parents would love this kind of thing.

I like this site a lot. It looks like Ted keeps it fresh and tends to the coding.

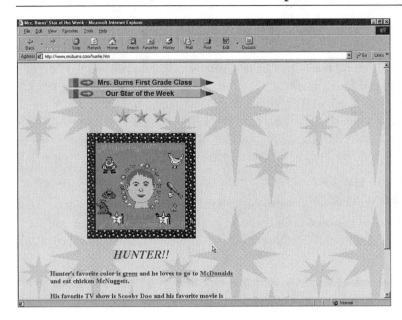

Figure 8.20
Way to go, Hunter.

Concern: I tell this to all of my classes. I think that Ted has also taken this concern into account. This actually should be a praise, but I wanted to make a concern so that it would be set apart from the long text above. I am not a fan putting small children's faces on the Web.

Ted has illustrated just about everything I would tell someone to do on a site involving small children. If you're going to put children's images on the Web, put only group photos and never put a name to a specific face. I see that Ted took this into account because his Stars of the Week pages only show cartoons of the children. That's good. Those who should know the child do, those who don't know the child, cannot.

I'm sorry to bring this up when discussing such a well-written, happy site, but there are just some very bad people out there and it's darn important to not give them any more advantage than the Web itself already grants them.

Suggestion: Ted has done everything right in terms of the children's faces. Just keep in mind that if you are going to put a child's face on the Web, do not attach a name, likes, dislikes, or locations. That could make the child a target. A sick individual could use this information to pinpoint that child's daily whereabouts and then lure the child into a false sense of comfort.

It's awful that I have to write that, but I do.

Concern: Ted, you have a selection of Midi music on just about every page. I listened to "Message in a Bottle" and "Takin' Care of Business" too many times. Your coding was set

273

up so that a plug-in window didn't open. I was forced to listen because I couldn't shut it off. Yes, you only looped the songs through once, but Ted, they were pretty long songs.

Suggestions: My guess is that those two songs have special significance or you wouldn't have used them. Background music is a real black or white deal. People either love it or hate it. My suggestion would be to either lose the songs altogether or make a point of telling me why you're playing them. If there's no reason for the songs other than you like them, then maybe they don't really belong there, but I bet they have significance—so tell me what it is.

Oh, and if you're only going to play them through once, shorten them up a bit. I can get the idea after only 10 or 15 seconds of music.

Concern: What is the difference between your Guestbook and your email? I went and entered some information so I know the Guestbook posts and the email just makes communication.

Suggestion: I would make that a little clearer by using text like, "Sign our Guestbook so everyone can read what you wrote."

Overall: I would have liked to have written more concerns, but they would have been picky and this site doesn't need to be nit-picked. Okay. One nit-pick. Some of your image rollovers are out. Fix them!

The site has won a series of awards (I see you put all the awards on a separate page—smart). You deserve every one of them. This is a solid model of what a school's or class's Web site should do and how it should perform.

Ted took the time to stop, think, and decide who the audience for this site would be, the parents. He plays to them with pictures, contact information, and praise of their children.

This is why I don't have kids. People would expect me to write Web pages for my kids' classes.

3. The {Not So} Daily Press/Author: Sarah Gates

`http://users.cnu.edu/~sgates/`

Load Time: 11 Seconds 57kps modem, cleared cache, 7/18/00 9:41AM.

My Screen Size: 1,024×768

Browsers Used: Internet Explorer 5 and Netscape Navigator 4.5

Figure 8.21
Ah, the morning paper...
(Color Plate C.24)

Concept: In the spirit of The Onion, Sarah Gates and some of her college friends decided to create a fake newspaper that would be filled with basically silly and goofy stories and just general ramblings about what they liked and disliked. Why not? I think it's a great idea. Who other than a few college students would have the time to actually keep up such a site? That's just the question...did they keep the site fresh?

I wish I knew. As you can see from the initial site figure, this is the final edition. My guess is Sarah graduated and abandoned the idea. I wouldn't. The Onion (http://www.theonion.com) started pretty much this same way and look at it today. You may want to think about grabbing a domain name and taking a real shot at turning this into a money-making venture.

Either way, let's look at the site.

Praise: I have done just this. I have written Web pages that were specifically designed to look like newspaper pages. If you think it's easy, give it a shot. I did mine the same way Sarah did hers—with big, involved tables. If you undertake such a project, follow this advice: Put a lot of comments into the code to remind yourself just where the heck you are on the page.

The masthead text is great. It looks like a newspaper. I'm also pleased you didn't go goofy with images but rather used only the bars or color. My newspaper had the weather report on one side of the banner headline and the price, free, on the other. It was too much.

Your use of links is good. I used the bylines when I did it. Yours are just as accessible.

The format looks good. I didn't really understand the content at all times, but I'm not 19, either.

Concern: You built this page with an 800×600 browser size in mind (see Figure 8.22).

Figure 8.22
Looks good...

In my larger monitor setting, the page seemed a little spread out.

Suggestion: You have the format inside of tables anyway, so use a WIDTH attribute inside of the main table flag and set the width to 750 so that it fits on larger monitor settings just as it does on the 800×600 it was designed for.

Concern: Your TITLE doesn't match the page. Remember that when someone bookmarks, it is the title text that is used to set the bookmark. Yours reads, "Updates Somewhat Less Than Daily." I get the joke and I see how it relates, but I lost your page because of it. When I was writing this book, I created huge bookmark lists of pages I wanted to use. I wanted to review your site from the get-go, but after bookmarking, I lost you. The text wasn't representative of the site.

Suggestion: I would change the text so that it describes the site. How about, "The {Not So} Daily Press"? That would work.

Concern: Bulk up the space between the columns. Your gutter is only the space allotted by the table border you've set to zero. It isn't so bad in the newspaper text itself, but down in the credit area, below the main text, the words from one column seem to run right into the next.

Suggestion: Again, since you're in a table format, it's easy to fix. Do one of three things, bulk up the cellpadding, bulk up the cellspacing (much different look), or add a very tall, thin cell between the content cells containing text. In that tall thin cell, put a line. The easiest way it to create a black image that's one by one pixel and through HEIGHT and WIDTH attributes, stretch that line to the correct heights. You've done a marvelous job of getting the columns all the same height, so the lines, too, will all be the same height. If that's a little rough then just bulk up one of the two padding areas. Do them both and see which you like better. One affects the text and the other won't. That's the basic difference.

Concern: You state that the site is updated now and again. That's not good. People only stop back to check so many times if they don't have a regular schedule to follow.

Suggestion: Try to set a timetable for updates. Once a week or even once a month is fine. I have a few sites that only update once a week or once a month that I go into all the time. I just know that it's Monday so these bookmarks are updated or it's the first of the month so these bookmarks must be updated.

Overall: Don't let this idea die unless you are so sick of it that you'd rather jump off a bridge than do the site anymore. You may be able to build it into something more than just a college fun site. If you do decide to try to make a go of it, get a domain, get a staff of writers who share the same dream, and pick a timetable to update the site.

Who knows, maybe you could write goofy news and commentary for the rest of your life. How fun would that be?

Chapter 9

Outside HTML

Over the years, I have been called a few names because of my stance on the newer tricks of the trade. Once the World Wide Web started to become the monster it is today, I began to dislike what I saw was happening.

The reason I am so gung ho about the Web is not that it offers information, but rather because it is a form of communication. I think the greatest thing about the Web is that it's little more than people making contact with others for no other better reason than they can. All the pages and the sites and the search engines are just methods of people letting each other know they are out there. What is important to me is important to someone else. We should find each other.

My first Web site included a page dedicated to my two cats. A few people in the computer department at my school frowned upon the page. They didn't feel it was an important enough topic for the Web. The fact was, my users did. That was the page that received the most email messages, and that's when HTML Goodies was just getting started.

We were ordinary people communicating over this Web of computers for no other good reason than we could. That was the great joy of the Web; we could communicate. This new programming language, HTML, was within the reach of just about anyone who could spell H-T-M-L. The language was so simplistic that often computer people would argue that it shouldn't even be considered a computer language. They wanted it called a mark-up language.

Heck, I'll call it Fred if you want. Who cares about the name? The language was within the grasp of the Weekend Silicon Warrior. We could all play. We could all be in the game. The Web was for the people. Personal computers were now becoming more than game-playing machines in people's homes.

Sometime in 1995, the rules began to change. Microsoft decided that the common 16-bit Windows for Workgroups operating system wasn't the best anymore. Bill Gates was going to take the Internet to a new level with this new 32-bit Windows 95 system. As a carrot on a string, he made an alliance with Sun Microsystems to push this new programming language called Java.

Design Goodies Survey

HTML Goodies Survey Question: How often do you enter a site that contains elements that you cannot run?

Often	15%
Sometimes	52%
Rarely	28%
Never	5%
N=497	

That 15% are the people that grab the latest technology first. The remainders are your users.

The change to Windows 95 took a toll on the Web. For the first time, there was a rift. There were people who could run everything, and there were people who could not. Those that held firm to their Windows for Workgroups never got to see Java Applets running. They would get errors.

Before that point, the only errors one would see were if someone had poorly coded a Web page. Now errors were flying around even though the coding was correct. The user was now the problem. The errors meant the user didn't have the correct updated equipment. I wrote long essays for classes and publication about how this change had hurt the Web. Surfing had all of a sudden taken on a kind of class-system mentality. There were the Windows 95 haves and the Windows 95 have-nots.

By the way, before you Mac fans out there explain that you were up to date all along, sorry, you weren't. When applets first came out, older operating systems, even though 32-bit, couldn't run them. It wasn't nearly as prevalent as the IBM wrangles, but it was out there.

The next rift came when Microsoft introduced Internet Explorer as a competitor to the greatly loved Netscape Navigator. Once the new browser hit the market, a new term began to fly around, proprietary.

Design Goodies Survey

HTML Goodies Survey Question: Have you ever entered a Web page where elements overlapped or ran into each other?

Yes   76%

No   24%

N=497

It's not an error, but the newest tricks of the trade can destroy your design if used incorrectly.

Proprietary basically meant that the command would work on only one browser or the other. The first big one was the Internet Explorer Marquee flag. Just that one simple flag would create a scroll across the Internet Explorer screen. To get an equal scroll, Netscape needed this new language called JavaScript, which they invented, by the way. It wasn't quite as usable on Internet Explorer as of yet. If you were using the right browser, the effect was displayed. If not…well…tough. A Marquee on Netscape Navigator simply posted text. Sorry, nothing will be scrolling today.

If you'd like to get a better idea of just how proprietary the Web has become, see my What-With-What tutorial online at `http://www.htmlgoodies.com/tutors/whatwithwhat.html`.

Back in 1997, I wrote that the computer geniuses were trying to take back the Web. With this blur of new commands, new flags, new languages, Web programming was becoming something that was getting out of the reach of the Weekend Silicon Warrior. In order to create an up-to-date Web page, not only must one know HTML, but also a knowledge of cross-coding, making sure your pages work on both browsers. In addition, JavaScript prowess was becoming a requirement.

In 1997, it was becoming so goofy on the Web I wondered if people weren't leaving because of it. There was a rivalry between Internet Explorer and Netscape Navigator users. Fans of one or the other would install JavaScripts that would post messages decrying you for using one browser or the other. There were even scripts that shut down your browser if you were using one the author didn't like. How stupid was that?

The best you could do was shake your head at the entire ordeal. Surfing could either be an enjoyable experience or it could be an error-filled romp. It all depended on what browser version you had. They were coming out at the rate of one every six months and each could do ten things the one before it couldn't do. If you had browser version 2 and the author had written a page specifically for browser version 3 then you were out of luck.

I often wondered why the people who created the browser didn't think about what would happen to someone surfing with a browser one level below what was required. The errors that would be produced were often silly, messing up the entire page layout, or throwing gray error box after gray error box.

Maybe the browser programmers wanted it that way so that it would force someone to go and download the latest browsers. Who knows?

That rift still exists today but not to the extent that it did a few years back. People do upgrade their browsers and the problem has become so well known that often designers compensate for it. However, you can still run into problems when you are using a browser that's one version too low or is incorrect for the proprietary commands the author has put on the page.

Today there's a new concern when surfing. If you cannot run something, you probably don't have the correct plug-in.

To their benefit, the browsers of today will at least attempt to go and get the plug-in for you if you'd like. You're not just left high and dry. That's a vast improvement over what used to be the case. In 1996, if you couldn't run an element, tough. It was up to you to get the fix. Now, at least, the browser will attempt to fix the problem.

The use of the latest and greatest technology can create stunning, interactive homepages, but they can also cause big headaches for the people you're attempting to serve. The purpose of this chapter is to discuss the latest and greatest tricks of the trade, how you can implement them and how you can use them, or not use them, to your advantage.

You Have Three Choices

When it comes to using the latest and greatest tricks of the trade, you really have three routes you can go. It all depends on your site, the technical level you want to reach on your site, and your attitude toward your users.

When considering each of these paths, just keep in mind the paramount concerns. The site is not for you as much as it is for your audience, your users. Content is the most important part of your Web site.

Content Path #1: Go with the Latest Stuff—The Audience Will Catch Up

This is a prevalent thought process on the Web today. People who follow the newest technology are inclined to jump on it immediately. When a new browser comes out, they get it and quickly start to implement all of the new tricks the browser can perform. To those who feel the same and have grabbed the proper browser and updated plug-ins, the page is fantastic. It jumps and twists and dances and everyone is impressed. To those who didn't upgrade, the page is error filled or static, or just plain doesn't display.

Design Goodies Survey

HTML Goodies Survey Question: Once you hear of a new browser version, do you:

Download it right away	17%
Get it when I have the time	41%
Wait a while to download	20%
Do nothing	22%

N=492

Almost half of your users are simply not moved to grab the latest browser versions. Of those that said they would download the new browser version, only 60% said they download it specifically for the newest Web page tricks.

Now, please, do not get me wrong. I don't believe this is a poor choice to make. It just all depends on what your site is for and who you expect will visit your site. HTML Goodies is always making a point of showing the latest stuff. If your site is dedicated to the latest technology or is a help site to get people up and running with the latest technology or your site is meant only for people who carry the same get-it-first mentality, go for it. Jump on those new events, offer links to plug-ins, offer examples, incorporate like crazy.

If your site is dedicated to your best chocolate-chip cookie recipes then you probably don't need the Flash introduction and DHTML-driven bowl of batter flying around your screen.

Just so we're all on the same page, Flash is a new style of animation. The program that creates these little animation is actually called Flash, thus the name. Think of it as a gif animation taken to the wildest extremes. People are now making multiple-minute movies using Flash animation. If you'd like to see a few, check out `http://www.shockwave.com`.

There are always some good ones there. You'll need to have the plug-in, though. Don't worry. You'll be offered the software once you log in.

It's actually a little tough to get a handle on DHTML because it's beginning to mean different things to a few different people. The actual term stands for Dynamic Hypertext Mark-up Language.

The essence of the term stands for almost any coding that creates movement or interactivity by employing the standards of the 4.0 level Netscape and MSIE browsers, but there was movement before with animation and interactivity with forms. Yeah, see...that's the rub. For something to be considered DHTML it has to employ version 4.0 browsers. Again, an argument I've heard is that DHTML is only viable if it occurs within the Explorer 4.0 browser. I've heard DHTML discussed as being PowerPoint for the Web. On the other hand, some people have stated that DHTML includes Netscape's Layering Commands. The best description I can offer is that DHTML is any combination of Style Sheets, JavaScript, Layering, Positioning, and Page Division (see the Positioning tutorial for more on this), at the 4.0 browser level, intended to create movement or user interactivity.

Above all else, if you decide to place some of the latest and greatest, stop and ask yourself, "Does this really add something to the page?" Don't rationalize an answer, either. Be honest to a fault. If the answer is yes then use the technology. We'll get into how in a short while.

If the answer that keeps coming up is, "I want it because I think it's cool," you probably shouldn't use it.

Okay, it's example time. Let's not talk about a huge DHTML event. Let's start small. The simplest and best example of employing technology that's not actually adding to a page that I can think of is the use of a clock. It's new. It's hip. It's going to look great having a running digital clock on your site, right? Figure 9.1 shows Rey B. Seno's page at `http://www.geocities.com/reyseno/`.

I like this page. It's kind of fun, so I have to ask, why the clock? What is it adding to the page? I feel it's actually taking away from the page not only because it isn't needed, but moreover because it's in a text box and draws the eye almost immediately. It's so different that it takes away from the remainder of the page.

When I ask students why they have the clock, they often answer that it would be a help to the user. I guess there's some logic to that, but keep in mind that while I am looking at your Web page, I am sitting at a computer terminal. I already have a clock. I already have the date. Now, if the time or date has some relevance to the page, then by all means use it, but if the clock is just there because you can put up a clock, or because you feel the user would like a clock, think twice about using it.

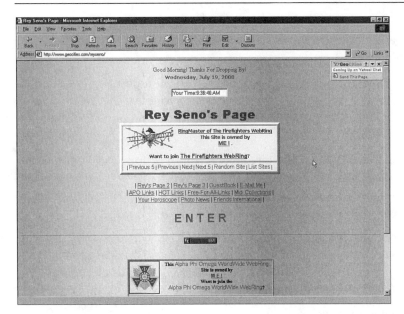

Figure 9.1
It's 9:38—do you know where your Web page is?

It's the same with all new technology. If it adds to the page, use it. If not then don't. It's pretty much that simple.

I know a clock is a small thing, but take this example as a method of thinking about any JavaScript, Java, DHTML, Flash, or whatever advancement. Does it add to the page? Is it redundant? Is it whiz-bang for the sake of whiz-bang? Finally, does it go to the killer app and help the user? If the answer is yes then keep it.

But if you keep it, how do you stop it from throwing errors for those who are not running the proper browser?

You accomplish it by following path #2.

Content Path #2: Use a Redirect JavaScript

I know people that just hate to do this because it involves a ton of extra work. If you don't remember what a redirect is, it's a small script that acts as a homepage. The user logs in and the script looks at the browser. If the user is running Internet Explorer, the script redirects him to a page specifically created for Internet Explorer. If the user is running Netscape Navigator, a redirect occurs and the user heads off to a Navigator optimized page.

I discuss it in greater detail, including the code that gets the job done, in Chapter 3, "Begin the Design."

The user never sees the script and it's one way I have found that allows you to use proprietary commands to death and not throw errors. The browser that cannot run the commands never sees the commands.

Redirect scripts, sometimes called browser detect scripts, are very common and can go from extremely simple little creatures to very involved monsters that not only check the browser type, but also its version number. That makes for a very long script and, of course, a lot of extra pages.

Rather than get into it here, if you'd like to see a redirect script in action, and maybe take it home with you, stop by the HTML Goodies Script Tips page at `http://www.htmlgoodies.com/stips/`. Script Tip number ten is a very simple redirect script. Script Tip 13 is a big ugly monster of a redirect script.

The downfall of the redirect script is that you put yourself in a page-writing corner. You really have no choice but to create one page for Internet Explorer and one page for Netscape Navigator. If you intend to continue using proprietary commands all the way through the site then you have to create duplicate pages each time you make a Web page.

In fact, you may have to make three. There are browsers out there that are not Internet Explorer or Netscape Navigator. There are text-based browsers that don't understand either browser's proprietary commands. These browsers include Opera, Cello, and Lynx. Browsers other than Internet Explorer or Netscape Navigator make up almost seven percent of the visitors to my Web sites. The redirect script must be set up to catch and serve these kinds of browsers as well.

Oh, yes. It can get quite time consuming, but if the effect is worth it then this is the way to go.

I have seen people set up two completely distinct directories. The redirect simply sends the user to the index page in whichever directory is appropriate and then the site works internally from there. That's not a bad method of setting up the system.

I've never done that because I feel it's a great deal of work and a huge use of space that I could be using for something else.

In terms of design and the latest and greatest, here's one more path you can take.

Content Path #3: Write Simply—Don't Use the Latest Technology

This is my favorite and this is why I catch grief for my views. I believe that content is the most important thing a Web page can deliver. I am often asked to look at Web sites that have so much extra baggage attached that the baggage starts to take over the page.

Animations are flipping around, clocks, dates, counters, new windows, JavaScript prompts, and the like are all going nuts while I am trying to read the pages.

Write simply. Use basic HTML and basic inline images. Use commands that are understood by the largest number of browsers. Wait on new technology until the vast majority of people actually have the browser that can run it.

That's usually a good long time after the browser has come out. Make an effort to write your pages so that they can be read and understood by the whiz-bang computer genius down the street and your Aunt Dolores in Cleveland.

I've said this before and I'll probably say it again. You cannot be hurt by what you don't use. If you do not put the latest stuff on your site, you won't get errors. If you do, you might. No one has ever entered a site and thought, "Gee, this is a great site with a lot of fantastic information. I just wish it had a clock."

In some people's minds there is a belief that new is better, that new makes the page better. It doesn't. If the content isn't there, no amount of programming can save it.

If you remember nothing else from this chapter, remember this:

I can only say "Oooooo!" once. From that point on you must either give me something new or I will become bored with the same fancy effect over and over again.

I might return to see an effect a couple more times, but that's about it. In short, I want the content but you keep throwing this thing at me. Very few fantastic effects can stand the test of multiple visits and still seem welcome.

Forced Interaction: JavaScript

With all of that said, let's talk about some of the tricks of the trade and the thought processes you should use when deciding whether to incorporate the trick or not.

Let me say again that I am not attempting to talk you out of or talk you into using any of these tricks. My goal is to give you the tools to make a correct decision when deciding to use any of the following elements.

There is no such thing as a truly bad design decision. Under the right set of circumstances and the right topic and the right audience, just about anything goes.

Just keep in mind the Lawn Ornament effect. I'll tell you what that is at the end of the chapter. Don't look! That's cheating.

Prompts, Alerts, and New Windows

JavaScript is a programming language developed in the research kitchens of Netscape. It is an amazingly versatile language that contains a small enough number of commands as to be able to be grasped by the Weekend Silicon Warrior.

Note

If you're interested in learning some JavaScript, I have a 30-step primers series online at `http://www.htmlgoodies.com/primers/jsp`. Of course, I also have a book on the subject titled *JavaScript Goodies*. Either one will start you at ground zero and get you up and running.

JavaScript is certainly not part of the latest and greatest, but what events users create with it fall into this category. How one uses JavaScript and how it displays on the page can be either helpful or annoying to those who are visiting your site.

JavaScript's main advantage is user interaction. Web pages tend to be static. That's the main argument against straight HTML pages and one of the main reasons people often cite for wanting to put the latest and greatest on their pages.

JavaScript is perfect for manipulating user data and offering help along the way. JavaScript creates image rollovers that brighten a page and assist the user in navigation. I could go on and on. I love JavaScript. Interaction is good, unless that interaction is forced.

Dig Figure 9.2.

The following page is by Rohan Roy. It's called Scooby's Supermall and you can find it at `http://www.scoobysupermall.freeservers.com/`.

Notice the JavaScript prompt? It wants to know my name. I don't know whether I want to give it my name or not. While I know what the author is trying to do, those new to the Web might see this as more than an invasion. They might see it as fiendish. They might think that if they give out their name then somehow this author will use it to do bad things.

The problem with not giving it my name is that the big white section there requires the prompt information be entered for the page to load. If don't give my name, the page doesn't load. Okay, I'll play. I put in the name "Erik the Great." If the guy wants my name, the effect he's going to produce must be great, right? I might as well give him an important-sounding name.

The effect produced is so small that you may have missed it. The text is up there just above my cursor. It reads, "Welcome to Scooby's Supermall Erik the Great" (see Figure 9.3).

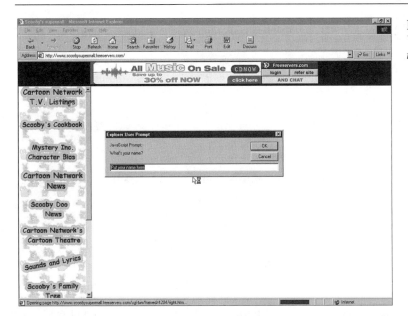

Figure 9.2
Why do you want my name?

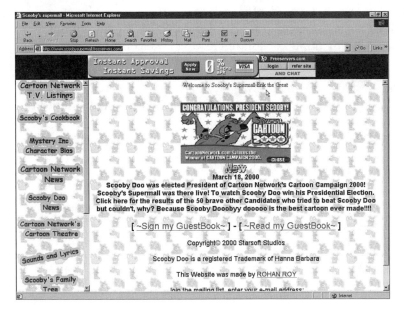

Figure 9.3
Thanks...

Design Goodies Survey

HTML Goodies Survey Question: What do you usually do when a JavaScript prompt pops up asking for information?

Enter the information	28%
Click Cancel	57%
Enter false information	15%

N=490

Is it that important to have the prompt when only 28% may even use it correctly while the rest dislike the effect?

Now, was that greeting really worth making a user stop and enter a name? If I didn't put in a name, the line reads "Welcome to Scooby's Supermall Null."

Who's this Null guy?

Null is JavaScript for nothing entered. Please don't think that I am decrying this effect because the text it produced was small. If you do, you might feel that I would be more impressed had it created much bigger welcome text. Throwing up a JavaScript prompt as a person enters the page is equal, in my mind at least, to creating a welcome page that greets the viewer and asks him to click to enter the site.

Why? Why did you stop me? Just let me come in. Would I have liked the site less had it simply read, "Welcome. Thanks for coming in"? No. I would have never actually noticed the text past a quick read. The prompt brought my attention to it and I actually felt let down. You created all that prompt concern for a simple greeting? I expected much more.

Figure 9.4 is another example of forced JavaScript interaction.

Being from Cleveland, I'm not so sure that the Vikings Rule, but what I do know is that that JavaScript alert doesn't. If the author, Laura Piper, wanted to tell us all that the Vikings rule, then why not put it on the page? It's a great page, too. It's very well done.

In fact, look again. Laura used JavaScript in a much better way at the top of the page. This is a football fan page. Football fans will come in. What does a football fan care about?

Uhhhhh...football?

Yes! Laura has put up a JavaScript that is offering a countdown to football's opening day. That is a correct use of a date function. The date means something to the page. The JavaScript that uses the date then offers good information to the users who stop in.

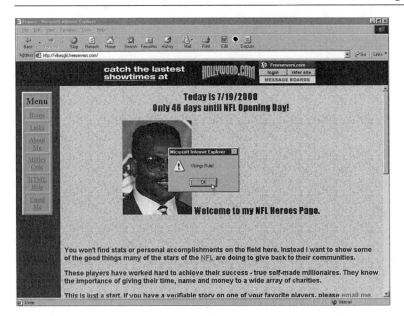

Figure 9.4
Well, I am Erik the Great!

Just lose that JavaScript alert at the beginning.

Figure 9.5 is another one.

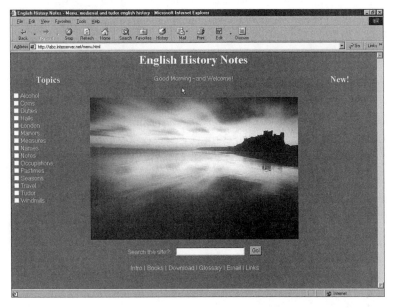

Figure 9.5
And Good Morning to you, too.

This is Andrew Burt's English History Notes page at `http://abc.interserver.net/menu.html`. The page told me good morning—and it actually is morning. I write early in the day when I can consume a lot of coffee.

I know it's a little thing, but it's helpful and it's not intruding upon the user.

So, When Do You Use the Prompt and the Alert?

When their name suggests. The prompt is meant to enter information. By setting up the prompt to pop up when a person enters a page, you are basically forcing the interaction. Prompts should be used when the user knows he is going to be prompted. Maybe you have a section on your page that will figure a person's age in dog years, or tell their sign. That's when you use the prompt and you only use it when the user says it's okay to use it. That means the user should have to click on something to trigger the prompt to display.

A prompt should pop up only when the person who will fill in the information requests it. That's about as clear as it gets.

As for the Alert, it should be used only when the name suggests, when the user needs to be alerted to something. That might include some dirty language is ahead or going into a certain page means a cookie will be set or that an appropriate plug-in is required for the next set of pages.

Alerts are also very good for helping a person fill out difficult forms or alerting people when the information they have entered isn't quite right. This is provided you don't use so many that it badgers the user.

It certainly isn't needed to let people know that the Vikings Rule.

Now, How About Those Pop-Up Windows?

I know you've made your way into a site that, upon entering, immediately popped up another window. Usually, it's a banner advertisement, or a contest, or a survey, or something else that the author wants to promote above all else in the site. The best example of pop-up window use is the free server Tripod (see Figure 9.6).

I had to laugh out loud when I saw this page first come up. This is a Bible study page by James Williams first found at `http://members.tripod.com/jesuslivestoday/`.

Notice the text under the pop-up window. It reads, "I wish I had said that." My first reaction was, "Said what?" I couldn't see the quote. That pop-up window sat right on top of it. Of course, James doesn't have a whole lot of choice in the pop-up window matter; the Tripod server forces you to put them up in return for free service.

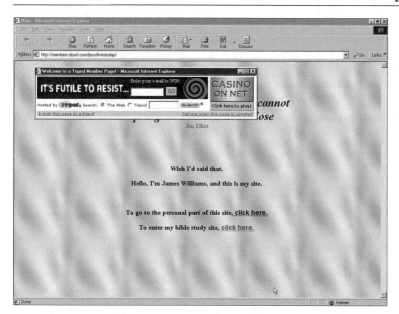

Figure 9.6
*What? Said what? What
are you talking about?*

Now, stop and think. How do you personally like it when a pop-up window appears without your requesting it? Do you welcome it or do you get rid of it straightaway?

If you're anything like those who responded to the HTML Goodies survey, you close it right away. In fact, over 70% of all respondents said they close the window without even caring to see what comes up. They often close it before it even has a chance to display its text.

One of the most common letters sent to the HTML Goodies site is a request for a JavaScript that will kill the pop-up windows on a Tripod, or now Geocities, site. If you dislike the window then why are you on the site? Is the free space really worth something you hate?

And if you hate the window so much, why would you think about putting one on your own site?

It's fairly obvious that people do not like forced additional pop-up windows. Unless you have a very, very good reason for using them, one of which I cannot think of right now, don't.

So, When Do I Use Pop-Up Windows?

The answer is the same as before, when the user knows it's coming. I have written numerous primer pieces that have little assignments at the end. You can grab the answer to the assignment by clicking a link. The link opens a new window that displays the answer. I actually go as far as putting the text "This will open in a new window" under the link text.

Many people use new windows when they offer links to sites off their site. CNN.com does this a lot. The purpose is to allow users to see the secondary site then easily return just by closing the window.

I followed this line of login on my wife's business site `http://www.streetartist.com`. After you arrive at a page, you can click on links to meet the artist. That artist page opens in a new window sized smaller than the main window so that you can easily close the new window to return to the paintings page. It looks like Figure 9.7.

Figure 9.7
Hello, Masri.

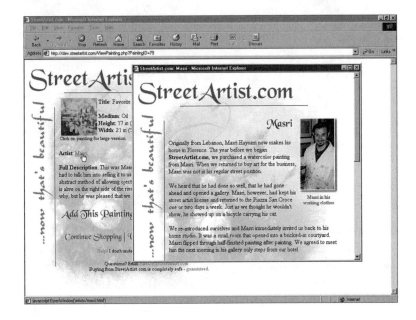

To be even more helpful, at the bottom of the page that opens, I offer a link that closes the window for the user.

That's important. Do not offer back navigation in a new window because often there is no Back. Back often means to return to the page that spawned the new window. You get there by closing the window.

There are many times I'll open some HTML code in a new window so that HTML Goodies readers can continue with the tutorial while referencing the code. However, the user always knows that a click will produce a new window before it does.

What should you do if this discussion has signed you off of pop-up windows yet you do have some information you want displayed right away? You cannot wait for the user to click and open a page. Whatever it is, it's really important!

Use the design of your site to offer and showcase that information. If you have something that is so important that you feel it belongs in a pop-up window, place that information on your homepage close to the top-left corner. Set it aside with color or inside a table cell so that the eye is drawn to it much more easily.

If you don't feel that is sufficient then have the information appear as a welcome page to your site. Yes, I know I rally against this and have said don't do it 505 times already, but if it's between creating a welcome page and using a pop-up window, use the welcome page. My first choice, however, would be to place the information on the homepage in the most important section of your design.

If you dislike pop-up windows when you surf, don't make a point of taking space on a server that has pop-up windows. Yes, the server may be free, but you're upsetting many of your users. Think about getting on a pay-for server.

Oh, one more thing about pop-up windows...

There's one use of pop-up windows that is disliked by an almost unanimous margin. That's the pop-up window that appears when the person tries to leave the site. Avoid using one of these at all costs.

Hey, you know what else would help bring attention to some text on your page?

Make it scroll.

Text Scrolls

Scrolling text is very popular. It's quick, it calls attention, it's unobtrusive to the remainder of the page, and it doesn't slow the page loading. It's a real win-win element to put on a Web page. Today, scrolls can go every which way. Java Applets allow text to scroll vertically, JavaScript and the Internet Explorer Marquee tag make scroll easy to put on the page. I'm a fan of text scrolls as long as a few simple rules are followed.

1. Make Sure It Scrolls

Remember that the Internet Marquee tag is proprietary. That means it works only in Internet Explorer. That was true at the time of this writing; it may be different now, but remember that even if the latest Netscape Navigator runs the Marquee, many earlier version do not.

What's the fix? The easiest is to use JavaScript to create the scroll. That works across browsers. It's either that or making a point of using a redirect script so that Netscape browsers do not get the chance to see the Marquee tag.

2. Easy on the Text

Don't make your scrolls overly long. Make the text no longer than twice the size of the window in which it will display. People will not sit through *War and Peace*–length texts be it a horizontal or vertical scroll.

3. Don't Offer URLs Unless the Scroll Is Active

If you put a URL, or an email address into a scroll but then offer no method of using or copying the link, that's frustrating. Make the scroll active or don't offer a link.

4. Think Twice Before Putting a Scroll in the Browser Status Bar

Figure 9.8 is the Uglysecretary. com homepage. It's quite a site, but that scroll…hmmmm.

Figure 9.8

Is the scroll getting in the way here?

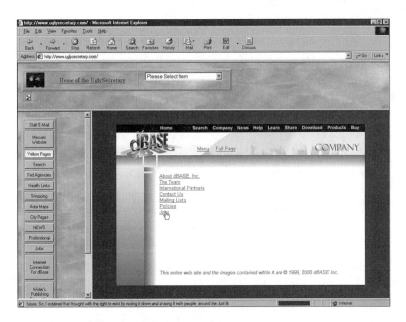

Two-thirds of the people that responded to the HTML Goodies survey suggested they want-ed to see text in the status bar when the mouse passes over a link. Those that answered that they wanted to see text overwhelmingly said they wanted to see the page URL. Others said they wanted text describing the page.

The scrolling text will always take precedence in the browser's mind. If you roll your point-er over the links, the URL will flash for a split second, but then the scroll will again take over.

Users want the URL far more than they want the scroll. If you want a scroll on your page, maybe you should put it on your page not in the status bar.

5. Give Me a Reason for the Scroll

As with everything else on your page, make sure there is a reason to use the scroll. If the only reason you're putting it on your page is because you think it's a cool effect then maybe you shouldn't use it. Remember that a scroll is motion on an otherwise static page. It will draw the eye. If you draw my eye and all you have to say is, "Hello, welcome to my page," then you might have just wasted my time.

Animated Images

Didn't this section belong in Chapter 7, "Images and the Visual"? Yes. In fact, I do mention animation a great deal in Chapter 7, but I want to return to it here for a moment. Animated images are items that add to a page but are not really required much like all of the elements mentioned above. Here's my take. I love animated images. I make them all the time. I find them full of life and great to add to a page. I have animation on my personal as well as my professional pages.

Animations are great, but they're often a lot like Halloween candy. You know you should only eat one, but two isn't so bad. Three is better. Four! Five! Wow! Look at my page. The whole page is just dancing around like crazy. I think I'm getting ill.

The more animations you put on a page, the more visual stimulation you are offering to your audience. Advertising banners are animated for just that reason. The banner wants to pull attention.

Animations are wonderful if used correctly. When deciding to use an animation, keep a few things in mind.

Animation Concern #1: The More Animations, the Less Attention Each Will Get

Since you know animations draw attention, why put so many on the page that they actually fight? Here is an example of an animation used correctly. Figure 9.9 is The Stancliffe Group site by Steve Finney at `http://www.thestancliffegroup.co.uk/index2.html`.

It's hard to display an animation in a static capture, but do you see the bar marked "News"? That bar has a blinking red light on it. That's the only animation on the page and my eye went to it immediately. That's what the author wanted to happen and that's what he got.

Figure 9.9
Blink, blink, blink...

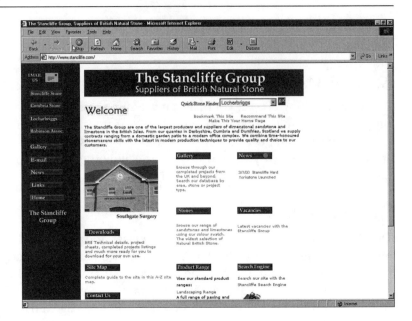

Now, those of you who enjoy a lot on animation might find this a little difficult to take, but stop and look at your page. What is the point of each animation? If you have Charlie Brown dancing and Hello Kitty stepping back and forth and your name flying around a small box, what are the reasons? If the answer is because they look cool, you may want to rethink your decisions.

Which leads me to my next item to keep in mind regarding animation.

Animation Concern #2: Don't Animate It If It Doesn't Need to Be Animated

Figure 9.10 is Wayne Morgan's site at Photo4u.com. Do you see the blurb just above Photography For Sale As Digital Images?

That's the name of the site, Photo4u, animated so that it spins in a big circle flying away and then back at you every second and a half.

That text is what I call the identifier of the site. It is what people will remember from the site. By animating it, you did call attention to it, but half of the time, I can't read it. Also, because of the size the image space required to fly off into the distance, a great deal of white space has been created at the top of the page, pushing the really important stuff down below the gatefold.

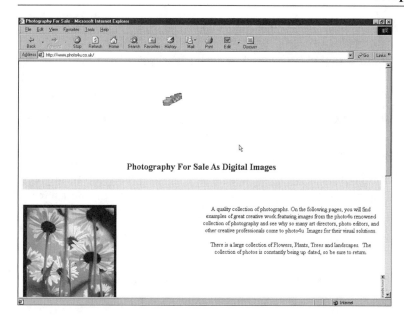

Figure 9.10
Photo4u, whee! Photo4u, whee!

Did this need to be animated? No. At least it didn't have to be animated to this extent. The animation could have been the letters changing colors or a flashbulb going off, or something else that had to do with the page. That way the identifier could have stayed stationary, always in view, and the remainder of the page could be brought up so that it appears on the page first thing when the site loads.

Animation Concern #3: Be Sure the Animation Fits in with the Site

This should go without saying, but I find proving my firm grasps of the obvious fun and challenging. It happens all too often that someone will build a wonderful site that will truly help others and then for some reason, sticks a little animated cartoon in one of the corners or down at the very bottom.

I understand that the cartoon is meant to be whimsical, but often takes away from the site. If your intention is to be whimsical then make the animation at least have something to do with the page.

I don't know who created the dancing Hobbes cartoon character animation, but it gets more play on more Web sites than any other animation I think I've ever seen.

I see that animation all over college Web sites and I don't mean just student pages, either. Someone will put up a page for the registrar's department and there's Hobbes. I saw another animation on the homepage of a school's business department where a little car kept driving across the bottom of the page. I'm sure there was a reason for the car, probably an inside joke, but I wondered what it meant. If I were the dean of the department, I would have asked that it be taken down. It took away from the grandeur the rest of the page attempted to create.

Search out an animation that is not only whimsical but fits. How about using a guy typing furiously on a keyboard for a computer store or a graduate throwing his cap into the air for a school page, both of which I have seen, by the way?

At this point, many of you are having the same reaction many of my students have after this discussion. They get a little miffed because they want their page to be fun and their site to be alive.

Note that I am not telling you to not use animation. I am suggesting that you use the animation correctly.

I brought up the dancing Hobbes animation because I actually had a student like the animation so much that she built a page specifically to use the image. It was a page dedicated to Calvin and Hobbes.

Perfect. Now it fits.

Animations, like a lot of other fancy Web page elements discussed here fall under the Lawn Ornament theory of life. Again, I'll tell you what that is at the end of the chapter. No peeking.

Speaking of animations, at the time of the writing of this book, the biggest animation program to date was beginning to take hold, Flash.

Flash Animation

Wow. What a program. At this point in time, I have only dabbled in Flash, but from what I can already see myself doing, I am just amazed.

Flash sites are out there and the number is growing everyday. The program is allowing tremendous interaction, sounds, new mouseover events, and movies to play over the Web. If I were to pick the next real wave to wash over the entire Web, it would be Flash.

Flash animation is used three ways as of the writing of this book. The first is opening a site with a flash animation. The second is using Flash in the navigation of a site. The third is building the entire site out of Flash (see Figure 9.11).

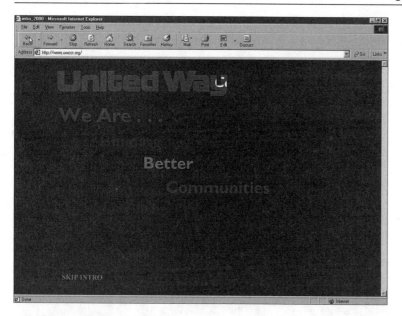

Figure 9.11
United Way of California at http://www.uwccr. org/main.htm.

Jeff Howes has to be proud of this site. The Flash animation that drives that opens the site is just fabulous. There's music, flying text, and effects just short of fireworks to get some-one psyched up to see the site.

Jeff used Flash as an introductory section. He did it correctly, too. Here's how:

- He used a small loading animation sequence so that the user wasn't sitting there star-ing at a blank screen. The loading sequence told people that something was coming.

- The Flash animation was small enough that the loading sequence didn't run through 50 times before the main sequence ran.

- The user was given a Skip Intro link so he didn't have to sit through the sequence every time they logged in.

- The main page was a separate page from the Flash animation so that that main page could be bookmarked skipping the entire animation.

- He carried Flash across into the site.

The last one is the one that often spells trouble for some sites using Flash animation. I have stated numerous times that using a Welcome Page that asks the user to click to enter the site is not such a solid idea.

Well, all too often people will set up a stunning Flash animation to run as a Welcome page. The animation runs and when finished, a basic Web site pops up. The animation acted simply as long welcome page. It is my opinion that you either go Flash or you do not go

Flash. Just sticking an animation at the front of your site acts a great deal like a Welcome Page. It stops me from coming in and slows down the loading of the site.

Where I feel flash is most useful to a site is within its navigation system. If you want to carry Flash into a site, your links are where it can be put to best use. If you use Flash to create a little movie while people are in your site, that little movie isn't much more than an animation.

This, of course, does not apply to Flash movie sites like Joecartoon.com where the main purpose is to play Flash movies.

Figures 9.12 and 9.13 are Jon Berry's Digibrill site at `http://www.hrfn.net/~digibrill/`.

Figure 9.12

After a short loading sequence, this navigation appeared.

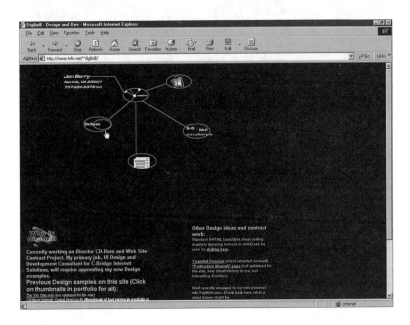

What you cannot see is the little animation that occurs after the click to display the text. It's quick and fun to watch.

I would suggest that an opening sequence is fun, and as long as you offer the elements Jeff offered previously, it can be useful, but if you're interested in getting Flash animation into your site, skip the opening sequence and work on the navigation first. This is where Flash really sings.

The third type of site I mentioned previously was the site made entirely of Flash. I'm impressed to no end with this type of site because I can only imagine the work and time it would take to build such an animal.

Speaking of animal, dig the longhorn in Figure 9.14.

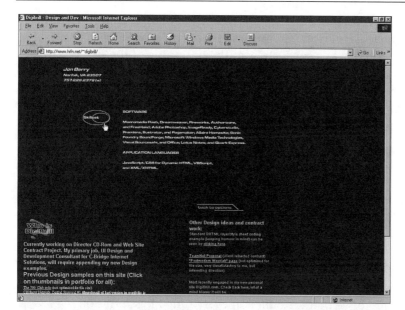

Figure 9.13
This is what you get after a click.

Figure 9.14
Powerlifting and a power site.

The Longhorn powerlifting site, located at the University of Texas, is Flash from front to back. It was written by Chris Kahanek and you can find it at `http://www.utexas.edu/students/power/index.html`. There was a small show at the beginning of the site, but that ended quickly and the remainder came in equally fast. The site offers everything a basic HTML-based site would offer, but this does it with an update appearance and far more user interaction. Movement from page to page is a show in itself. All the time you're surfing, the banner text continues to flow with color.

The site looks alive and it looks like it is playing with you rather than acting upon your wishes. I almost expect the computer to thank me when I click. I'm sure Chris could add a few commands and get that—although I wouldn't.

The odd thing is that I never tired of the Flash the entire time I was in the site. The events were so short and such a part of the site that they never seemed to get dull. Now, had a 10-second event occurred every time I clicked, maybe I would have grown tired, but this worked very quickly and without much pomp and circumstance.

The site is so self-contained that you never leave the main page. That seems to be its one very small downfall. I do hate to see that introduction every time I log in. It's only a few seconds long, but I would still put up a Skip Intro button.

Flash animation is the wave of the future and if you want to get into the programming, you should. Just remember that like any other programming that's new to the Net, you might run into a few problems. The first is that your users will require a plug-in to run the site. The plug-in isn't large, but if you throw a Flash-based site at someone that doesn't have the plug-in, an error message will pop up.

Flash is becoming so popular that as time goes on, more and more people will get the plug-in. Just fewer than 50% of those polled by HTML Goodies said that they get plug-ins when asked to. Almost 30% noted they do get plug-ins, but at a later time. Only 15% reported they would leave a site if a plug-in were required.

Handling this new technology is usually done one of two ways. The first is to hope people have the plug-in and just run the animation. I think this option will become more and more popular as Flash becomes more and more popular.

The second method is to stop the user at the front door and ask them which site they would like to see. Lori Sullivan went this route on her site Princessgeek.com (see Figure 9.15).

As much as I dislike Welcome pages, I am not against this one. It's saved an error and my thinking is that a page that stops you for a moment is a lot better than a page that might throw an error and beg you to download a plug-in.

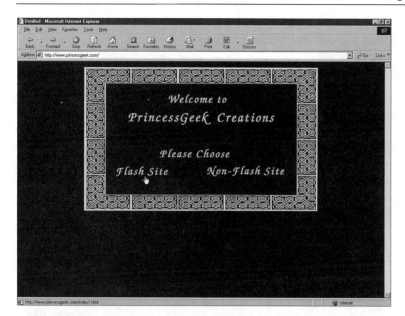

Figure 9.15
Your highness, I presume?

Note

A quick note about plug-ins

While going through the hundreds of sites that were sent in hoping to become part of this book, I ran into a lot of pages that asked me to download a new plug-in. Comet Cursor was the most popular.

If the new element that you want to run requires the user to download a plug-in, do not make that element a necessary part of your page. Most people won't download the plug-in just when you tell them to and many won't download it at all.

By not making the element a necessary part of the page, when it doesn't display, nothing is really lost from the page.

Flash is coming on strong and if you're a little bored with your Web site, give it a try. The animation program is like a big toy box. I found it pretty easy to wrap my brain around. You will, too, and soon your site will be fresh and new again.

Cascading Style Sheets (CSS)

I'll bet at least one person has noticed that up until this point in time, I haven't mentioned CSS. It's not that I dislike CSS; quite the contrary. I think it's spectacular. I think it's one of the greatest inventions to come to the Web to date.

The reason I haven't specifically talked about CSS is the same reason I haven't specifically talked about HTML coding. This is a design book, not a book devoted to coding.

The vast majority of the events, effects, and general page impressions I've discussed up until this point can be created using either HTML or CSS. Whichever you would like to use is fine with me.

Just remember that as with anything else in this chapter, CSS has a proprietary effect to it. Some commands work only on one specific browser or another.

The really good thing about CSS is that many of the commands that don't work on one browser or the other, don't also throw errors. They are what I have termed ignored commands.

For example, at the time of my writing this book, Internet Explorer allowed for the command, hover. Used correctly, hover would change the color of a link when the mouse pointer sat on top. Netscape Navigator didn't support the command; thus, there was no color change.

That's it. No color change. There was also no error or real problem for the site. That's what I call an ignore command.

So, long story short, CSS is a great way to get many of the effects described in this book, but if you never use it and always get the effect you want through HTML, all the better. It really comes down to whatever works for you. If you make a point of always checking your pages in two different browsers before taking them live, then you'll see where one command worked and another one is needed. You may have to go with CSS or you may have to go with HTML to get the effect you want across browsers. It's all about what works and what makes the page display correctly cross-platform.

DHTML, XML, XHTML, and All the Little MLs

Between 1999 and 2000, new, and supposedly better, programming languages started coming out that all claimed they would eclipse HTML and push the Web in a new direction.

Before you jump on a new format for your writing, remember that any new language that makes its way to the Web immediately carries problem baggage with it. DHTML (Dynamic HTML) only works on Internet Explorer 4.0 and above. Some claim that Netscape's

Layering function is also DHTML. Even if you accept that that is the case, the problems still remain. DHTML commands are proprietary. Layering does not work on Internet Explorer and the majority of the commands that would be referred to as DHTML do not run on Netscape Navigator (as of the writing of this book).

XML (Extensible Markup Language) is a coding format that is quite similar to HTML but is different in that it is far more strict. From a programming standpoint, that's perfect. XML can be used to create better Web pages that can be catalogued much more specifically within search engines. The language would allow searches like "dog" to only find the four-legged animal without bringing up all those pages that have the word "dog" in another context.

In order to run XML, you must be using Internet Explorer 5.0 or better. XML is becoming an accepted language behind the scenes of the Internet. Search engines and programming houses are setting up their systems to run off of XML. In fact, the company that I work for, EarthWeb, will be taking their entire operation to XML very soon.

Note

As of this writing, the site had gone completely XML just before being sold to Internet.com. Some examples can still be found by visiting http://www.developer.com.

Will XML make its way to the mainstream and will the average Weekend Silicon Warrior begin using it? I honestly doubt it. It's too restrictive and zaps a lot of the fun out of building a Web page. I see HTML being the preferred language of the Web for a very long time.

XHTML is, in my eyes, a compromise. Those in the know understand that XML will not easily make its way into the mainstream so XHTML was created to help it along. Depending on whom you speak to, XHTML is either HTML with XML extensions or it's XML with HTML 4.0 stuck inside. I don't know that it makes a difference which ML comes first. The outcome is still the same. What I do know is that one must be running a higher version of Internet Explorer to see XHTML pages.

By the time you read this, another ML version might very well be making some smaller headlines across the Web. While each of these languages has its good and bad points, I think the main thing you should be concerned with is the audience's browser's ability to read the languages.

The one good thing about each of these languages is that they in no way expect to completely overtake HTML. That would be quite foolish. There are so many HTML pages out there on the Web that to all of a sudden proclaim them all dead would be foolish.

When you put your site together, not only do you have to choose what elements will be included, but now also have the choice of what language you would like to use.

Again, the choice depends a great deal on what you would like to do with the site and who your audience is most likely to be. When I was researching for my short piece on XML at `http://www.htmlgoodies.com/tutors/xml.html`, I went to numerous sites that were written fully in XML. That made sense. The purpose of the site gave rationale to using the language.

I would wonder if a page dedicated to the local bowling league would benefit from a site built out of XML?

Probably not.

The Lawn Ornament Theory

All the way through this book, I have continually hit upon the fact that there really is no incorrect coding, color, or image use as long as the site that will present the effect is supported. What works for one site may not work for another site. If an effect works for your site, use it. If it doesn't but it's a really cool effect, don't use it.

Well, allow me to complete this discussion of the newest tricks of the trade with what I call the Lawn Ornament Theory. It goes:

> "One is charming. More just starts to get silly."

If you place a single lawn ornament, it looks charming. A little ceramic rabbit, or a dragon-fly made out of wire (I have this one) by itself looks great. I think you can even get away with a gnome or gazing ball if that's the only thing in the yard.

It's when you begin to have a gazing ball, a bunny, butterflies up the wall, the wooden cutout of the woman bending over so you can see her bloomers, a turned-over bucket of dirt with flowers planted in the dirt, and a black silhouette of a man leaning up against a lamp post smoking a pipe that it all starts to go downhill.

> "One is charming. More just starts to get silly."

It's the same with your Web site. The effects that the latest and greatest allow are really neat, but not all at the same time.

If you have a single animation, or a single JavaScript effect, or a single scroll, or a single Java Applet, then it's something that adds without taking over the most important part of the page, the content.

It's when you log into a page that has numerous animations, a counter, three scrolls, a JavaScript prompt, and a pair of eyeballs following your mouse all around the browser screen that it just starts to get silly.

Here it is as plainly as I can put it. Content is the most important thing on your site. Everything else is simply support.

Period.

Site Critiques

1. Zentropa/Author: Peter Thorn

`http://www.zentropa-film.com/`

Load Time: 24 Seconds 57kps modem, cleared cache, 7/21/00 9:00AM.

My Screen Size: 1,024×768

Browsers Used: Internet Explorer 5 and Netscape Navigator 4.5

Figure 9.16
Welcome to Zentropa. Got 4.0? (Color Plate C.25)

Concept: The site is a little difficult to get a handle on. The programming is different from any site I've run into before or since. Zentropa is a collaboration between director

Lars Von Trier and producer Peter Aalbæk Jensen who worked together on a film titled Europa. The English title is Zentropa.

I wrote that earlier because that's what the site had written to it. The problem is that the entire time I was within the site, I got the feeling that I was being taken, that this was a bit of a joke and I was falling for a little too much of. There were images of Von Trier with Bjork, but they looked a little doctored like they were built for the site. There were links to many different movies and a Web design company, but I never got the feeling any of the links were quite on the up and up.

That, to me, was the real draw of the site. I liked going from link to link wondering whether the authors were giggling at me the entire time. If they are not, and all this is for real, then I say, Bravo! Too often people build sites that are to be outside the mainstream but fall short. This site has all the elements of being against the grain and outside the traditional programming of a Web site. It is rebellious like Nirvana in the '90s rather than Pat Boone in the '50s.

Praise: I was almost turned off by the site at first because they had a welcome page, which you see in Figure 9.16. The page appears quite stark, but seemed to take forever to load. The page is filled with browser tests to see whether I was a Mac user and to see color levels. Plus there's a counter on the page but the author, Peter Thorn, has hidden it by setting the height and width to one each.

Where the site just begins to come alive is after you click to enter. It looks like Figure 9.17.

Figure 9.17
I've got a Mac desktop on my IBM.

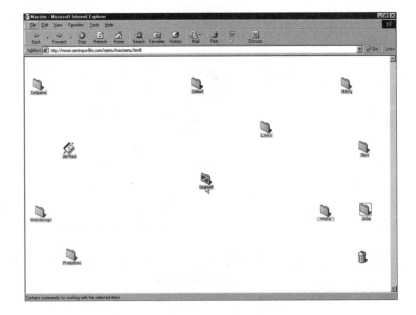

The desktop idea is great. I have numerous friends that are Mac fans and this is what their desktop looks like. We IBM people like our icons all lined up nice and pretty. Mac users, for some reason, want their program icons to be all over the place. The page resized nicely and every icon has its own rollover function popping up the "Z" as you can see in Figure 9.18.

For fun, even the trash icon is active. It takes you to a page that has a sendup of the movie *The Matrix*. You can click either the red or the blue pill. You'll just have to go and see what happens.

As far as I saw, that was the only link that opened in the same window as the Mac desktop. Past that, the site works like an operating system. The author set up each link so that it would open in a new window giving the impression a new application had opened (see Figure 9.18).

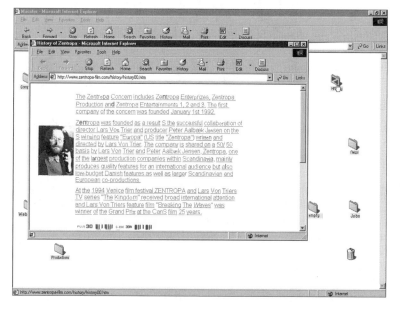

Figure 9.18
The history link opened.

Each of the pages that open are either colored wildly or the text is hand-drawn by what looks like an eight-year-old.

It works.

The page that opens when you click "companies" looks innocent enough until you click the link inside. Then you get a mosaic built out of new windows. I had to close the windows and see it a couple more times to really marvel at the effect. I had never seen anything like it before (see Figure 9.19).

Figure 9.19
Look at the windows as a whole. They make an image.

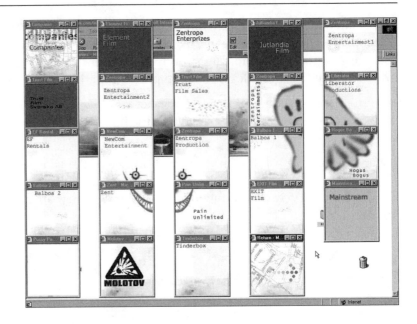

That effect had to take a good long while to work out, but the time seems well worth it.

The Zentropa site is a fantastic piece of work simply because it breaks every rule of traditional Web site design, but it works. The desktop idea is wonderful, but I do have a concern. I'll address it in a moment.

Undertaking a site like this would be an involved task, but the results would serve to set your site apart from all of the rest. I don't mean that you should copy the site; I mean that you should take the time to stop and think if your Web site idea could possibly use a design so far out of skew with the rest of the pages out there that wrong would become right.

Concern: Copyright. I think you actually used Mac icons. I'll bet you got them from simple screen captures. I've seen that done with IBM icons, also. People have used the folder icon or the Notepad icon to make a point. Those elements are copyrighted and Apple may not take too kindly to your using them. Yes, your site might not be that big or get that many viewers, but keep in mind that copyright law reads that a company may forfeit their protection if they do not take steps to enforce copyright. That means the biggest will have to come after the smallest if the copyright is to be upheld.

Suggestion: Ask permission to use the elements. Until you receive permission, either put up folder images of your own creation or put up a statement saying that the images are copyright Apple. The first is the one I would follow. Using without permission and hoping a simple thanks will suffice may spell doom. Usually copyright wrangles begin with the owning party asking that the offender cease and desist. If that happens, don't fight it. You were in the wrong to begin with.

Concern: You probably wanted this effect, but I had no idea what to click on first. There didn't seem to be any one icon that jumped out and grabbed me right off. The trash was the only different icon so I went for it first. There was also a get Flash icon, but I knew what that did and didn't click. I think that led to my being a little confused about what the site is actually about.

Suggestion: Set aside a single link in some way. Make it a different color or a little bigger or place it in the upper-left corner. Make that the icon that offers the description of the site and offered help with navigation.

Again, you may not do this because maybe that is just the effect you're shooting for.

Concern: The Companies page that opens all of the smaller windows is great, but once I see the effect, then I have to close every window. I looked at your code and saw how you placed each window. Clever. What I didn't like, then, was I had to close every window.

If you opened them all, you could close them all through a similar JavaScript format using the `window.close()` statement. You have a space open in the lower-right corner. Put a button in there that reads "Close Them All." That would help.

Concern: You have a smaller window open up that has some rather dirty images and text. I blanked it when I made the screen capture.

Suggestion: I am not a prude by any stretch, but the dirty stuff didn't fit with the rest of the site and actually lowered my thinking of the site. Yes, a few teenaged boys will giggle at the image and text, but women and older persons will probably not find it as amusing. Your site is irreverent enough without having to resort to bathroom-level humor.

Overall: I dug this site. The design alone kept me clicking along. Except for the one page with the numerous smaller windows, I didn't even mind having to close window after window. That was part of the site and it was fun.

I would concern myself with making navigation a little easier on the users first. Past that, lose the unrelated dirty stuff and this site will sing.

2. MASter's Homepage/Author: MASter (Mohammed A. Al-Shaikh)

`http://snap.to/MASter`

Load Time: 19 Seconds 57kps modem, cleared cache, 7/21/00 10:43AM.

My Screen Size: 1,024×768

Browsers Used: Internet Explorer 5 and Netscape Navigator 4.5

Figure 9.20
Thanks. I will. (Color Plate C.26)

Concept: This is the personal homepage of "MASter." That's the name Mohammed A. Al-Shaikh has derived by pulling letters out of his name. Actually, Figure 9.21 is the homepage of MASter.

In terms of personal homepages, this one is very well done. The images he used are quite nice and produce a pleasant rollover. The images suggest MASter might still be living in North America; apparently he spent some time in Arkansas. The pinecone, needles, and maple leaves are traditionally U.S. or Canadian plants. The truth is that MASter is in Saudi Arabia.

There are hints to that throughout the site. Images of his family in traditional clothing line his pictures page, which offered fast-loading thumbnails linked to larger images, by the way. Like most young men, MASter is most proud of his car, which he devotes a page to explaining how the car has one name in the United States, but is called something else in Saudi Arabia.

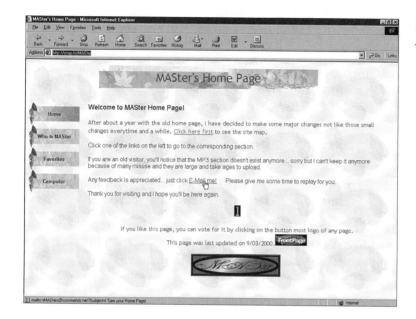

Figure 9.21
Ah. Much better.

In addition, you can vote for MASter to become part of the Saudi Arabian Top 100. I voted for him. I'm sorry to say I didn't see him on the list, but if we all go and vote...

One more thing that impressed me about MASter's page was his This Site page. Not only was it a site map, which I very seldom see on a personal homepage, but it also explained a bit of the site design. For instance:

"There isn't things that require special plug-ins or a specific browser to work probably...I'm considering using MS Vis Act but if I do so, the page will still work fine with Netscape Navigator and other browsers but without those vizacts :-)"

I left the English as he wrote the text. I think his use of the language is charming. I can hear a heritage in the words. I liked reading it very much. If you're thinking he put those lines in there for me thinking I might review the site, I don't think so. I believe that was there before my call for sites came along. The site is simply too well designed for those lines to be added later. He put too much thought into the process.

Concern: The first is the JavaScript Alert that greets me as I attempt to enter.

Suggestion: Lose it. It doesn't add to the page and actually, I think, takes away from a very nice site.

Concern: Your homepage completed and displayed, but there were errors on the page. It took me a little time to figure out where the errors were coming from, but I found it. It's your image-based counter.

Suggestion: The counter is for your own purposes. Unless you have a very good reason for keeping it, I would lose it altogether.

Concern: You followed a format I am seeing a little too often. Your page is actually in a frames format yet one would never know that without looking at the code. The format you chose is not intended to move people through windows-keeping navigation; it is specifically created to keep the URL in the location box the same throughout the site.

Let me explain. MASter has set up his page so that there are two frames. You'll never see the one frame because it doesn't exist. MASter has set the main frame to 100% and the smaller frame to zero. The entire site displays in just that one frame but because the frame is the full browser screen, it gives the appearance that there is no frameset to speak of.

You may be asking, "Why do it if I never see the second frame?" The reason someone would use this is because the URL that appears in the location bar at the top of the browser will never change. After all, the location is pointing to a frames page, not to the page that is displaying in the window.

Confusing? You bet. Just try to bookmark a page. You'll get the same bookmark every time—the frames page. It never leaves the foreground. MASter has just set it up so that it appears to leave the foreground.

My guess as to why MASter did this is that his page is actually located at a place different than what shows in the location bar. Right now, the location reads `http://snap.to/MASter`.

That's not really the URL. That's a handle applied to the URL so that the address will be smaller and easier to remember. You see a page on Geocities can have a very long name employing many subdirectories. By Geocities applying a handle to that long address, people can more easily pass around their URLs.

The problem is that the handle doesn't always stay in the location bar. Once you arrive at the homepage and click, the handle is gone. The real address pops up. Many people, including MASter, are interested in keeping that short URL handle all the way through the site so they set up this 100% frame window and the handle never leaves the location bar.

Get it?

Suggestion: My first suggestion would be that if you're that interested in your site's location, then get off of the free server and get your own URL or go for it all and buy your own domain. The handle system was not meant to make your site a domain. It was set up for ease of communication regarding URLs.

By creating this frames format, you have made it impossible for anyone to bookmark any part of your site except the homepage. In regard to a personal page, that may not be so bad, but if you ever take this page to a different level or decide to build a commerce page, you'll probably run into much bigger problems.

(To the reader: Yes, I know that Internet Explorer 5.0 bookmarks inside of frames. Don't rely on that. IE5.0 is not the most-used browser on the Net.)

Overall: You state on the site page that this is your first site. Gosh. My first site was just terrible compared to this. You obviously have a talent for design. My suggestion would be to now go on and build other sites. Too often one can get bogged down fixing and primping and changing a single site. Make a few changes and go on. Build something else. Broaden your horizons in terms of topics. Try to build a page for a business. Who knows, maybe you can make a living at this. It's been known to happen.

Heck...I do it.

3. Love.../Author: Ross Lasthero

http://www.mindspring.com/~lasthero/msiepage.html

Load Time: 19 Seconds 57kps modem, cleared cache, 7/21/00 10:43AM.

My Screen Size: 1,024×768

Browsers Used: Internet Explorer 5 and Netscape Navigator 4.5

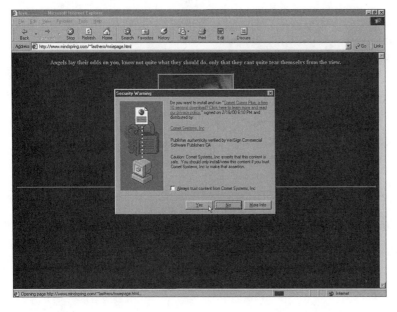

Figure 9.22
Uh-oh. What am I going to get with this? (Color Plate C.27)

I am going to place three figures right off the bat in critiquing this site. The previous figure is what greeted me when I logged into the site. Right off, I am a little nervous. I know what Comet Cursor will produce, a cursor, but I don't know that I really want yet another thing with its hand in my computer. Just for the book I said yes.

Figure 9.23 is the page that displayed.

Figure 9.23
This is just wonderful.

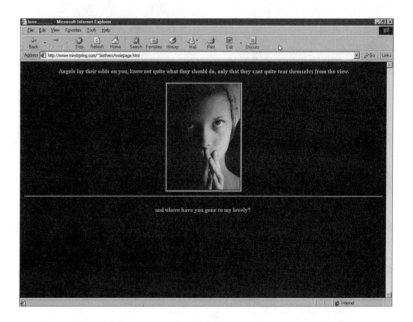

Look at that picture. I am mesmerized by it. It evokes just the perfect emotion for the site. The quote is lifted higher because of the image. The text below the picture is perfect. I know this is a welcome page to the site and I have to click on the image to enter, but I love it.

Notice also that the cursor downloaded through Comet Cursor is not on the screen capture. It is in Figure 9.24.

My image, my beautiful, beautiful image. The black-and-white still photo that brought so much emotion now has a little, beating, cartoon heart sitting on top of it.

Aw, shucks.

I think the entire feel of the page and the entire reason for putting it there has been blown. It's like sticking Daffy Duck in the middle of a Rembrandt.

Happily, I could see that the red heart would not follow me to the next page because as it loaded I was not reasked any plug-in questions, but other things did happen.

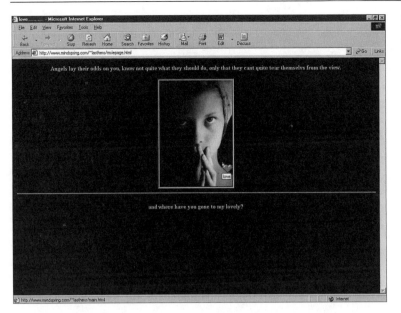

Figure 9.24
Aaaaaaaauuuuuuuuuuuugh!

For one, notice the address. See the name of the page I'm looking at? It's msiepage.html. The author set up a JavaScript that checked my browser and sent me to a page that is built specifically for my platform.

That's a correct use of the latest and greatest.

Concept: This is a personal page. It shows the likes, dislikes, and opinions—he calls them revelations—of the author. I read a good many of the pages and I liked the person I met through the site. His coding is wonderful. He was able to take very difficult JavaScript and incorporate it so that it not only aided the viewers, but entertained them as well.

Praise: The welcome page, past the beating heart, was wonderful. What's more, when I did click to go to the real homepage, the pages melded into one another using a very fancy JavaScript. It looked like Figure 9.25. The fade fit the page and fit the movement from page to page. It only happens that one time and it's what makes it even better in my eyes. An effect that happens again and again is an effect that gets overplayed way too soon. The homepage is a series of nine images set into a checkerboard pattern. As your mouse rolls over each active section, other sections pop up as in Figure 9.26.

Figure 9.25
Correct use of an effect.

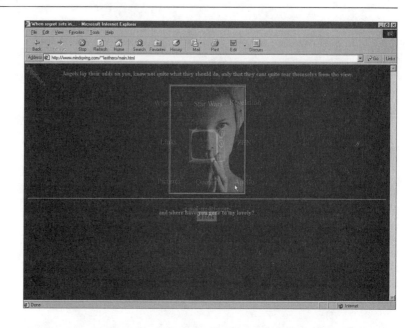

Figure 9.26
Heavy coding, nice effect.

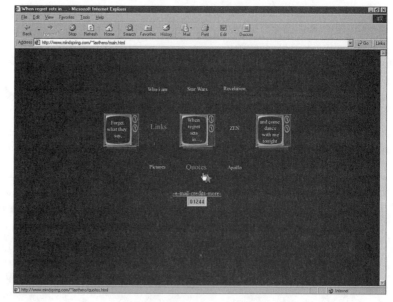

The methods to getting this double and triple image flip can get very involved, but the author wrote and created the effect so that it assisted the view and basically put on a show. I wanted to run my pointer over each of the links simply to see what each of them did.

Sometimes they popped up in color, sometimes not. It seems random but it isn't. It's just that well done.

That seems to be the conundrum that hangs over this site. The author is obviously a person who likes the latest and greatest and wants to incorporate it all. The problem is that it doesn't all fit.

The fade from welcome page to homepage was perfect. The cursor was just not needed. There are a few other examples that I'll get into. Suffice to say, this author is in a rather interesting place in terms of his Web site. Most people are in dire need to make additions to their Web sites. He needs only to cut away. However, choosing what to lose may be harder than choosing what to keep.

Concern: Wow, does this guy love the cursor effects. On the main page there are a series of five stars that just won't leave me alone. They follow me everywhere and actually make it hard to click on a link every now and then. It looks like Figure 9.27.

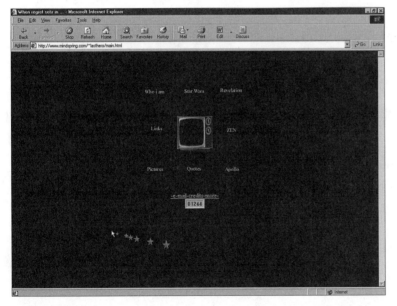

Figure 9.27
Run away! Run away!

Suggestion: Lose them. In fact, this site is so good by its lonesome that the last thing it needs is another effect piled on top. Lose the Comet Cursor and lose the DHTML cursor star trail.

I am starting to see those trails all over the Web. Hopefully, they will go out of fashion quickly. It's one of those effects that people will put on their own Web site, but will complain about when they see it on someone else's site.

Concern: You have kept the black background throughout the site and that's good. However, many of your pages have information that someone might want to print.

Suggestion: Offer a link to a page that's the traditional white background with black text so that people can print if they want to. I am talking about your revelation and quotes page specifically. You'll also find that offering a print button actually causes more people to print. Putting the idea in their minds will force a few printings.

Concern: I really don't know your name. I'm guessing from your email submission that it's Ross. I looked at your Who am I page. Not there. Your friends are all named, but not you.

Suggestion: I would suggest getting your name in at least that page. You should also think about signing your revelations. I worked radio for a while and one of the hardest things to get in a new disc jockey's mind was that he had to say his name, a lot. Often, new jocks and Web designers see saying or writing their name as egotistical. It's not. People want to know the name of the author. They want to know whom they're reading. Get your name up there a couple of times.

Concern: There is only one place on the site that offers email. That's the homepage.

Suggestion: Add email to each of the subpages as well. I would put it at the end of the link of links that sit at the bottom of each page.

Concern: Your revelation page has a feedback mechanism. The problem is that it offers no place to put in a name or an email address. There's simply a text area box and a submit button.

Just as people want to know who you are, when you ask for their input, they want you to know who they are. Give them the opportunity to do that.

Overall: The site is good, darn good. There are just a few too many lawn ornaments on the property. You have more effects than you need and it's harming the page and getting in the way of navigation. Look the site over carefully and choose the elements that truly add to the site. Those that do not add to the site, lose them. May I suggest the cursor effects might be first to go?

Chapter 10

Promoting Your Site

At this point, you should have a site that is finished, tested, and ready to go. The site should be complete. There should be no errors of any sort on any browsers. All of the images should load correctly. Each of the subpages should be complete. The site should be free of Under Construction images and "Coming Soon" massages.

So, it's done. You post it to the Web at your chosen ISP and there it sits.

Now what?

Well, now you have to get visitors. Remember, this site is far more for the visitors than it is for you, so you need visitors. You need traffic. You need people coming to the site, thinking it's wonderful, and telling other people about the site.

That's called promotion. When a new business opens, they usually have some kind of advertising, or contest, or big to-do to get the name of the business out there. You must do the same when it comes to your Web site.

Promotion of a site is pretty much a full-time job. There's a big push at first, but after that, you need to make a point of telling people about your site at just about every turn. You need to make it so those who like your site can tell other people about it. That's what you're looking for, the word-of-mouth effect.

HTML Goodies became wildly popular quickly. I really didn't have a time when I felt visitors were down far enough to think about quitting. As I look back, I realize that the site became popular for two reasons.

First, I had a good product. That is paramount. I had what people wanted. It was different from anything else out there and it was helpful. People wanted to visit. Then they wanted to visit again. They told friends and those friends wanted to visit.

Second, I was a promotion machine. I didn't set out to be a promoter, I just believed in the site so much that every chance I had, I would get the address in front of people. I had business cards. I created press releases. I wrote articles and submitted them to publications. I attached information to emails, newsgroup posts. I had banners people could download. I traded links. Whatever I could do to get the address of my site in front of another pair of eyes, I did.

Some of you believe that promotion costs money. Some of it does, but promoting HTML Goodies never cost me a cent. It's not that I was cheap—it's that I was a graduate student. I didn't have enough money to eat well, let alone push a new Web site. The promotion that I did was free and much of it is still available to you today.

If I were to break promotion down into any sort of specific categories, I would have to broadly break it into promotions that are free and promotions that cost you money.

At this point, I have both. I pay for promotion and I still do free promotions. They both have their place and they are both effective. In this chapter, I lay out for you a series of promotions that will help to get your Web site up and running from the first day and keep it running throughout its lifespan.

You've built the site. That was the fun part. Now it's time for a little work.

Opening Day

I have now had four live parties for four sites I helped to launch. My fifth is coming up in about a month from the time I am writing this chapter. A live party is a party that you throw starting the night before your site goes live. At midnight of the first full day, upload the files and cross your fingers. You're live.

Right now, some of you are saying that your site is just a personal site, or just a little site you put together for a church, or just a little site you built for your company.

So?

Is your site any better or worse than sites built by the big boys? Is it important to those who are represented by the site, your family, your church members, and your fellow employees? Of course, it is.

Every site will have an opening day and that opening day should come after the promotion has already started.

Pre–Opening Day

To begin with, you should have a place to post your files already set up and ready to accept posts. Now, pick a date when your site will go live. The first of a month is good, or if your site is represented by a specific date, use that. Either way, pick a specific date.

On the site, post a page that states the site is coming soon, but make it more than that. Post a great deal of information. Tell people what the site will be about. Let them know what they can expect from your site. Maybe give a small piece of the text they can expect, or a couple of images.

Always offer en email link. Suggest that people can write with questions or members of the media can write to request an interview. Do you think the last one is silly? No media is going to call.

Bunk. It has happened and it has happened to me.

Last, make sure that the page has the live date posted very clearly (see Figure 10.1).

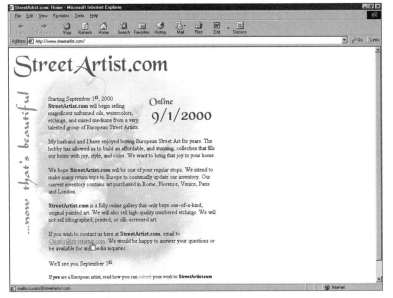

Figure 10.1
When does this site go live?

Before you say that what is mentioned previously is nothing more than a big "Under Construction" image, it isn't. What is mentioned previously is part of promotion. It is not a simply lack of completing a page. What is mentioned earlier was done on purpose rather than as a result of not completing a Web site.

The page you build will sit for about a month. Any longer and people may lose interest. During that month, you cannot just rest and wait for the clock to tick down. You need to be generating interest in the site. You want to build some anticipation.

If you followed the format outlined in Chapter 2, "Before You Write a Word," you already know who your audience will be. You need to make a point of reaching that audience. Start by creating a one-page advertisement for your site. Call it a press release if you'd like.

The page should have your site's name and address most prominent on the page. The text should be short, concise, and to the point. You see, you're going to send this one page out to media, other sites, and other publications that might be interested in knowing another great site is going up.

Keeping your words brief is of the utmost importance. Having worked in the media for a long while, I know that press releases and notes to the editor are very commonplace and each day a slew comes rolling through the door. You need to make a point of keeping your words so small and so succinct that your text can be read almost at a glance.

I've found that bullet lists are more easily read than paragraphs. Use bold to draw out specific words. Make sure your site name and address are most prominent. That's the most important thing, right?

Make a point of including your name, email, and phone so someone can contact you if they want to gather more information. Make it known that you have the ability to talk for the site.

A press release is a very tricky thing. The steps to writing one would fill a book. In fact, they have. I suggest that you check into a book specifically geared to helping you write a better press release. Run your release past friends and colleagues and get their feedback. Take all comments to heart and create the perfect one-page invitation to the opening of a great new site.

Okay, stop rolling your eyes. Those of you with a business site think this is great. Those of you who are just putting up a recipes site, or a site with your poetry, or a site dedicated to Britney Spears think this is a bit overblown.

It's just a recipe site, right? Where could you send a press release?

Hmmm…how about *Redbook, Better Homes and Gardens, Reader's Digest,* or any other number of magazines that print recipes? Better yet, offer somewhere in your press release that you would like to be interviewed about what it's like putting such a site together. That's a great story. A real person discusses creating a site that will be for other real people. That's a winner.

How many places print poetry? Well, send to them. How many sites dig Britney? Send to them.

The darn thing is, it probably won't even cost you a stamp. Many of these places already have a Web site where you can email the editor. That's perfect. Email the editor. Send your press release digitally. Yes, they do read their email. I contact editors all the time.

If your site has local appearance only, there's the local paper. If you are creating a site for a church, there are bulletins, and publications, and any number of outlets that will reach people who will be interested in what your site has to say.

At this point, someone usually asks, "What if people don't read the press release?"

Here's my answer, "What if they do?"

Who is to say that your site is any more or less deserving of attention than any other site? No one. So, at least try. The worst that can happen is that your press releases yield nothing and you're right back to where you started. Not trying is the dumb choice in my mind.

Now, send out those press releases. Send to any and everybody and any place you can think of. If you hear nothing back in two weeks, send it again.

The next step is to invite a few friends, serve up some soda and chips, and wait until midnight.

Once the site is live, it's not a bad idea to send another version of your press release off to your lists of receiving places. Your first press release said you were opening soon. This one will say that you're open.

Okay, You're Live—Tell the Search Engines

Congratulations. You're a Web site. Now it's time to get your pages on the search engines.

Some of you may be asking why I would wait until after the site is live to register with search engines. The reason is simple, because the site is live. You can't register something that's not live. Furthermore, you shouldn't register something that isn't done.

If you send your site into a search engine and that search engine catalogues all of your pages for you, and your site isn't done, that's big trouble. From this point on, you will now have pages in that search engine that read, "Coming soon!"

That's not inviting to someone who wants to visit. In fact, it's harmful. Even before a user visits, he or she knows you don't have a completed site.

"But now I do!" you proclaim.

Tough. You submitted early and that's what the search engine has logged for your site. You can attempt to alter the listing, but that's such a long shot that I wouldn't even waste my time.

After your site is finished and still off-line, you need to make a point of getting your pages ready to be submitted to the search engines. Search engines work in fairly logical fashion so you can easily create pages that play to that logic. To begin with, write down a few words. The content of the words you write will soon become what are known as META tags and those META tags will help the search engines to find your page when someone searches.

Keywords

A keyword is any word that describes your site or any word that can be used to find your site. The last time you went into Yahoo! or AltaVista or the like, you entered a keyword. By creating a list of your own keywords and putting them on your pages, you'll be in a sense, assisting the search engine to find you.

Now, don't be shy and don't be humble. List every word you can possibly think of that would be used to find a site like yours. Use words that exist on your site as well as overriding general words. Use differing tenses of words, use multiple spellings if there are some. This is not a time to be shy.

To give you an idea of how many keywords can be used, here are the keywords from the HTML Goodies pages:

> html tutorials editor code help frames beginner's guide helpers tags programming forms letters color sounds charts tables backgrounds tutor tool basics design script beginner flags primers lessons buttons 4.0 cascading style sheets freeware shareware downloads directory reference resource example sample htmlgoodies cgi script creating banners image maps style sheets web pages learn javascript java applets passwords programs dhtml layers goodies webmaster tips online services guestbook dhtml script client-side image maps commerce community content hex codes embedded systems video goody information technology it professionals link buttons implementation strategies millennium bug positioning preloaded images library searchable database software development top ten sites joe burns vb scripts css properties banner primers aligning images adding text motion getting advertisers beyond html ask Joe Script Tips Users Choice active x goodies to go reference pieces active server pages developers meta commands Active X web development EarthWeb htmlgoodies.com earthweb.com

How about that, huh? The concept is to create a list of keywords that cover every possible keyword search that someone could possibly make.

Get the keywords that you feel will be most common higher up in the list. Give the words a hierarchy. That could also help on your getting displayed by the search engine.

A Few "Don't Dos"

It's only a matter of time before someone tells you how you can get around the system by not playing fair. People will suggest you mess around with your keywords and trick the search engine into picking you first. The following tricks should be avoided at all costs, because not only will they not work, but they will most likely get your site banned from the search engines for good.

1. Do not write a keyword numerous times.

Don't do this. If your site is about Buffy the Vampire Slayer, don't write "buffy" 100 times and expect that it's going to help. It's considered spamming and will get you kicked off the search engine. I suggest finding more keywords rather than doubling up on keywords.

2. Do not put in keywords you know will be searched but have nothing to do with your site.

Again, this is playing games and will most likely get you kicked off. If you put the keywords, "Yahoo" and "Playboy" and "Microsoft" on your site simply to have it pop up, forget it. If you do get listed and someone searches "Playboy" and you pop up with your site all about the Cleveland Browns, that person will think pretty ill of your site. There won't be a lot of conversions from Playboy to Browns fans today.

Some try to get away with this trick by putting links to those major sites on their pages and stating that the keyword is now valid because the page's content reflects it.

Gimme a break. Knock it off.

3. Don't put keywords on the page again and again.

Here's another trick you might want to avoid. Have you ever been to a page that is only about a browser screen long, yet goes on for three with just blank space? What's that all about?

The author is attempting to trick the search engines to pick his or her site by putting keywords on their pages time and time again. They probably have the same keyword a thousand times, set to minus-five font and set to the same color as the background so the text doesn't show up.

The author of such a page is playing to the search engine's methods of searching. Usually the page that has the keyword listed the most times gets listed highest. Even though you cannot see the words on the page, the search engine can. This, too, is considered spamming by the search engines and can get you kicked off.

Next time you run into one of these pages, look at the code. It's insane and really doesn't help all that much.

Description

Now that you have a long list of words, let's set about creating a description to your site. This is exactly the opposite of keywords in terms of length. In keywords you are attempting to get as many as possible. Here, you need to stay around 25 words.

Can you describe your site in around 25? Sure you can! Think about what is really important. What is the thing that your site offers that sets it apart?

Write that.

Remember that this description is going to display as a description of your site when your link pops up on a search engine, so write with action words. Draw the user. Give them a feeling that this is a site they must see. Maybe even invite them to come. Make the text come alive.

Just do it in around 25 words. These 25 words should be your killer app. They will be the words someone reads when your site comes up in a search engine.

I know it seems rough, and it will take up a good bit of your time, but take that time. You have to get this one right. I suggest you go to some of your favorite sites and see how they did it first. How did the pros describe a site? Here's how it's done on HTML Goodies:

> Free html tutorials from industry expert Dr. Joe Burns. Featuring extensive tutorials on tags, programming, basics, script, frames and more. Our weekly newsletter provides the latest html information, available only at htmlgoodies.com

Quick-eyed readers will probably note that this description is over 25 words. Yep. It is. The reason is that the number of words each search engine will display varies greatly. Some only offer a few, some offer more, some will print it all.

Notice how the description is broken into three sections. The first sentence can stand on its own if the search engine prints only the first few words. The next sentence adds and the third is helpful, but not really needed.

Depending on the search engine, some or all of the description will display. Try to write yours so that the same some-or-all format can be followed.

Now that you have the words, you'll want to place them on every page on your site. It's important that each page carries these keywords because you'll want to submit every page on your site to the search engines, not just the homepage.

Here's the format you'll follow:

```
<META NAME="keywords" CONTENT="key,word,key,word">

<META NAME="description" CONTENT="Great page! Come see!">
```

Put those two lines between the `<HEAD>` flags on your page. Fill in your keywords and the description with the text you just created.

There is a whole slew of META tags that will help search engines with categorizing your pages. Here are three others that I have used in the past.

```
<META NAME="generator" CONTENT="Notepad">

<META NAME="author" CONTENT="Some Body">

<META NAME="copyright" CONTENT="Copyright © 1997 Me">
```

Make a point of following the formats and add them in between the `<HEAD>` command following the first two.

Get the Page to the Search Engine

When I first wrote this chapter, almost all of the search engines, even the big names, allowed free submissions. I'm sorry to say that that is now no longer the case.

Many of the biggest search engines on the Web now ask for money in order to be listed. Yahoo! is one search engine that has gone to a pay-for scheme. It now (5/6/01) costs $199 (U.S.) to have your site considered for posting at Yahoo!.

If you're interested in why many of the search engines have gone to a pay-for format, I wrote a newsletter on the topic. You can find it at `http://www.htmlgoodies.com/letters/124.html`.

This is not to say that there aren't still numerous search engine sites out there that offer free submissions—quite the contrary. There are a lot. Go to any major search engine and search "Search Engine" and you'll get a list a mile long. The majority of them will accept free listings.

I suggest you make a point of getting on as many free search engines as you can as long as the search engine deals with the topic your site deals with. Don't post a page dedicated to Led Zeppelin on a search engine that deals with car parts. That's not very nice and it won't help you, either.

As for the pay-for sites, I'm afraid my advice is to pay the fee if you can do it. It may very well be the only way to get on the search engine.

If I were to suggest the search engines to be most concerned about listing your pages, I would say Yahoo! and LookSmart. Yahoo! is still the number one search engine and shows no sign of slowing down anytime soon. I mentioned LookSmart because it is what is known as a feeder. The LookSmart database is used by other major search engines such as Webcrawler and AltaVista when they perform a search. If you get on LookSmart, you get on others as well.

I have heard that submitting to Google might help with getting a page onto Yahoo! since one feeds the other. At the time of this writing, Google accepted free submissions. They may not by now. Check the site carefully.

No matter what happens in terms of paying for a search engine or not, the fact remains that search engines are, by far, the number one method people use to find information on the Web. If you are building a personal homepage, you may want to think long and hard about paying those fees. You may not need them. You may be the best reason someone comes to your personal site.

If you are a business or e-commerce site then you need visitors. Look upon the fees as a business expense and pay them. That's about as cut and dried as I can be.

Now that you have the META tags on the page, you need to let the search engines know about them. I was told one time that all one really had to do is sit and wait and the search bots would come and find me. You may not know this, but search engines often patrol the Internet looking for new pages and add them as they go along.

You can wait if you want, but I'm an active guy. I submit.

To this point, I have followed two general methods of submitting pages to search engines. At first, I would set aside a weekend just about every two months and visit my long, long list of search engines and hand-submit each page.

Submitting to sites that still accept free submissions is usually so easy it's silly. For the most part, you enter your site's URL and leave it at that. The search engine not only grabs the page you submit but also all the pages links from that page. One submit. Many pages.

Other sites require you to put in your keywords and description to the screen because they don't search your pages but rather their own database. Yahoo! works like this.

Either way the search engine does it, it's usually easy and quick. When you arrive at a search engine's homepage, look for the icon or text that asks whether you want to submit a site.

I actually didn't mind putting in my new pages every couple of months. It was a way to watch a football game and relax. But I know there are some of you out there who lead a much more interesting life than I do, so you might be interested in the multiple submission sites.

These are sites that take your information once and then submit to multiple search engines for you.

Usually you can get a few for free just to try out the service, but past that there's a cost involved. To be honest, I now pay one of these services to submit for me. My sites have become too large to do it by hand.

Try these out and search for others if you'd like. They're out there.

- Submit-it: `http://www.submit-it.com/`
- Add-Me: `http://www.addme.com`
- Postmaster: `http://netcreations.com/postmaster/`

Those are the three that I have tried and liked. I use one of them full time.

Keep a Record

Your pages are not always cataloged right off the bat when you submit. It can take three days to two weeks to see results. Keep a record. Write down each search engine you submitted to and when you submitted.

Each week, check back. Perform keyword searches to find your site. If you cannot find the site after two weeks, submit again.

If you pay to have your site posted to a search engine, you should be vigilant. You paid your money, now they should keep up their end of the bargain. Make sure your site gets listed. If you do not find your site, write and find out why. You did pay, after all.

Keep this up until you see your site on each and every search engine you made contact with.

Shameless Self-Promotion

Okay, you're up and running and your pages are at least in the search engine mix. Now what?

Well, there's not much more you can do on the technical side of things, so let's start looking at method that you can undertake to continually promote your site.

When I started HTML Goodies, I made a point of attaching the name and the URL to everything I wrote and everything I posted.

My email signature file had the URL. No matter who received the email, they had to look at the URL. The one concern you should keep in mind is to not allow the signature file to get too long. A short signature file will get more attention than a very long file made up of numerous quotes and funny phrases. Remember, you are pushing your site here.

If you want people to come to your site, go to where those people are. Join discussion groups that deal with your site's topic. Enter chat rooms that do the same. Once there, only offer your site when it is appropriate. Too often people will enter the Goodies' Discussion Groups and leave a post that reads, "Check out my site!" No one ever does and the person who left the post often gets flamed for making such an intrusion. When you enter a newsgroup or a chat room, get a feel for the room and offer your site as help in response to a question or as somewhere that information can be gathered. Offer it when it can help. People will be more willing to come to a site that isn't forced upon them.

Many discussion groups offer signature files. Place your URL in that signature file.

If you're going to promote, promote. Get that URL in front of people. Just don't force it down their throats.

Promote Cross-Traffic

A good many people see this method of gaining visitors as the most important. I can see their point, but there is a downside to it.

The basic concept is that you find a site, or sites, that would attract roughly the same audience as your site and suggest to the Webmaster that you trade links. You put a link to his site and he or she puts a link to your site. The trade can be either a straight text link or an ad banner trade.

If all goes according to plan, people that visit your site will also visit the linked site and vice versa. This cross-traffic effect will build both of your numbers.

The problem is first finding a site that will trade with you and second, finding a site that will trade fairly. Be honest. If you trade a link with someone, don't you want your link to be top center on the homepage, but would like the other site's link to be buried three floors down in yours?

Don't feel bad. It's a common tale. You faithfully trade links and you display the other site's link so all can see it. You check the other site and your link is buried down deep.

When trading links, make a pact with the person regarding placement and time length. If that person doesn't keep to his or her end of the bargain, drop the link. It's that simple.

You just make a point of keeping to your end of the link bargain.

The thought process has been taken to a new level through what are known as Web rings (see Figure 10.2).

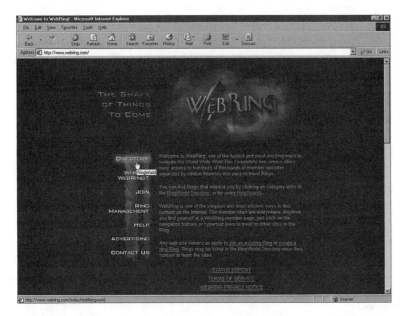

Figure 10.2
Webring—still the biggest and best. Find it at http://dir.webring. yahoo.com/rw.

A Web ring will attach your site to a list of other sites that all share the same general topic. You needn't worry about placement because every site is required to have the Webring code on the homepage. It's usually low on the page, but at least it's equal coding on all pages.

Your page will allow people to move throughout the ring as will everyone else's. That promotes a pretty fair use of cross traffic. If you can find a Web ring that fits your site, I would get on it until you are established.

Many people try to create cross traffic through banner trade sites such as LinkExchange, now available through http://www.bcentral.com/. Some people claim they work, but I have never been sold on them. The reason is that the exchange is never equal. LinkExchange itself offers a 2:1 ratio. Your site must show two banners before your banner is shown once. That doesn't seem like a fair exchange to me. I certainly wouldn't accept it from another site—why accept it here?

In addition, there have been numerous cases of people putting up suggestive banners and those banners running on sites that really shouldn't be displaying them. I don't mean the banners were dirty, just suggestive and if I posted a site dedicated to my new baby daughter, I don't want that on the site.

You also have no control over placement on the page. I can hide the banner or I can display it proudly. Hopefully, you get on a page that displays, but you just don't know.

If you do a quick search using "banner exchange," you see numerous sites that offer such exchanges. Note that some of them are far more specific in their focus than others. If your site falls under the umbrella of one of these specific link exchange rings, you may want to give that a shot, but one of the nationals is really a shot in the dark in my opinion.

When all is said and done, the best method for creating cross-traffic is to get hooked up with other sites you know are just as interested in making it as you are. Make deals with those sites to trade links and/or banners and start promoting cross traffic that way.

Only when you have a modicum of control over the situation can you really feel safe in posting links that will probably take people off of your site.

You see, that's the downside of cross traffic. The traffic doesn't stay. It crosses. It's called the "flight-effect." In order to gain more traffic, you are offering a method for people to leave your site. Hopefully the site you've trading links with is also experiencing the effect. That's about the only way you will both win, if people leave both of your sites.

Strange, isn't it?

Bring 'Em Back Alive!

One of the greatest methods to gaining more traffic to your site is to get those who are already stopping by to continue to stop by again and again.

I've talked about how a site is ever evolving and growing. To that end, what are you doing to bring a user back? Do you update your site? Do you offer some daily things such as a horoscope or a puzzle or some other new information?

If not, think about what your site could offer on a regular basis that would be new information. Make a point of offering that information on a set schedule, every day, every week, every month.

Also, make sure your users know that the information is available and that they know it's new. Promote the new information on the site. Ask users to sign up for mailing lists so you can send them email telling them when something new is up and running on the site.

Create a page, or a portion of the homepage, that specifically lists the newest elements on the Web site. I have a page I call The New Page at HTML Goodies. You'll find it at `http://www.htmlgoodies.com/new.html`. Go there first and you'll find links to the newest stuff.

Offer something new, and make sure your users know it.

If you keep me coming back, I'll think your site is pretty useful and you know what? I may tell a friend.

Tell a friend? That's great!

Word of Mouth and Word of Link

If I were to choose one form of promotion that made HTML Goodies a success, it would be word of mouth and word of link. The problem is, you can't buy this kind of promotion. You can't force this kind of promotion. It happens all by itself. Well, almost all by itself.

Word of mouth and word of link occur when a user from your site likes it so much that he or she either tells a friend to go or posts a link to your site out of the kindness of his or her own heart. I would even suggest that someone setting you as a bookmark falls under this heading.

Anyone even remotely knowledgeable regarding advertising will tell you that there is no stronger sell than a good friend suggesting a site. If I see an ad banner, I might look at the site. If a friend emails me and suggests I look at a site, I go. It's really about that simple and that clean.

So, since you cannot force people to create word of mouth or word of link, you just sit back and hope it happens, right?

No way. You can't force it, but you certainly can suggest it.

If you want someone to do something, you should make a point of suggesting it. There is nothing wrong with putting the text "If you like this site, tell a friend" on the homepage. If people write you a letter, make a point of replying and asking them to return. Let them know when the new stuff is posted. Ask them whether they would like to be on a mailing list to receive update information.

If you want people to bookmark your page, ask them to bookmark your page. Internet Explorer 5.0 allows you to create a link that will set the bookmark for the user. I have the code right here: `http://www.htmlgoodies.com/beyond/addtofavs.html`.

If you want people to link to you, ask them to link to you. Offer them the code so they can just copy and paste it from your page to theirs. Offer ad banners in many different sizes free. Offer to run the banner from your own site. All the person has to do is copy and paste some code. Your server will do the rest.

I see people going as far as asking users to set their page as their browser's "Home" page. I think that might be asking a bit much, but why not? What could it hurt? Try it. Again, IE 5.0 offers code to do it for the user. Grab that here:
`http://www.htmlgoodies.com/beyond/homepage.html`.

The only thing you really need to be careful of is to not appear as if you're begging. Place the text lower on the page than the important content. If you create links that set your page to favorites or to the homepage, don't push it on the people. Put the links further down the page.

If you offer banners, create a page specifically for those banners. Don't put them on the homepage. Let the user click to see the banners and decide for him or herself.

Asking is not a sin and it can be very productive. Just don't go overboard. Remember, content is most important. If what you have is good, people will link without your having to ask.

...but asking doesn't hurt.

A Couple of Other Ideas

I've seen these options used at many different sites. Sometimes they were done correctly and sometimes they, well, weren't. If you can undertake one of the following successfully, give it a try. Just remember that if you get started, you cannot just stop. Commit to doing the following if you choose to try it.

Offer Giveaways

If your site lends itself to giveaways and you have a budget then go for it. Giveaways don't have to be huge. A two-dollar key chain would be enough of a prize in most cases. Maybe you can work out a deal with another site where you can both go in on a prize and get something bigger and better.

Better still, maybe you can get a sponsor. Would you play around in a Web site if you could win a subscription to *Rolling Stone*? Talk to a local business. Maybe you can trade some prizes in return for putting an ad banner up on your site. Restaurants, amusement parks, and local sports arenas might all be interested. It's free advertising for them and you get prizes. What a deal.

The big thing to keep in mind regarding prizes is that the Web is global and prizes will most likely have to be mailed. If your site is in Cleveland, Ohio, will you mail a prize to Argentina? Think about it. Maybe you could give away something that doesn't have to be mailed, like some software.

If you create a giveaway, make it beneficial to your site first. That's the purpose. Remember? Make it so people have to register. That way you get their email addresses. Make sure you ask the person whether you can have permission to put them on a mailing list. Just don't take their email and then send them tons of stuff.

Make the contest something that requires people to move through your site. Put a word at the bottom of every page and then have the users gather the words and build a sentence out of them.

Make the user look at every page and place them in alphabetical order by page title.

Tell the user that there is a clue on every page and, with all the clues, they can find an answer that will win them the prize.

Just keep in mind that the prize must be available to everyone, there cannot be a purchase involved, and there must be an actual prize to win. Don't offer fake contents where no one wins. It's a lousy thing to do and could get you sued under the U.S. FCC Lottery Laws. Really...no kidding. See `http://www.fcc.gov/cib/consumerfacts/contests.html`.

Do it right, and a contest could start a buzz around your Web site. Just remember to send that press release out telling the media that you're running this contest.

Oh, here's another thing. Prove to your users that people actually win. Post the user's name and email (if you can get permission). Some of the best promotion I ever did during my years in radio was telling my audience the winners of my contests. It proves the contest is real and that people actually win.

Set Up a Club

Remember when you were younger and being part of a group really meant something? You had to be part of the in crowd. Well, set up your site so that people who visit are part of the in crowd.

Give your users names and allow them to communicate with each other through email addresses, chat rooms, or discussion groups.

Have people register and give them password and special information that only members can know. Set up emails back and forth among members. Allow the members to help you further design the Web site by making suggestions.

However you design it, just make it so that there is good in joining the club. If nothing else, there should be contact with other members.

Just be very careful. There are some bad people out there who would like to get into a club simply to gather names and addresses. If you set up the club, ask and offer nothing more than first names and email addresses. Never post street addresses, phone numbers, or any other contact information.

Sign Up for Awards

There are sites out there that give out awards. Go get them. Sign your site up to be considered for the prize. Often when you win an award, you site is posted as the winner. That's a pretty nice link to have.

When you win, you're often asked to post a link in return. Do it—just post it on its own page rather than on the homepage.

Try a site call The Awards Jungle at `http://www.awardsjungle.com/main.htm`. They'll sign you up for multiple awards in one shot.

Give Out an Award

You may want to wait until you're a little bigger than just starting out before starting this one. An award coming from a site that itself has no visitation seems pretty hollow.

If you decide to give an award, above all else, be sincere. Give the award because a site deserves it, not just because a link back would be nice.

There are times I receive awards from sites that I know are only doing it for the link back. The award itself is little more than a black square with some white text. The award image probably took an entire five minutes to build.

These types of awards never actually explain what I won for, just that I won and can I please put the award up on the site. Please?

Nope.

If you give an award, lay out the criteria first. Keep the criteria close to what your page is about. Truly seek out pages that fit the criteria. When you offer a site an award, tell the site author why he or she won. Tell them why you are even in a position to give out an award. Make the award more than just a futile attempt to get a link.

Payment Due in Full: Advertising

It is only recently that I got into purchasing advertisements for any of the Web sites I helped create. HTML Goodies was long since successful before I started to buy ads. In fact, I was selling ads before I was buying them.

I suggest you think about buying advertisements for your site if you require the site to gain visitors very quickly. Yes, I know that everyone wants visitors quickly. I'm talking about a commerce site, a site that may be part of your livelihood, a site that has to work pretty quickly or you're going to have a heck of a time paying back that bank loan.

I've been there. I know.

Once you set aside a budget for advertising, it's up to you to first determine where that ad budget will be spent. Will you spend it apart from the Web or spend it on the Web?

That all depends on what audience you're attempting to reach. There's an old saying that goes, if you want to get to come to a Web site, advertise to those already on the Web. That makes sense. An ad banner has a better chance of immediately getting someone to your site than does a magazine or television advertisement.

In the past, I have purchased magazine, newspaper, and direct marketing as part of a site launch. The reason was that the audience I was attempting to reach was not a traditional Web audience. However, the budget I spent off of the Web was always less than the budget I spent on the Web.

Please understand that your site will differ from the sites I have posted in the past. I would suggest that you consult someone in your field that knows your audience before making any final decisions on what amounts of money to put into what areas.

As for the Web, here are a few things to be concerned about.

Ad Banners

There are only a couple of things I can tell you for sure in terms of an ad banner. Past that, the sky's the limit in terms of packages, prices, and methods of payment.

To begin with, let's talk size. The standard ad banner is 468 pixels wide by 60 pixels tall. That's the standard. I'm not sure how that became the standard, but that's it.

When you purchase ad banner space, you will need to keep to that size and usually a few other parameters. The most common are, the ad banner cannot be greater that 10,000 bytes and can have no more than five panels in the animation. Those rules can vary, but I'll bet what you'll get is close to that.

Lately, smaller ad banners have started to come into the picture. These often run down the side of a screen and are less obtrusive than the main ad banner. That doesn't mean they aren't as successful—they just aren't as noticeable right off.

See the big ad banner up at the top of Figure 10.3? There's another smaller ad there where the mouse pointer is. It depends on your point of view. Some believe the smaller ads are better because they more easily gain attention rather than screaming for it. That's up to you to decide.

When you build an ad banner, no matter what the size, you need to make a point of that ad banner representing your site. Your text will be minimal and so will your number of animations panels, so think less about the flash of the ad and more about what the ad will look like and what you can say in about 15 words.

Figure 10.3
Does the ad grab your attention? Does it belong?

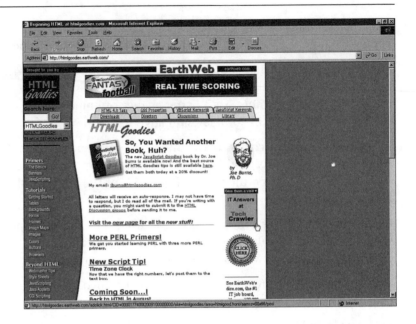

No matter what you say, make sure it is legible. Too often, people use small text to cram more words onto an ad banner and that just kills the effect. I can't read it so I won't click. That's money down the drain.

Can you offer me a real reason to click in your ad banner? I just arrived at this page. Why would I want to go to your site? I just got here.

An ad banner is no place to be clever. State your sales pitch on the first animation panel. Don't hold back information hoping it will draw in the audience. It won't. Tell when you want me to know quickly and right up front.

Color is important. Action colors are bright colors. Dark colors don't carry as much attention-grabbing punch.

You may also want to make a point of calling for action. The words "Click Here" never hurt.

That's the conundrum of putting an ad banner together. My suggestion is to create three or four and to test that with people who understand both your business and the World Wide Web. I always run my ads past a select group of people who are brutally honest. You should do the same.

Test, test, test. Take all comments seriously and build the best ad banner you can. Each time it displays, it costs you money.

How Will You Be Paying for This?

That will all depend on the seller. How can I pay for it?

Once you've decided to spend money on ad bannervertisements, you should start looking for sites that would be best for your ad. You don't want to randomly place an ad banner on the Web—that's not a good use of your money. Find sites that cater to people that would be interested in your site. You can come up with a pretty large list pretty quickly.

Once a site is on your list, look for a link on that that offers to tell you how to buy advertising on the site. I guarantee you it's there. Follow it and fill out the form to request an information packet, called a Media Kit. It will arrive via email very soon after you ask for it.

That media kit will break down deal after deal and offer a rate card showing how much each deal is worth. Different sites will offer different methods of paying for the ad banners you buy. Here are the most common:

CPM

The most common form of buying advertisement on the Web today is what's known as CPM or Cost Per Thousand. The letter M means 1,000 in Roman numerals.

The thousand usually means impressions, or pairs of eyeballs that see the ad.

Let's say a site has a cost of $10 per thousand. That's low actually. CPM can range anywhere from $10 to $90 depending on the site and the makeup of the people who visit. A more narrow, specific audience will carry a higher CPM while a broad audience will cost less. Nonetheless, if you spend $1,000.00 at a $10 CPM, you will be guaranteed 100,000 impressions for your money.

That's a good bit actually. The CPM is usually discussed in terms of a time span, also. You'll get 100,000 impressions in a month, or a week, or some other time span.

It's possible to make it so that your banner displays across an entire time span. If you want an ad to display 100,000 equal times over a month, the server computer will figure out how many displays that is per day and show you only so many times that the 100,000 spans the entire time period.

When you pay that way, once your banner had displayed however many times you paid for, it's pulled out of the rotation. Ad banner software packages can pull an ad after any number of hits it's set to.

You can also pay for your advertisement with a CPM that is tallied up at the end of a time period, usually a month. The site simply bills you for however many impressions your ad received. It's a floating monthly number and can be a little hard on sites with set budgets.

Click-Through

This is becoming less and less prevalent on the Web. A click-through ad campaign is one that has the advertiser pay only when a user clicks on the ad. The amount of money can range from around fifty cents to up to three dollars per click-through depending on the site.

Time Buy

You pay an amount of money and your ad banners runs for a set amount of time. How many times it displays is dependent upon the number of advertisers and the number visitors.

Inside of each of these pay formats are usually deals upon deals. You can expect to pay less or more depending on a great many factors including placement on the page, if you're on the homepage or not, size of ad banner, and availability.

Search engines are a very popular place to put ad banners. The number of users coming through those sites is staggering. The concern is that just randomly shooting into a group of people doesn't mean you will hit those that are interested in your site, but you can narrow your audience a bit if you use your search engine buy correctly.

If you purchase space on a search engine, make sure your ad is attached to certain keywords. That means the ad will only come up when one of your chosen keywords is entered.

If not, your art gallery site might pop up for a guy looking to purchase a small black Chevy. I don't see him clicking.

You may have to pay a bit more for the use of the keywords, but it's worth it in the long run. The only problem I ran into was that the keyword I wanted was sold out. I had to go with a different word.

How Long Should I Advertise?

I would suggest you should never stop. The Web is a place where name recognition is everything. When people sit down to surf, you want your site's name to be foremost in their minds. That's what advertising will do. It will help to keep your site fresh in people's minds. There's an old advertising adage that goes, "When things are good, advertise. When things are bad, advertise more." It's not a bad idea.

You should also advertise as long as it is working for you. If your ad bannervertisements are bringing people to the site then you will be most likely able to buy more advertising.

Obviously, not every site can keep a blitz of advertising going nonstop. If that's the case then the main concern is to get people to the site when it opens. Concentrate on getting people there early and attempt to keep them there using many of the free methods discussed earlier in the chapter.

The Final Decision

The whole world will give you an opinion if you ask them. In the end, though, it is your site and it is your money. Your advertising budget should be spent how you feel it should best be spent. I have used advertising agencies and I have used my gut instinct and I didn't see a difference in the results.

Pick your locations. Make your deals. Buy your ads and continue to run the best site you can.

Remember, no matter how much advertising you buy, it just won't matter unless your site is as good as the ad made it out to be. The ads simply get the users there. Once they arrive, it's up to your content and design to keep them.

e-Commerce

I wanted to wrap up the book and the site critiques by touching on e-commerce and some of the elements that make an e-commerce Web site so good or so bad.

e-Commerce does not require any special new rules or any special new design formats. If you follow the parameters set aside in the book and apply them to an e-commerce site, you should have just as much success as the site that is dedicated to Mom's latest chowder soup.

Yes, there are a few elements that you'll find on an e-commerce site that you won't find on a personal site, but the parameters still apply.

I was once asked to address a small group of people that all owned businesses that wanted to get online. It was my job to quickly get them up to speed or at least let them know what they were in for. I found that the lecture quickly turned on one gentleman's question about what he should expect that no one told him about. What was going to come out of the blue? What should he have known going in?

Immediately after the lecture, I sat down and answered his question. I came up with ten things that you'll probably wish you knew going into starting your e-business. These items are easily enough to fill a book. However, I'm almost at the end of this one so I leave you with these thoughts.

My guess is that you've heard a few of them before, someplace earlier in this book.

The Top 10 Things They Never Seem to Tell You About Starting an e-Commerce Site

1. You Must Acquire Your Own Domain

You're never going be taken seriously in the world of e-commerce until you are www.*something*.com. This is the big one! Make a point of picking a name that can be easily spoken and understood. Avoid these pitfalls:

Do not use numbers. If you must use a number, buy the domain name with the number both spelled out and as a number. For example: 2dogs.com and twodogs.com. Either way, the people come to you.

Avoid hyphens. They are often misunderstood when people first hear a Web address.

Do not include words such as *the* or *a* if you can avoid it.

You want a domain name that is short, easy to speak, and hard to hear incorrectly. You may also want to make a point of buying the .net, .org, .tv domains.

If your domain has a word that can be easily be misspelled, buy the domain with the misspelling. You can always set those misspelled domains to the correct domain.

Network Solutions, `http://www.networksolutions.com` is where I've purchased all of my domain names.

2. Speed Is Your Main Concern

Remember that the vast majority of Web users are on AOL or are running a dial-up modem. Pages load slower on their machines than your Ethernet-driven Pentium Pro. An Internet user gives pages an average of 15 seconds to load before they leave. Shoot for content, not flair.

The most important part of a Web page is the content. If you do not have the content then no amount of images, pretty colors, or computer wizardry will help your site to succeed.

3. The Cheapest Server Probably Isn't the Best

I use to pay just under $250 per month to have my own domain. For my money, I am on a state-of-the-art, very fast, machine. I don't share hard drive space with any other business. Problems are fixed immediately and I know the server's owner by name. Twenty bucks won't buy you all that. A free server certainly won't buy you all of that.

Buying space on the Web is like buying a storefront for your business. You wouldn't buy a storefront with broken sidewalks, and a door that's hard to open, would you? Then, why buy Web space that's slow and hard to use?

Talk to numerous service providers. Try to stay local so you actually know the person who takes care of the server. Be vigilant. Get the best deal, but remember that the best deal isn't always the cheapest.

4. Unless You Know What You're Doing, Get Help Building Your Web Site

Your e-commerce Web site is no place to begin your Web site construction process. That's what a personal page is for. Your business Web site must be professional. It cannot look like your first attempt at building a Web site.

Depending on your budget, get help. If you have a small budget, contact a local university and ask for their Web-Wiz kid. If you can afford it, get professional help. Either way you go, make your Web site every bit as professional as your brick-and-mortar store.

5. Users Want Their Email Returned

Not returning an email is the Web's equal to being ignored by a clerk. I don't mean setting up a program that sends a nice form-style thank-you-for-writing letter. Users want an answer from you.

Your Web site must be seen as an extension to your business, not just something you create and leave alone. Web customers are customers just the same as if they walked into your front door.

6. Most of the Biggest Search Engines Now Want to Be Paid to List Your Site—Pay Them

It is a cost of doing business. The general fee today is $199 to be listed in 48 hours or less. Think of the money as advertising. Yes, you can still submit to many search engines for free. However, it may take up to eight weeks to be listed. The amount of business and traffic you will gain over those eight weeks of waiting is more than worth the $199 you will pay to the top three search engines: Yahoo!, AltaVista, and LookSmart.

7. You Will Need Visitor Software

How many people come to your site? From where? What hours of the day? What pages are the top referring pages for your site? What browsers are used most by people who come to your site? Are you being visited by students more than homes or businesses? Find software that will answer these questions. Many packages will offer daily, weekly, or monthly statistics from your site that can be sent to the client over email without your doing anything.

8. 10,000 Visitors per Month Is the Advertiser Plateau

This is the minimal number of visitors that must be coming to your site before most advertisers will think about including you in their advertising budget. Please understand, I mean ten thousand individual visitors per month. Not ten thousand hits, or ten thousand page views, but ten thousand people.

Think before you start putting ad banners on your site as a means to bring traffic. Usually those banner exchange sites are set up so that your site must display two of their banners before they will display one of yours. That's just not a very good deal.

There are better methods to building traffic. Don't use ad banners unless you are the one being paid for their display.

Here are a couple more hints when it comes to offering ad bannervertisements.

Cost Per Thousand (CPM) is the best method of selling advertising. I feel the relationship between my site and a client was most fair when I charged a specific dollar amount per thousand banner views (a user seeing the advertising banner) with a guarantee that a certain plateau would be met. For example, $15.00 per 1,000 page views with 100,000 guaranteed.

You will need advertising banner software. Soon you will have advertising banners on your site. Advertisers will want to know picky little things like how many times their advertising banner was viewed and how many times it was clicked. Most will want exact banner display numbers when you send a bill for payment. The software you use must randomly post banners to pages on the fly. Assigning specific banners to specific pages is not a good idea. It makes the site appear static. There are many different software packages to choose from. Pick one that can back up their claims with testimonials and references.

9. You Must Accept Credit Cards

You may hear that accepting credit cards is no longer needed because of services like PayPal, http://www.paypal.com. This is simply not true. Go to any major e-commerce site and see whether they accept PayPal or whether they accept credit cards. Credit card payment allows for impulse buys. It allows immediate sales.

If you do accept credit cards, you must take the steps to accept them in a secure, encrypted environment, what's known as a Secure Socket Layer (SSL). This type of programming is well out of the reach of the first-time programmer. Ask your Internet service provider for help or consult a professional for help.

10. Make It As Easy on Me As the Corner Drugstore or I Won't Be Back

If you take nothing away but this, I'll be happy. When creating your site, program it so that the user can easily find his or her way around. Make it obvious how to make a buy. Make the buying process easy and quick.

In short, make as easy on me as the corner drugstore or I won't be back.

Think about it. What does the corner drugstore offer? I can find what I want easily. I know where to go when I'm ready to check out. At checkout, no one asks for strange information. I pay with a traditional form of currency. After I pay, someone says, "Thank you." I feel secure.

I'll try to drive my points home using three critiques of e-commerce.

Remember…corner drugstore.

Site Critiques

1. The Clown Store/Author: Leah Morrison

http://www.theclownstore.com/
Load Time: 19 Seconds, 57kps modem, cleared cache, 7/12/00 12:07AM.

My Screen Size: 1,024×768

Browsers Used: Internet Explorer 5 and Netscape Navigator 4.5

Concept: The Clown Store offers a lot. At first I thought it was going to be a simple gallery; then I noticed it actually was an e-commerce site. Then there were recipes, and other Southwestern art. There are numerous artists and other persons represented on the site, but Leah does all of the artwork and HTML coding. It is an in-house operation. I know what you're going through, Leah. Let's look into the site.

Praise: One of the biggest concerns I have about e-commerce is that the sites must be at least as easy as going to the local store. If not, why would I come to the site over the local store? The site will make me wait to get the item; the local store lets me walk out with it.

Figure 10.4

e-Commerce from The Clown Store. (Color Plate C.28)

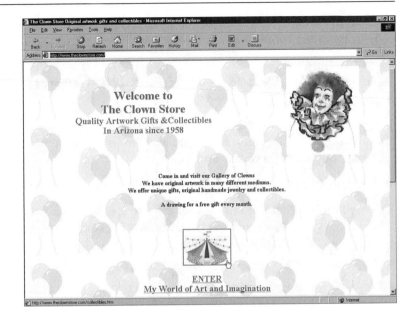

The Clown Store seems to recognize that and is actually pretty easy to navigate. The links offer what they say and the subpages are fairly blatant. This is the "Gallery of Clowns." It's a look at some of the art that is for sale on the site (see Figure 10.5).

Figure 10.5

Pick a clown, any clown...

Once you click on the clown image, a larger version pops up and you get the basic facts about the painting.

There are other galleries that offer other forms of art that all act the same way. Ah-ha! There must be something to it.

Concern: I helped put together an art site once so I was interested in how the author would set up the actual sale of the art. The Clown Store did not make it as easy as going to the local store. In fact, it was a bit of a pain.

I found out that you couldn't buy a painting from the galleries. The thing that tipped me to that fact was that some of the art was marked as sold. I went in to see the sold pieces and then made it my chore to find out how people actually bought the art.

You must go to the Gift Shop to buy the art. Once in the gift shop, you look for the painting you found in the gallery and buy it. In effect, each purchase required two searches.

Suggestion: That is simply too hard. I know it seems easy, but remember that ease of use is very important in e-commerce. Also keep in mind that the impulse buy must be catered to. When I am looking through the galleries and see a painting I like, I should have the ability to buy that painting right away. If I have to go to another place, search again, and along the way see even more paintings, I could pretty easily change my mind. You could have had the sale, but you made me work for it. That gave me time to think it over and maybe not pull the trigger.

I would lose the Gift Shop idea altogether. Make it so that when someone browses the galleries, they can buy right from there.

And what is up with saying that something is sold? Are you trying to make me feel bad? Do you want me to think that I'm a dolt because I wasn't the first on scene?

K-Mart doesn't put up a sign that tells me something is sold. If something is sold, it isn't on the shelf. Follow that thinking here. It's sold. I can't buy it. Don't show it to me.

Concern: There are a few places where the HTML coding gets a little sloppy. Each of your active images has that dreaded blue (or pink, or green) border around it indicating that it is a link.

Suggestion: You need to lose that completely. Add the attribute BORDER="0" to your IMG flags. Those borders are just not acceptable anymore.

Poor coding gives a users a sense that the site does not take itself seriously. It shows a lack of professionalism. This is a site that is expecting people to make a purchase. I don't know that I want to give my money to a site that doesn't fill me with an air of being professional.

If you don't take enough care to keep your basic coding correct, why should I believe you will act professionally with my credit card number?

Concern: I think you have way too much going on for this site's own good. The front page suggests this is a site that sells art and crafts. That's great. Stop there. There's no need to do anything else.

In addition to the art, you have links, recipes, and a writer's corner. In addition, on some of the galleries, there are features other than the art. For example, on the page showing the clown art, you have something that turns a picture of a little boy into a clown. It is cute, but it doesn't fit.

Suggestion: If you want all of these elements on a page, that's fine, just do your readers a favor and put them on a separate site. The Clown Store sells art and crafts. That's all. The other information may be very helpful and great for people to have, but it muddies the water at The Clown Store.

What if you went to K-Mart to buy a chair and along the way someone asked if you wanted your face painted? Another person tried to get you to take home a recipe. Yet another tried to get you to discuss your feelings for the store.

Stop! I came here for a chair! Let me buy my chair!

Set up other sites for other information.

Concern: Because the site offers so many different types of art, you really need to make a point of carrying something across from page to page. You can't really do it with that balloon background because much of the art doesn't lend itself to that balloon imagery.

Suggestion: Why not use that Clown Store logo you have on the main page (see Figure 10.6)?

Carry that logo across from page to page. Put it in the same place on every page, top and center. That way, even if the background images change, the user will still know they are within the boundaries of The Clown Store.

I have written that I am against changing backgrounds, but here it might work. The Clown Store identified would keep the consistency. If I am looking at clown art then reinforce that with a clown background. If I am looking at cowboys then reinforce that. Southwestern art would have a different background.

The background would reinforce the painting category while the logo would reinforce the site itself.

Overall: Here's to The Clown Store! I have nothing but good things to say about a person who takes the plunge and attempts to start their own business. My wife and I have done it four times. Three failed, one didn't.

Figure 10.6
The Clown Store logo.

Just keep in mind that when you jump onto the Web to sell something, you have placed yourself into an arena that requires a certain level of ease and professionalism. If you can rewrite and make it so that I can buy as soon as I see the painting, that will be the best step you can take for this site. Past that, clean up the HTML, carry something across pages for consistency, and you'll be well on your way to a great e-commerce site.

Apparently, it's already a welcome site. I noticed a lot of paintings were sold. Darn. And I wanted that one, too.

2. Computer Books Online/Author: Jill Armour

http://www.computerbooksonline.com/
Load Time: 16 Seconds, 57kps modem, cleared cache, 7/25/00 10:46AM.

My Screen Size: 1,024×768

Browsers Used: Internet Explorer 5 and Netscape Navigator 4.5

Concept: Hooray for anyone who would go online with a business. Further hooray for anyone who would go online with a business that go head to head with some monster sites. Computer Books Online is just such a site. With Amazon looming large, Jill Armour posted the site and is making a go of it. Good for her. I wish her nothing but the best.

Figure 10.7
Want a book? Buy it online. (Color Plate C.29)

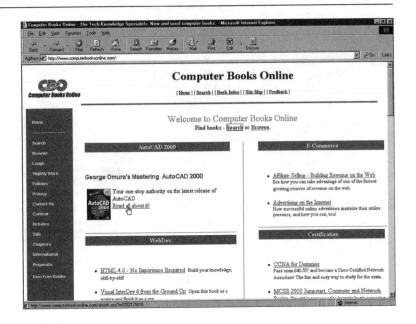

Praise: The site is sleek and loaded very quickly. It is certainly not labor intensive and I found it fairly easy to get around in. The left menu helped me most of the way. Like many other online bookstores, I find the text that makes up the main page is just the owners pushing a particular book. When I arrive looking for a book, I want the search feature right away. I found it right off. It's the first link (after Home, of course) on the left. That placement put my eyes right to it.

I did a search for, what else, my Goodies books. The search turned up three books including that Mac book that took the word "Goodies" and used it. The search results were very basic, but look what happened when I chose to look at one of the results (see Figure 10.8).

This was something I hadn't seen before. A secondary window opened and the search results displayed. If you clicked on one of the links, the page appeared in the main window. I thought that was very clever and very helpful to the user. That second window allowed you to roll through your results without constantly going back to the display page. I would just make a point of stating that a new window will open under the button that fires a search function.

The site uses familiar terminology to represent the sales process. Users will put items into a shopping cart and go to the checkout to purchase. The pages made the process quite obvious and I never found myself in any trouble understanding how to go through the buying process.

354

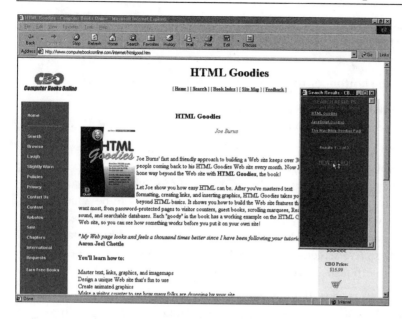

Figure 10.8
No going back!

The first thing I wondered when coming to the site was why I would use this site over Amazon.com? What did this site offer that Amazon did not?

The prices were the same. I checked a bunch of books and I didn't see a difference in price, so that can't be it. Then I found it in Figure 10.9.

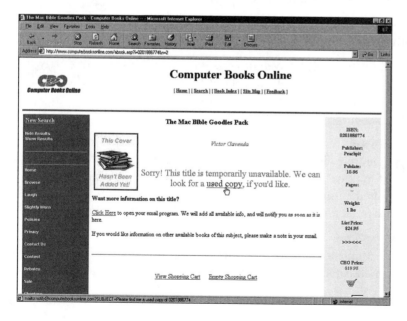

Figure 10.9
A used copy? Cool.

You have used computer books? Cool. I want that first. I think that's your biggest selling point over the other bookstores online. So, I did a search for "used" on the homepage since I never saw it.

It's there, but it's almost at the bottom of the page, which leads me to my first concern.

Concern: It is my opinion that your homepage is modeled after other stores on the Web and because of that, you do not separate yourself from the other stores on the Web.

Suggestion: You need to look into a new design that immediately moves you away from the others online. That used-book deal is a great selling point. I would get that up high. Pushing certain books if fine, but most people will come looking for what they want rather than those books that are offered. Your "Book Services" area looks to me to be what sets you apart from other sites. I would suggest you go as far as to make each of the headings you have into links rather than filling the page with text. Right now, your homepage scrolls three pages long. It'll go five screens on 800×600. Cut it down so that it goes less than two and get the elements that make you different up higher.

You have a link way at the bottom that denotes your return policy. I cannot tell you how important people feel that policy is to a purchase. They want to know that they can get their money back if the book is not what they were hoping for. You explain it very well. It's just that the link is so far down the page that I don't know that anyone would get there.

The "Recent Additions" section is one that should be trumpeted as well. That's something that shows that your site is updating, that it is different from the last time someone stopped in. That's a key to repeat visits and repeat customers.

Concern: Your links on the left, in the blue bar, have no rollover or activity to them at all. They are simply white active text.

Suggestion: That's very odd in the world of Web design. Static text links are not overly popular. In addition, you have them pretty well spread out. That also adds to the length of the page you've created. Try to make the navigation bar shorter so the entire page can be shorter.

Concern: I don't really like to say this is a concern because it could have just been the time of day or that your people were cleaning the system, or a hundred other things, but when I performed a search, it took well over a minute to get the results. That's a long time in the world of the Web. I waited a minute to add a book to my shopping cart and it never did submit. I tried three times in all and the server never entered the item. It just sat on the page.

Suggestion: Tell your server people about the time problem and perform searches regularly on your own site. If the search is too slow, get them to speed it up. If they can't, find someone who can. People simply won't wait a long time for every search to complete. There are sites out there that won't make them wait.

Concern: You have links that you titled "Fun Stuff." I went to them. They had nothing to do with the site. They were just as you titled them, fun stuff.

Suggestion: People might say that I'm being dull here and that the links are just fun but I have to say this is an e-commerce site, not a personal homepage. People came for books. They came to shop. I would lose the links altogether. The time people spend reading anagrams is time they are not shopping. That may sound terrible and capitalistic, but think about why you put the site up in the first place. If I'm digging your links, and I don't buy books, the site won't be up for long.

Overall: I would have liked to go the entire way through the process and actually buy something to see what your receipt page looked like, but I couldn't. The server fought me all the way.

Past that, I think you really have something here. The concept of used books and buying and selling books is different from what's out there right now, yet I never saw that when I first arrived at the site. Push that. Push the differences between your site and the Amazons of the world. What makes you different? Why should I come to you rather than go where I've been ten times before?

You site is a winner. You just need to make a point of telling people why it's a winner. I think once you trumpet the correct elements, you'll see business increase dramatically.

3. Barbara Allen Hats/Author: Patrick Lockwood

http://www.barbaraallenhats.com/
Load Time: 25 Seconds, 57kps modem, cleared cache, 7/25/00 10:46AM.

My Screen Size: 1,024×768

Browsers Used: Internet Explorer 5 and Netscape Navigator 4.5

Concept: How about a hat, a Barbara Allen hat? The author of the site, Patrick Lockwood, put the site together for his mother's millinery business. That's a good son. If my Mom ever goes into business, I'll make her a site, too. The site is there to sell hats, nothing more, nothing less.

Praise: You simply have to love that background. It's two-shade pink and just tells of another time when hats were *the* fashion accessories. I was drawn to the site not only because of its design but also because my wife is just one of those people that looks good in hats.

Figure 10.10
Hats by Barbara Allen.
(Color Plate C.30)

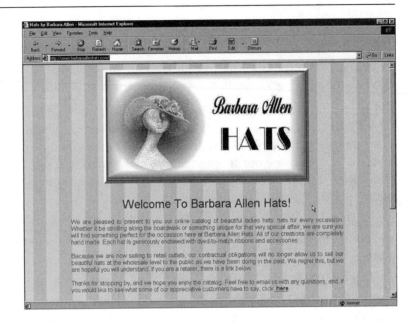

The images and background are very supportive. They were well chosen and add a great deal to what the site is all about.

The site was fairly easy to navigate and I found myself clicking a lot. That's a good sign. I looked at different hats, turned them around, and checked for colors. I had a good time.

Once inside the catalogue, you can look at each hat on its own. I happen to like the crusher style shown in Figure 10.11.

You obviously see the hat, but then there's a back view and a choice of colors. You even get the price, which all too often, business Web sites tend to hide until you make a purchase. A little description and the page is complete.

It's a nice system. Each hat is displayed the same way offering the same views and colors.

The best praise I can give is I lost track of time in the site. I surfed numerous hats and looked at all the views. I enjoyed the site and was moved to buy a hat until one mistake stopped me cold. We'll talk about it in a minute.

I'll start with some of the design concerns first.

Concern: The large image on the homepage is waaaaay too big. It takes over the page from the text and the links below. Furthermore, the image is vital to the page. It describes exactly what the site is all about. Since it loaded last, I was a little lost at first.

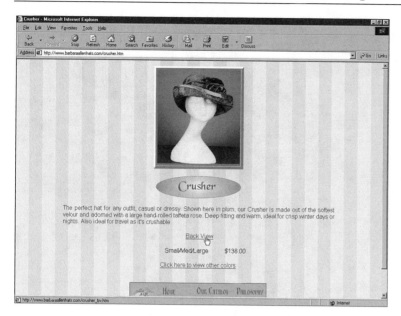

Figure 10.11
Oh, crusher... (à la Bugs Bunny).

Suggestion: Make the image much smaller. Get it to pop up fast, fast, fast. It's the banner image and should be there.

Concern: Your pages are almost all stacked works. There is no left-to-right eye movement to them. I have to scroll to get anything new.

Suggestion: Look for a way to get some elements up against each other, especially the links image. Redesign that so it is vertical rather than horizontal so that it can sit higher on the page. As it stands now, your links are always last and always off the browser screen. That's not overly bad within the site, but on the main page, the links are so well hidden that I had to go looking. Get them up higher and in turn, attempt to place elements next to one another so that I don't have to always move vertically.

Concern: Where's the background on Mom's page and a couple others? You lost it.

Suggestion: That background is a dream. Keep it on all the pages.

Concern: You made it a little difficult on me to buy, but not too bad. I can click on a page that contains a hat that I like and get to another page that starts me on the buying process. I think I understand why you stop me. It's to explain sizing, return policies, and the like. That's not a bad reason for stopping me. I think most people can accept that.

This is where I ran into my major concern illustrated in Figure 10.12.

Figure 10.12

The name doesn't match the security certificate?

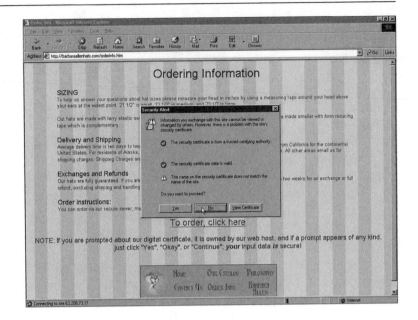

That error message came up when I attempted to buy a hat. I know what I'm doing and it stopped me cold. I had to read your certificate and found why the alert and felt fairly safe going on.

The problem is that not everybody knows as much about the Web as you and I, and this Alert will kill the sale completely.

Yes, yes, I see on the page that you attempt to explain the alert before it happens. It reads:

> "NOTE: If you are prompted about our digital certificate, it is owned by our web host, and if a prompt appears of any kind, just click 'Yes,' 'Okay,' or 'Continue;' your input data is secure!"

No way, Ray. I would wager that 50% of those that see this warning go no farther. You may say to me that you do get a lot of sales. Well, think how many more you could be getting.

People are nervous enough about sales on the Web—do not give them even more to be concerned about.

Suggestion: This site is nothing if not a winner. The product, the design, the method of display, and so many other elements are coming together. Yes, some tweaking is required, but all in all, you have a real jewel here. Your Mom's hats are great and they should sell with no trouble.

Do yourself a great favor. Find another server. Get on a business server that will set up a Secure Socket Layer system to accept credit cards that will allow you to buy your own certificate. I cannot emphasize how important I think this will be to the site.

After following the link despite the concern, I found your order form to be extremely easy to follow and whoever designed it did a wonderful job of walking the user through the process.

You just need to get that major hurdle out of the way. Believe me, I wouldn't suggest the time and the money that will go into getting on your own commerce server if I didn't believe it was the very best thing you could do.

Index

X-Z